HOME
EMERGENCIES

Other Publications:

AMERICAN COUNTRY

VOYAGE THROUGH THE UNIVERSE

THE THIRD REICH

THE TIME-LIFE GARDENER'S GUIDE

MYSTERIES OF THE UNKNOWN

TIME FRAME

FIX IT YOURSELF

FITNESS, HEALTH & NUTRITION

SUCCESSFUL PARENTING

HEALTHY HOME COOKING

UNDERSTANDING COMPUTERS

LIBRARY OF NATIONS

THE ENCHANTED WORLD

THE KODAK LIBRARY OF CREATIVE PHOTOGRAPHY

GREAT MEALS IN MINUTES

THE CIVIL WAR

PLANET EARTH

COLLECTOR'S LIBRARY OF THE CIVIL WAR

THE EPIC OF FLIGHT

THE GOOD COOK

WORLD WAR II

HOME REPAIR AND IMPROVEMENT

THE OLD WEST

HOME EMERGENCIES

TIME-LIFE BOOKS
ALEXANDRIA, VIRGINIA

Fix It Yourself was produced by
ST. REMY PRESS

MANAGING EDITOR	Kenneth Winchester
MANAGING ART DIRECTOR	Pierre Léveillé

Staff for *Home Emergencies*

Series Editor	Brian Parsons
Editor	Elizabeth Cameron
Series Art Director	Diane Denoncourt
Art Director	Odette Sévigny
Research Editors	Donald Harman, Michael Mouland
Designer	Julie Léger
Editorial Assistant	Gerry Wagschal
Contributing Writers	Iris Clendenning, J. Serrentino
Electronic Designer	Robert Paquet
Contributing Illustrators	Gérard Mariscalchi, Jacques Proulx
Technical Illustrator	Nicolas Moumouris
Cover	Robert Monté
Index	Christine M. Jacobs
Administrator	Denise Rainville
Administrative Assistant	Natalie Watanabe
Coordinator	Michelle Turbide
Systems Manager	Shirley Grynspan
Systems Analyst	Simon Lapierre
Studio Director	Maryo Proulx

Time-Life Books Inc. is a wholly owned subsidiary of
TIME INCORPORATED

FOUNDER	Henry R. Luce 1898-1967
Editor-in-Chief	Jason McManus
Chairman and Chief Executive Officer	J. Richard Munro
President and Chief Operating Officer	N. J. Nicholas Jr.
Editorial Director	Richard B. Stolley

THE TIME INC. BOOK COMPANY

President and Chief Executive Officer	Kelso F. Sutton
President, Time Inc. Books Direct	Christopher T. Linen

TIME-LIFE BOOKS INC.

EDITOR	George Constable
Executive Editor	Ellen Phillips
Director of Design	Louis Klein
Director of Editorial Resources	Phyllis K. Wise
Editorial Board	Russell B. Adams Jr., Dale M. Brown, Roberta Conlan, Thomas H. Flaherty, Lee Hassig, Donia Ann Steele, Rosalind Stubenberg
Director of Photography and Research	John Conrad Weiser
Asst. Director of Editorial Resources	Elise Ritter Gibson
PRESIDENT	John M. Fahey Jr.
Senior Vice Presidents	Robert M. DeSena, James L. Mercer, Paul R. Stewart, Joseph J. Ward
Vice Presidents	Stephen L. Bair, Stephen L. Goldstein, Juanita T. James, Andrew P. Kaplan, Carol Kaplan, Susan J. Maruyama, Robert H. Smith
Supervisor of Quality Control	James King
Publisher	Joseph J. Ward

Editorial Operations

Copy Chief	Diane Ullius
Production	Celia Beattie
Library	Louise D. Forstall
Correspondents	Elisabeth Kraemer-Singh (Bonn); Christina Lieberman (New York); Maria Vincenza Aloisi (Paris); Ann Natanson (Rome).

THE CONSULTANTS

Consulting editor **David L. Harrison** served as an editor for several Time-Life Books do-it-yourself series, including *Home Repair and Improvement*, *The Encyclopedia of Gardening* and *The Art of Sewing*.

Joseph Truini is Shop and Tools Editor of Popular Mechanics magazine and specializes in home improvement articles for do-it-yourselfers. He has worked as a home improvement contractor, carpenter and home remodeler.

Richard Day, a do-it-yourself writer for over a quarter of a century, is a founder of the National Association of Home and Workshop Writers and is the author of several home repair books.

Kathleen M. Kiely was a Series Editor of *Fix-It-Yourself*. She has worked as a writer and editor for other Time-Life Books series including *Home Repair and Improvement, Your Home* and *Planet Earth*.

Library of Congress Cataloging-in-Publication Data
Home emergencies.
     p. cm. – (Fix it yourself)
   Includes index.
   ISBN 0-8094-6280-X
   ISBN 0-8094-6281-8 (lib. bdg.)
1. Dwellings—Maintenance and repair—Amateur's
   manuals.
2. Home accidents—Prevention—Handbooks, manuals, etc.
   I. Time-Life Books. II. Series.
   TH4817.3.H645   1989
   643.7—dc20   89-4623
                                 CIP

For information about any Time-Life book, please write:
Reader Information
Time-Life Customer Service
P.O. Box C-32068
Richmond, Virginia
23261-2068

CONTENTS

HOW TO USE THIS BOOK

Home Emergencies provides you with information that can be indispensable, even lifesaving, in the event of a household emergency. The chapter entitled Prevention and Preparedness focuses on preventing emergencies—and on ways you can be prepared to handle emergencies. Each other chapter offers a comprehensive approach to troubleshooting and handling a specific type of home emergency—from family first aid to cleaning up after a major fire, water or environmental disaster. Take the time to study each chapter *before* you need the important advice it contains.

Pictured below are four sample pages from the chapter entitled Fire, with captions describing the various features of the book and how they work. For example, if flames or smoke come from an electrical outlet, the Troubleshooting Guide on page 56 will direct you through the quick-action steps to take and refer you to detailed procedures in the chapter and elsewhere in the book. You will be instructed to have someone call the fire department immediately and sent to page 61 for information on controlling the electrical fire using a fire extinguisher rated ABC or BC. If the fire is not small and

Introductory text
Describes emergency prevention measures, most common emergency situations and basic approaches to coping with an emergency.

Tools and supplies
Present suggested safety devices for preventing emergencies and any specialized tools and equipment required for coping with emergencies.

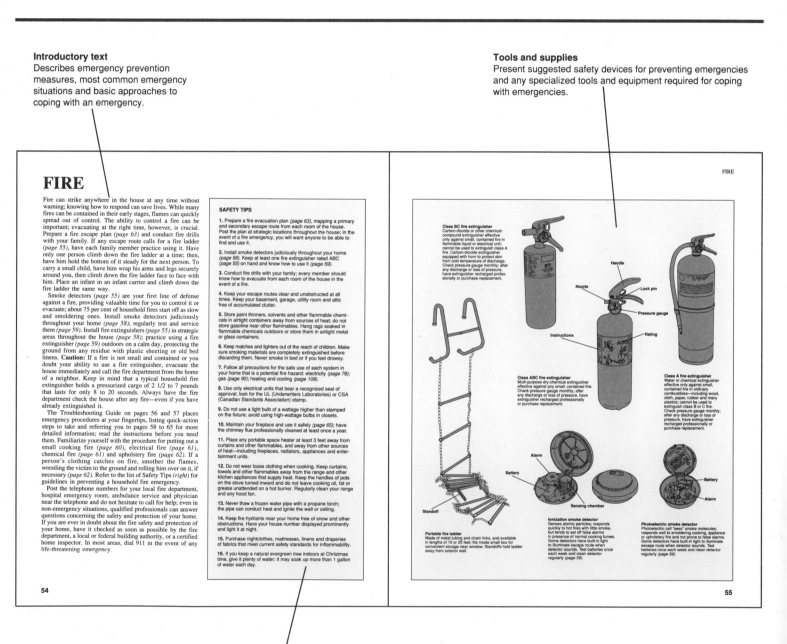

Safety Tips
Cover guidelines for preventing emergencies; offer advice on coping with an emergency.

contained or if flames or smoke come from the walls or ceilings, you will be instructed to evacuate the house and sent to page 63 for information on using a primary escape route; page 64 for information on using a secondary escape route.

The Safety Tips in each chapter cover guidelines for preventing and coping with an emergency. Step-by-step procedures and sidebars in each chapter present greater details; for example: installing smoke detectors (*page 58*) and using a fireplace safely (*page 65*). Suggested safety devices for preventing an emergency and any specialized tools and equipment required for coping with an emergency are shown at the beginning of each chapter.

Take the time to familiarize yourself with each system in your home and the special hazards that may be associated with it; the effort you make could save a life. Locate and label or tag the main shutoff for each utility: electricity (*page 82*); gas (*page 92*); propane (*page 93*); water (*page 99*); oil (*page 111*). Post emergency telephone numbers by each telephone; note that in most regions, you should dial 911 in the event of any life-threatening emergency.

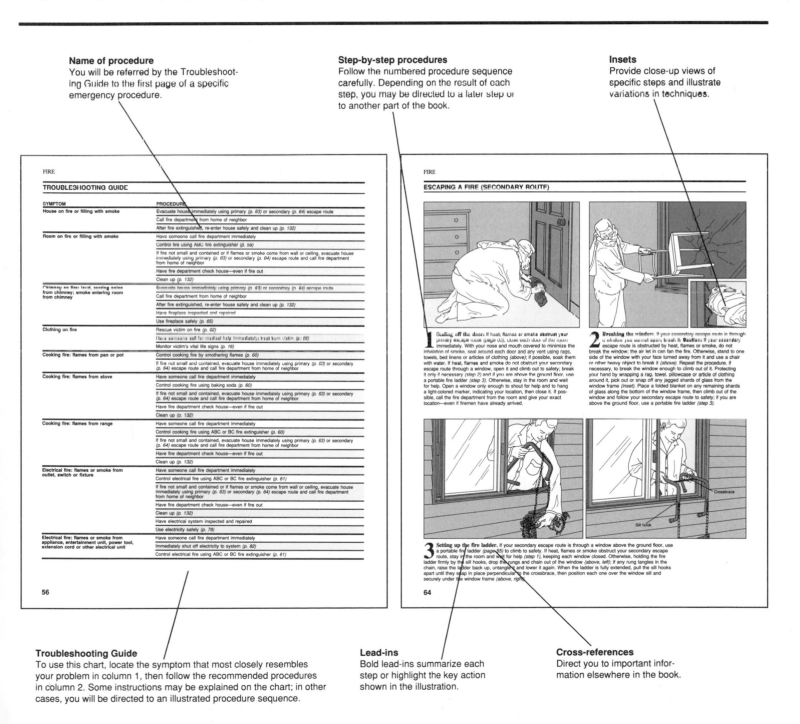

Name of procedure
You will be referred by the Troubleshooting Guide to the first page of a specific emergency procedure.

Step-by-step procedures
Follow the numbered procedure sequence carefully. Depending on the result of each step, you may be directed to a later step or to another part of the book.

Insets
Provide close-up views of specific steps and illustrate variations in techniques.

Troubleshooting Guide
To use this chart, locate the symptom that most closely resembles your problem in column 1, then follow the recommended procedures in column 2. Some instructions may be explained on the chart; in other cases, you will be directed to an illustrated procedure sequence.

Lead-ins
Bold lead-ins summarize each step or highlight the key action shown in the illustration.

Cross-references
Direct you to important information elsewhere in the book.

PREVENTION AND PREPAREDNESS

There is no place like home; however humble, it is the environment in which you and your family share much of your lives—and keeping it safe requires emergency prevention vigilance. However, even with the best of efforts at prevention, emergencies can and do occur; your preparedness for them can save lives and help minimize the damage to your house and possessions. Refer to the illustration at right for guidance in establishing the focus of the emergency prevention and preparedness measures appropriate to your home. Keep in mind the outdoors around the house as well as the interior of your home and its systems and utilities: water, electricity, gas, plumbing, and heating and cooling. Consult the Troubleshooting Guide on pages 10 and 11 for the list of prevention and preparedness measures appropriate for each type of household emergency you may be forced to confront—and to the specific chapters for more detailed information on the special tools and supplies you should have on hand and the steps to take in handling an emergency in the event one occurs.

Keep a well-stocked first-aid kit *(page 13)* on hand and equip your home judiciously with the many safety and security devices, detectors and equipment on the market, most of which are readily available at a building supply center or hardware store. Smoke detectors *(page 55)* are your first line of defense against a fire, providing valuable time for you to control it or evacuate *(page 63)*. Keep at least one fire extinguisher rated ABC *(page 55)* in your house and know how to use it *(page 59)*. Regularly inspect and maintain the systems, utilities and appliances of your home; have your heating and cooling systems professionally inspected at least once each year. Be sure to locate and label or tag the main shutoff for each utility in your home: electricity *(page 82)*; gas *(page 92)*; propane *(page 93)*; water *(page 99)*; oil *(page 111)*; in the event of an emergency, you will want anyone to be able to find them quickly and shut them off.

Post emergency telephone numbers near each telephone in your home— including your local hospital emergency room, poison control center and physician, your local fire and police departments, the water and electricity utilities, the gas or oil company, a 24-hour plumber and your insurance agent. If your telephone has a programmable memory, store the numbers and identify the code to use in each emergency. In most regions, dial 911 in the event of any life-threatening emergency. If you are ever in doubt about the safety of your home or your ability to handle an emergency, do not hesitate to call for help; even in non-emergency situations, qualified professionals can answer questions about the health of your family and the safety of your home.

Water *(page 66)*
Each spring and fall, routinely inspect your roofing and siding system—the attic, the vents, the siding material, the roofing material, the gutters and downspouts, the flashing, and the fascia boards. Have any repairs required undertaken as soon as possible. Keep a roll of heavy-duty plastic sheeting on hand for use as a temporary water barrier in the event of an emergency.

Environmental disasters *(page 118)*
Safeguard your home and possessions in advance of an environmental disaster. Make sure your homeowner insurance policy provides adequate coverage and prepare panels to protect windows against strong winds. Keep an emergency survival kit on hand.

Household security *(page 46)*
Lock the doors and windows of your home and keep the area around each entry to the house well lit at night. Install security locks and devices judiciously throughout your home and install outdoor lighting fixtures around the perimeter of the house.

Hazardous materials *(page 42)*
Store hazardous household products in a locked cupboard, well out of the reach of children. Read the label on the container of any household product and follow the manufacturer's instructions for its use.

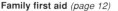

Family first aid (*page 12*)
Keep a well-stocked first-aid kit in a convenient, accessible place in your home. Childproof your home and ensure any swimming pool is fenced in with the gate kept locked when the area is unsupervised.

Fire (*page 54*)
Have at least one fire extinguisher rated ABC on hand and know how to use it. Install smoke detectors judiciously throughout the house. Keep your fire escape routes clear and unobstructed at all times.

Electricity (*page 78*)
Know how to life safely with electricity, both indoors and outdoors, and take measures to protect your children. Install electrical safety devices such as ground-fault circuit interrupters (GFCIs), surge suppressors, plug covers, cord shorteners and safety caps judiciously throughout your home.

Plumbing (*page 76*)
Do not use a toilet as a waste basket or rinse foods, grease, fats or coffee grounds down a sink drain. Do not leave a hand-held shower attachment in a filled bathtub or a garden hose in a swimming pool.

Heating and cooling (*page 108*)
Keep furniture and curtains away from the registers of an air distribution system and make sure any electrical baseboard heater is unobstructed. Store paints, solvents and other flammable materials away from gas or oil burners and electrical heating elements.

Gas (*page 90*)
Keep gas appliances clean and have them serviced regularly. Make sure each family member is familiar with the distinctive odor of natural and propane gas. Install natural and propane gas detectors as well as a carbon monoxide gas detector.

PROTECTING YOUR HOUSE AND POSSESSIONS

Insurance coverage. A homeowner insurance policy is one of your first lines of defense in emergency preparedness, protecting you from any liability in the event of medical injuries and property damages suffered by a third party and protecting your house and possessions in the event of any loss or damage. A basic homeowner insurance policy typically provides coverage for a wide variety of misfortunes, from break-ins, theft and other violations of household security to fire and certain types of water-related emergencies; usually the expense provisions included are broad, ranging from rebuilding of the house to temporary lodging.

Assess your insurance needs, however, and update your homeowner insurance policy regularly. Make sure your insurance coverage is extensive enough for the household emergencies you may be forced to confront and high enough in relation to the dollar value of your house and possessions. For example, any loss or damage incurred as a result of an earthquake or flood is not covered by a basic homeowner insurance policy. Consider obtaining extra insurance coverage for any environmental disaster to which the area you live in may be vulnerable; a flood insurance policy, for instance, may be available from a private insurance company or through a government-sponsored program such as the

TROUBLESHOOTING GUIDE

EMERGENCY	PROCEDURE
Family first aid	Basic homeowner insurance policy usually covers third-party liability
	Keep well-stocked first-aid kit on hand *(p. 13)*
	Practice monitoring vital life signs *(p. 16)*
	Practice administering artificial respiration: adults and children *(p. 17)*; infants *(p. 19)*
	Take course in cardiopulmonary resuscitation (CPR)
	Practice applying recovery position *(p. 20)*
	Childproof home *(p. 39)*
Hazardous materials	Basic homeowner insurance policy usually covers fire loss or damage caused by hazardous material; does not cover cost of eliminating source of indoor pollutant
	Identify sources of indoor pollutants *(p. 44)*
	Install carbon monoxide gas detector; natural and propane gas detectors *(p. 44)*
	Use chemical products safely *(p. 45)*
	Keep fire extinguisher rated ABC or BC *(p. 55)* on hand *(p. 58)*; know how to use it *(p. 61)*
Household security	Basic homeowner insurance policy usually covers loss or damage of appliances, furniture and clothing; add special endorsements for valuables such as artwork, jewelry, silverware and heirlooms
	Install security locks and devices *(p. 47)* judiciously throughout home *(p. 49)*
	List valuables and their serial numbers, credit cards and their account numbers; keep list hidden
	Engrave valuables with driver's license number; photograph or use video camera to record valuables that cannot be engraved
	Form neighborhood watch group
Fire	Basic homeowner insurance policy usually covers loss or damage caused by fire
	Install smoke detectors *(p. 55)* judiciously throughout home *(p. 58)*
	Keep fire extinguisher rated ABC *(p. 55)* on hand *(p. 58)*; know how to use it *(p. 59)*
	Prepare fire evacuation plan *(p. 63)* and conduct fire drills with family
	Maintain fireplace and use it safely *(p. 65)*
Water	Basic homeowner insurance policy usually covers water loss or damage caused by faulty appliance or plumbing system; does not cover costs of repairs to appliance or plumbing system
	Locate and label or tag main water shutoff valve *(p. 99)* and valve or valves for fixtures *(p. 100)*
	Locate and label or tag main circuit breaker, main fuse block or service disconnect breaker of electrical system *(p. 82)*
Electricity	Basic homeowner insurance policy usually covers loss or damage caused by faulty electrical system
	Locate and label or tag main circuit breaker, main fuse block or service disconnect breaker of electrical system *(p. 82)*
	Map circuits of home and label service panel *(p. 84)*

U.S. Flood Insurance Program. And while a basic homeowner insurance policy normally covers the full replacement value of common household possessions such as appliances, furniture and clothing, special endorsements are often necessary for valuable possessions such as artwork, jewelry, silverware and heirlooms. Notify your insurance agent of any upgrading or addition to your house and of each expensive new possession you acquire; ensure your homeowner insurance policy is appropriately adjusted. Avoid the temptation to under-insure your house and possessions—it could result in an increase to your hardship at a time when you need the most help.

Take steps to protect yourself before you need to file an insurance claim. Prepare a written inventory of your possessions along with their model and serial numbers; include your credit cards and their account numbers. Have valuable items engraved with the number of your driver's license to make them easy to trace; take photographs or use a video camera to record valuable items that cannot be engraved. Keep a copy of your inventory in a safety deposit box or at the office. In the event of any household emergency involving loss or damage, notify your insurance agent as soon as possible; an insurance adjuster will be assigned to assess the situation.

EMERGENCY	PROCEDURE
Electricity (cont.)	Install electrical safety devices (p. 79) judiciously throughout home
	Inspect plugs and cords (p. 85)
	Prevent electrical emergencies (p. 89)
	Keep fire extinguisher rated ABC or BC (p. 55) on hand (p. 58); know how to use it (p. 61)
	Have emergency energy supplies on hand (p. 128)
Gas	Basic homeowner insurance policy usually covers loss or damage caused by faulty gas system
	Locate and label or tag main gas shutoff valve (p. 92) or main propane shutoff valve (p. 93) and shutoff valves for appliances (p. 92)
	Install carbon monoxide gas detector; natural and propane gas detectors (p. 44)
	Keep fire extinguisher rated ABC (p. 55) on hand (p. 58); know how to use it (p. 59)
	Have emergency energy supplies on hand (p. 128)
Plumbing	Basic homeowner insurance policy usually covers water loss or damage caused by faulty appliance or plumbing system; does not cover costs of repairs to appliance or plumbing system
	Locate and label or tag main water shutoff valve (p. 99) and valve or valves for fixtures (p. 100)
	Locate and label or tag main circuit breaker, main fuse block or service disconnect breaker of electrical system (p. 82)
Heating and cooling	Basic homeowner insurance policy usually covers loss or damage caused by faulty heating or cooling system
	Locate and label or tag main shutoff for each utility: electricity (p. 82); gas (p. 92); propane (p. 93); water (p. 99); oil (p. 111)
	Install carbon monoxide gas detector; natural and propane gas detectors (p. 44)
	Keep fire extinguisher rated ABC (p. 55) on hand (p. 58); know how to use it (p. 59)
	Have emergency energy supplies on hand (p. 128)
Environmental disasters	Basic homeowner insurance policy usually covers loss or damage caused by environmental disaster; earthquakes and floods require special insurance coverage
	Keep well-stocked emergency survival kit on hand (p. 122)
	Locate and label or tag main shutoff for each utility: electricity (p. 82); gas (p. 92); propane (p. 93); water (p. 99); oil (p. 111)
	Practice taking shelter quickly (p. 122)
	Prepare evacuation plan (p. 123)
Cleaning up	Basic homeowner insurance policy usually covers loss or damage caused by water, fire or environmental disaster; earthquakes and floods require special insurance coverage
	Locate and label or tag main shutoff for each utility: electricity (p. 82); gas (p. 92); propane (p. 93); water (p. 99); oil (p. 111)
	Have emergency energy supplies on hand (p. 128)

FAMILY FIRST AID

Many household medical emergencies are not life-threatening; equipped with basic first-aid techniques, the homeowner can be prepared to handle most of them. However, in the event of a major medical emergency, the correct action taken quickly can maintain a life until medical help arrives. Familiarize yourself with the signs and symptoms of major medical emergencies *(page 16)*; before a major medical emergency occurs, practice monitoring vital life signs—checking for breathing, taking a pulse and taking body temperature. Keep a well-stocked first-aid kit in your home *(page 13)* and know how to use the supplies it contains; refer to pages 28 to 34 for the use and application of dressings and bandages.

The Troubleshooting Guide on pages 14 and 15 puts procedures for family medical emergencies at your fingertips; it provides you with quick-action steps to take and refers you to pages 16 to 41 for more detailed information. Familiarize yourself with the procedures for administering artificial respiration to an adult or child *(page 17)* and an infant up to 1 year old *(page 19)*. Know how to treat a choking adult or child *(page 23)* and a choking infant *(page 26)*. Practice placing a person in the recovery position *(page 20)*. To be fully prepared for a major medical emergency, you should take a course in cardiopulmonary resuscitation (CPR), offered by the American or Canadian Red Cross and the American or Canadian Heart Association. CPR requires hands-on training and the guidance of professional instructors; administer it only if you are qualified.

The list of Safety Tips at right covers basic guidelines to help prevent household medical emergencies. Refer to page 23 for details on preventing falls; page 39 for information on preventing accidental poisoning. Keep at least one fire extinguisher rated ABC in your home and know how to use it *(page 59)*. When confronted with a medical emergency, stay calm; the first step in providing assistance to a victim is clear thinking and an unpanicked response. For example, if you must rescue a victim from contact with a live current, do not touch him or the electrical source; use a wooden broom handle or other wooden implement to knock him free *(page 88)*, then monitor his vital life signs. Or, for instance, do not attempt to remove an embedded object from the skin; immobilize the short *(page 33)* or long *(page 34)* embedded object, then seek medical help immediately.

Post the telephone numbers for your local hospital emergency room, poison control center, physician, ambulance service, police and fire departments, and pharmacy near the telephone; in most regions, dial 911 in the event of a life-threatening emergency. If you must cope with a major medical emergency, first treat the victim, then call for medical help; if possible, instruct someone else to call. In the event of any medical emergency, do not hesitate to call for help; even in situations that may not be life-threatening, medical professionals can answer questions concerning proper first-aid techniques and follow-up treatment.

SAFETY TIPS

1. Keep a well-stocked first-aid kit *(page 13)* on hand and store it in a convenient, accessible place in your home. In the event of a family medical emergency, you will want anyone to be able to find and use it.

2. Do not attempt to move a victim if a spinal injury *(page 16)* or broken limb is suspected or if he complains of extreme pain. Cover the victim with a blanket to keep him warm and call for medical help immediately.

3. If a victim has no pulse or his pulse is weak or irregular, administer cardiopulmonary resuscitation (CPR) only if you are qualified. An unqualified person who attempts to administer CPR risks harming the victim more than helping him; place him in the recovery position *(page 20)* and call for medical help immediately.

4. Store medication and potentially harmful household products well out of the reach of children—behind a locked door or in a locked drawer. Do not give a victim of ingested poison anything to eat or drink and do not induce vomiting unless instructed by a medical professional.

5. Carefully read the label on the container of a medication or household product. Follow the manufacturer's instructions and heed specific health or safety warnings.

6. Store knives and other sharp implements out of the reach of children. Never leave tools or other sharp objects on the ground where they can be tripped over or stepped on.

7. Uproot poisonous plants around your home; to avoid skin contact, wear heavy work gloves, a long-sleeved shirt and long pants. Have a lawn care professional remove poison ivy, poison oak or poison sumac if you are allergic. Do not destroy poisonous plants by burning them; inhalation of the smoke may result in poisoning.

8. In snake-infested areas, wear protective boots; carefully watch where you step and reach with your hands.

9. During a heat wave or unusually high temperatures, avoid strenuous physical activity. If you must venture outdoors, stay in the shade and wear a hat to protect your head against the sun. Dress properly for hot weather—do not wear heavy clothing. To reflect heat and sunlight, wear light-colored clothing.

10. During extreme low temperatures, try to stay indoors. If you must venture outdoors, dress for the weather, guarding against frostbite of exposed skin or extremities—your nose, ears, face, hands and feet.

11. Childproof your home *(page 39)*. Take the door off a refrigerator or freezer when storing or discarding it, preventing a child from trapping himself and possibly suffocating.

12. Do not use any electrical unit near a toilet, bathtub, shower or sink, or around any other source of water.

13. Ensure that any swimming pool is fenced in and that the gate is kept locked when the area is unsupervised.

Reusable hot or cold compress
Applied to strained muscles to ease discomfort.

Medicine dropper
Calibrated tube for administering measured doses of liquid medication.

Medical tape
For securing gauze dressing or eye pad; hypo-allergenic type available for sensitive skin.

Adhesive bandage
Gauze dressing with adhesive strip for protecting minor cuts and scratches. Available in wide variety of shapes and sizes; butterfly-shaped used for cuts on hand or foot.

Gauze dressing
Used to cover wound; secured with medical tape or gauze roller bandage. Available in 2 by 2 inch, 3 by 3 inch and 4-by-4 inch sizes.

Eye irrigator
Filled with water; and used to flush foreign particle out of eye.

Tweezers
For extracting splinter or other small object embedded in skin.

Gauze roller bandage
Used to secure gauze dressing; roll about 5 yards long available in 2-inch or 3-inch width.

Triangular bandage
Multi-purpose bandage can be folded to make slings, swathes, ring pads or head bandages; measures about 55 inches across base and 36 to 40 inches along each side.

Medicine spoon
Calibrated tube for administering exact dosage of liquid medication.

Thermometer
Calibrated vial filled with mercury used to determine body temperature; use oral type *(bottom)* with adult or child, rectal type *(top)* with infant. Newer, electronic models give temperature reading on liquid crystal display.

Rubbing alcohol
Used to sterilize needles, tweezers and other first-aid equipment.

Ipecac syrup
Used to induce vomiting in victims of ingested poison. **Caution:** Administer only if advised by poison control center or physician.

Calamine lotion
Applied with cotton ball to soothe skin irritation from poisonous plant or insect bite. Can also use hydrocortizone cream.

Eye pads
Sterile pads taped loosely over eyes to protect them and prevent movement; also available as oval-shaped, self-adhering patches.

Cotton balls
For applying soothing medication such as hydrocortizone cream or calamine lotion to skin irritation.

Reusable ice pack
Applied to sprained joint to ease swelling.

TROUBLESHOOTING GUIDE

SYMPTOM	PROCEDURE
Heart attack suspected: tight pain across chest; labored breathing; weak or irregular pulse; cold or clammy skin	Monitor victim's vital life signs (p. 16)
	Have someone call for medical help immediately
	If no pulse or pulse weak or irregular, administer cardiopulmonary resuscitation only if qualified
	If no breathing or breathing shallow or uneven, administer artificial respiration (p. 17)
	Place victim in semi-sitting position
Stroke suspected: disorientation; paralysis on one side of body; speaking, swallowing, or breathing difficulty	Monitor victim's vital life signs (p. 16)
	Have someone call for medical help immediately
	If no pulse or pulse weak or irregular, administer cardiopulmonary resuscitation only if qualified
	If no breathing or breathing shallow or uneven, administer artificial respiration (p. 17)
	Place victim in semi-sitting position
Unconsciousness suspected: eye-, speech- or muscle-control loss	Monitor victim's vital life signs (p. 16)
	Have someone call for medical help immediately
	If no pulse or pulse weak or irregular, administer cardiopulmonary resuscitation only if qualified
	If no breathing or breathing shallow or uneven, administer artificial respiration: adult or child (p. 17); infant (p. 19)
	Place victim in recovery position (p. 20)
Spinal injury suspected: fall from roof, ladder or top of stairs	Do not move victim
	Monitor victim's vital life signs (p. 16)
	Have someone call for medical help immediately
	Treat fall victim (p. 22)
	Prevent falls (p. 23)
Shock suspected: injury; illness; sudden emotional upset	Monitor victim's vital life signs (p. 16)
	Have someone call for medical help immediately
	If no pulse or pulse weak or irregular, administer cardiopulmonary resuscitation only if qualified
	If no breathing or breathing shallow or uneven, administer artificial respiration: adult or child (p. 17); infant (p. 19)
	Treat shock victim (p. 22)
Electrical shock	If victim immobilized by live current, knock him free using wooden implement (p. 88)
	Monitor victim's vital life signs (p. 16)
	Have someone call for medical help immediately
	If no pulse or pulse weak or irregular, administer cardiopulmonary resuscitation only if qualified
	If no breathing or breathing shallow or uneven, administer artificial respiration: adult or child (p. 17); infant (p. 19)
	Treat shock victim (p. 22)
Fainting spell suspected: pallor; sweaty, cold or clammy skin; shallow or uneven breathing; dizziness; numbness or tingling	Treat fainting-spell victim (p. 21)
	Monitor victim's vital life signs (p. 16)
Adult or child choking: gagging; blue in face	Have someone call for medical help immediately
	Treat choking victim (p. 23); self-help (p. 26)
	Treat unconscious choking victim (p. 25)
	Place victim in recovery position (p. 20)
	Monitor victim's vital life signs (p. 16)
Infant choking: gagging; blue in face	Have someone call for medical help immediately
	Treat choking victim (p. 26)
	Treat unconscious choking victim (p. 27)
	Place victim in recovery position (p. 20)
	Monitor victim's vital life signs (p. 16)

SYMPTOM	PROCEDURE
Wound	Stop bleeding *(p. 28)*
	Apply bandage: leg or arm *(p. 28)*; hand or foot *(p. 29)*; head *(p. 30)*; arm sling, if necessary *(p. 31)*
	If bleeding persists or wound deep or gaping, seek medical help immediately
	If wound caused by rusty or dirty object, see physician for tetanus treatment
Object embedded in skin	Do not attempt to remove embedded object
	Immobilize short *(p. 33)* or long *(p. 34)* embedded object; make arm sling, if necessary *(p. 31)*
	Seek medical help immediately
Foreign particle in eye	Do not attempt to remove foreign particle if on cornea, embedded or adhered or cannot be seen; seek medical help immediately
	Remove foreign particle from eye *(p. 35)*
	Prevent eye movement using eye pads *(p. 34)*
Chemical splashed in eye	Flush chemical from eye *(p. 35)*
	Prevent eye movement using eye pads *(p. 34)*
	Seek medical help immediately
Burn	If burn severe, seek medical help immediately
	Treat burn victim *(p. 36)*
	Apply bandage: leg or arm *(p. 28)*; hand or foot *(p. 29)*; head *(p. 30)*; arm sling, if necessary *(p. 31)*
Exposure to extreme cold	Treat hypothermia or frostbite victim *(p. 36)*
	Monitor victim's vital life signs *(p. 16)*
Exposure to extreme heat	Treat heat victim *(p. 37)*
	Monitor victim's vital life signs *(p. 16)*
Skin irritation: contact with poisonous plant	Treat skin irritation *(p. 37)*
Snakebite	Treat snakebite victim *(p. 38)*
	Monitor victim's vital life signs *(p. 16)*
Insect bite or sting	Treat insect bite or sting *(p. 38)*
	Monitor victim's vital life signs *(p. 16)*
Animal bite	Wash wound with soap and water
	Apply bandage: leg or arm *(p. 28)*; hand or foot *(p. 29)*; head *(p. 30)*; arm sling, if necessary *(p. 31)*
	Monitor victim's vital life signs *(p. 16)*
	See physician for rabies treatment
Poison ingested	Treat ingested-poison victim *(p. 39)*
	Do not give victim anything to eat or drink or induce vomiting unless advised by professional
	Monitor victim's vital life signs *(p. 16)*
	Seek medical help immediately
	Childproof home to prevent accidental poisoning *(p. 39)*
Splinter	Pull out splinter *(p. 40)*
Cut or scratch	Stop bleeding *(p. 28)*
	Treat cut or scratch *(p. 40)*
	If cut or scratch caused by rusty or dirty object, see physician for tetanus treatment
Strain or sprain	Treat strain or sprain *(p. 40)*
Nosebleed	Stop nosebleed *(p. 40)*
Tongue or skin stuck to frozen metal	Warm tongue or skin *(p. 41)*
Fish hook embedded in skin	Remove fish hook *(p. 41)*
	If fish hook rusty or dirty, see physician for tetanus treatment

COPING WITH A MAJOR MEDICAL EMERGENCY

Monitoring vital life signs. In the event of a major medical emergency, immediately deal with the victim, then call for medical help; if possible, instruct someone to call. Reassure the victim that medical help is on the way. Monitor the victim's vital life signs: breathing *(step right)*, pulse *(step below)* and temperature *(page 17)*. Assess the victim's condition while waiting for medical help to arrive:

• **Heart attack.** A heart attack occurs when insufficient blood and oxygen reaches the heart. A victim of a heart attack may experience tight pain across the chest radiating to the arms, neck and shoulders, labored breathing, a weak, irregular pulse, and cold, clammy skin. Place the victim in a semi-sitting position, cover him with blankets and call for medical help; monitor the victim's vital signs.

• **Stroke.** A stroke occurs when a blood vessel of the brain bursts or an artery of the brain is blocked. A victim of a stroke may be disoriented, paralyzed on one side of the body, and have difficulty speaking, swallowing or breathing. Place the victim in a semi-sitting position, cover him with blankets and call for medical help; monitor the victim's vital signs.

• **Unconsciousness.** Loss of consciousness is a sign of interference with the nervous or circulatory system. A victim may be unconscious if his eyes do not open or open only to speech or pain, he does not respond or responds confusedly to speech, and his muscles do not respond or respond only to pain. Call for medical help and monitor the victim's vital signs.

• **Spinal injury.** A back, neck or head injury may cause spinal damage. A victim with severe pain in the back, neck or head, loss of feeling or tingling in the limbs, loss of bladder or bowel control, and clear liquid flowing from the ears or nose may have a spinal injury. Call for medical help and monitor the victim's vital signs; do not move him.

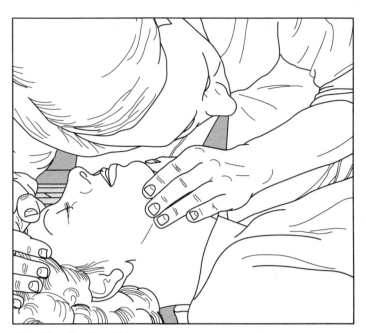

Checking for breathing. Look for a rise and fall of the victim's chest as he inhales and exhales—indicating he is breathing. Lower your head, placing your ear and cheek within 1/2 inch of the victim's mouth *(above)*, to hear and feel air being exhaled. Normal breathing at rest is quiet and regular with an even rhythm. If there is no breathing or the breathing is shallow or uneven, administer artificial respiration immediately *(page 17)*.

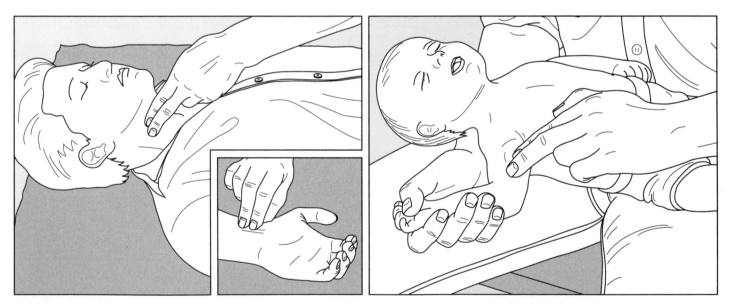

Taking a pulse. Place 2 fingertips about 1 inch above the creases on the inside of the victim's wrist *(inset)* to take his radial pulse; apply moderate pressure and move your fingertips until you feel the pulse. If the victim seems unconscious or you cannot locate his radial pulse, place 2 fingertips in the space between the windpipe and the neck muscle *(above, left)* to take the carotid pulse the same way. With an infant, place 2 fingertips on the inside of the upper arm *(above, right)*, pressing lightly and moving your fingertips until you feel the pulse. Do not use your thumb to take a pulse; it may give a false reading. A normal pulse is strong and regular. If there is no pulse or the pulse is weak or irregular, seek medical help immediately; administer cardiopulmonary resuscitation (CPR) only if you are qualified.

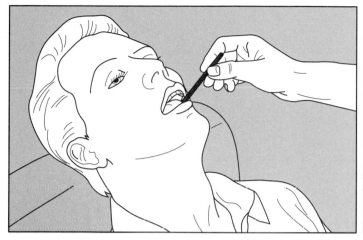

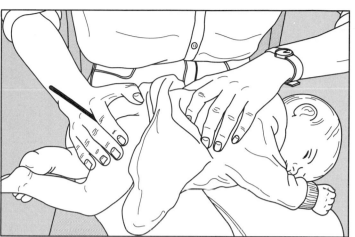

Taking a temperature. Shake the thermometer until the mercury is in the bulb, then rinse the bulb under cool water. Place the bulb of an oral thermometer under the tongue *(above, left)* and leave it in place for at least 2 minutes, with a child, you can place the bulb of the thermometer in an armpit and leave it in place for at least 3 minutes. With an infant, use a rectal thermometer, identifiable by its short, round end; insert it no more than 1 inch into the rectum *(above, right)* and leave it in place for 3 to 5 minutes. To read the thermometer, hold it up to the light and turn it slowly until you can see the mercury column and take a reading. Normal body temperature (98.6 degrees Fahrenheit) is indicated on the scale; a rectal reading is 1 degree higher than an oral reading. If the temperature of an adult, child or infant reaches 102 degrees Fahrenheit or more, seek medical help immediately.

ADMINISTERING ARTIFICIAL RESPIRATION (ADULTS AND CHILDREN)

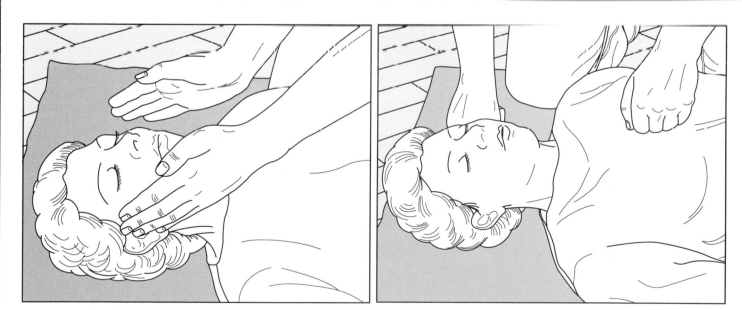

1 Checking responsiveness. Have someone call for medical help immediately. If the victim is an infant, check his responsiveness *(page 19)*. Otherwise, place the victim on his back and loosen his clothing at the neck, chest and waist. Kneel beside the victim and ask if help is needed. If the victim does not respond, lightly slap his cheeks *(above, left)*, then pinch an earlobe and ask again if help is needed. If the victim does not respond, rub your knuckles back and forth on his breastbone *(above, right)*. If the victim still does not respond, monitor his vital life signs *(page 16)*, checking for breathing. If there is no breathing or the breathing is shallow or uneven, open the victim's airway *(step 2)*. Otherwise, place the victim in the recovery position *(page 20)*.

ADMINISTERING ARTIFICIAL RESPIRATION (ADULTS AND CHILDREN) (continued)

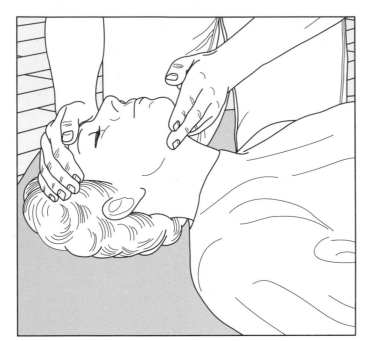

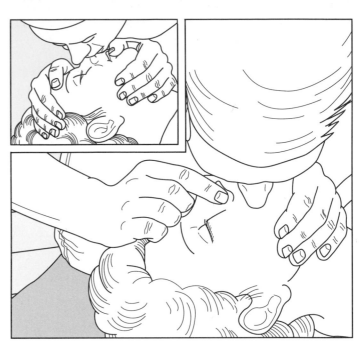

2 **Opening the airway.** Open the victim's airway by tilting his head back, gently lifting the chin and pushing down the forehead *(above)*; this action raises the lower jaw and draws the tongue away from the back of the throat. Drop the victim's lower jaw, opening the mouth, and check again for breathing *(page 16)*. If there is still no breathing or the breathing is shallow or uneven, blow air into the victim's lungs *(step 3)*. Otherwise, place the victim in the recovery position *(page 20)*.

3 **Blowing air into the lungs.** Holding the victim's lower jaw to keep his mouth open, pinch his nostrils to close them. Take a deep breath, press your open mouth over the victim's mouth, forming a tight seal, and deliver the full breath slowly *(above)*. Take another deep breath and deliver it the same way. If the victim has a mouth injury or you cannot form a tight seal over his mouth, raise his lower jaw to close his mouth and deliver 2 full breaths slowly through his nostrils *(inset)*.

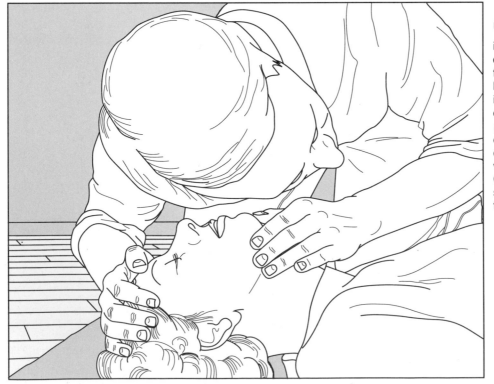

4 **Checking for breathing response.** After delivering 2 full breaths slowly, break contact with the victim, allowing air to flow from his lungs, and take a deep breath. Check for breathing response from the victim *(page 16)*, dropping his lower jaw to open his mouth *(left)*. If there is no breathing or the breathing is shallow or uneven, blow air into the victim's lungs *(step 3)*, delivering 1 full breath slowly every 5 seconds; if the victim is a child, every 4 seconds. Otherwise, place the victim in the recovery position *(page 20)*. Continue monitoring the victim's vital life signs *(page 16)*, checking for breathing and taking a pulse until medical help arrives.

ADMINISTERING ARTIFICIAL RESPIRATION (INFANTS)

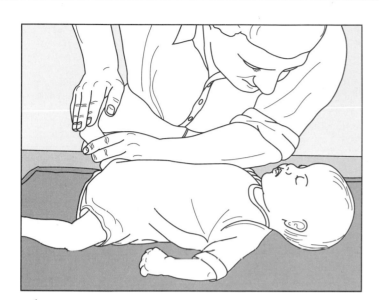

1 Checking responsiveness. Have someone call for medical help immediately. If the victim is an adult or child, check his responsiveness *(page 17)*. If the victim is an infant, place him on his back and loosen his clothing at the neck, chest and waist. Gently shake the victim; if there is no response, tap his foot *(above)* or hand and shout loudly. If the victim still does not respond, monitor his vital life signs *(page 16)*, checking for breathing. If there is no breathing or the breathing is shallow or uneven, open the airway *(step 2)*. Otherwise, place the victim in the recovery position *(page 20)*, keeping him from rolling onto his back.

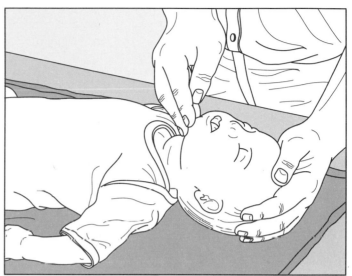

2 Opening the airway. Open the victim's airway by tilting his head back, gently lifting the chin and pushing down the forehead; this action raises the lower jaw and draws the tongue away from the back of the throat. Drop the victim's lower jaw, opening the mouth *(above)*, and check again for breathing *(page 16)*. If there is still no breathing or the breathing is shallow or uneven, blow air into the victim's lungs *(step 3)*. Otherwise, place the victim in the recovery position *(page 20)*, keeping him from rolling onto his back.

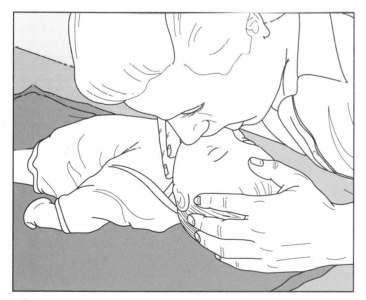

3 Blowing air into the lungs. Holding the victim's lower jaw to keep his mouth open, take a breath and press your open mouth over the victim's mouth and nose, forming a tight seal. Deliver the breath through the victim's mouth and nostrils slowly in 1 short blow *(above)*, without allowing air to flow from his lungs. **Caution:** Do not deliver a full, deep breath to an infant; air may be forced into his stomach. Take another breath and deliver it the same way. After delivering 2 breaths slowly, break contact with the victim, allowing air to flow from his lungs.

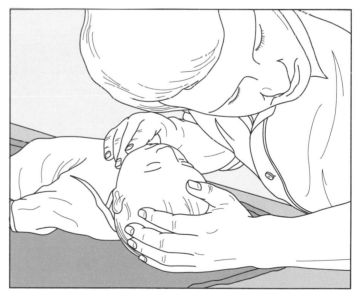

4 Checking for breathing response. Take a deep breath and check for breathing response from the victim *(page 16)*, dropping his lower jaw to open his mouth *(above)*. If there is no breathing or the breathing is shallow or uneven, blow air into the victim's lungs *(step 3)*, delivering 1 breath slowly every 3 seconds. Otherwise, place the victim in the recovery position *(page 20)*, keeping him from rolling onto his back. Continue monitoring the victim's vital life signs *(page 16)*, checking for breathing and taking a pulse until medical help arrives.

PLACING A VICTIM IN THE RECOVERY POSITION

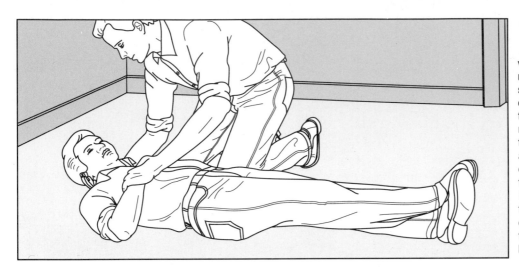

1 **Handling the victim.** Have someone call for medical help immediately. Monitor the victim's vital life signs *(page 16)*. **Caution:** Do not move the victim if a spinal injury is suspected. Otherwise, place the victim on his back and loosen his clothing at the neck, chest and waist; make each movement gently. Kneel beside the victim at his waist and cross his legs at the ankles, bringing the leg farthest from you over the leg closest to you. Tuck the victim's arm closest to you along his side. Reach one hand under the victim's head to support it at the neck and use the other hand to lay the victim's arm farthest from you across his chest, bending it at the elbow *(left)*.

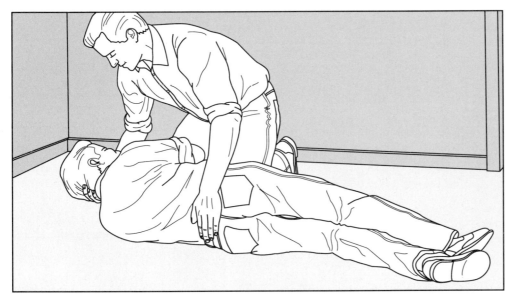

2 **Rolling the victim onto his side.** To roll the victim onto his side, place your knees as close as possible to his chest and abdomen. With one hand still under the victim's head, supporting it at the neck, slide your other hand under the victim's lower back on the side farthest from you; grip a belt loop or other part of his clothing to hold him securely, if necessary. Keeping your hand under the victim's head, supporting it at the neck, gently roll the victim toward you in one smooth but firm motion *(left)*. Stop rolling the victim when he is on his side, his chest and abdomen resting on your thighs.

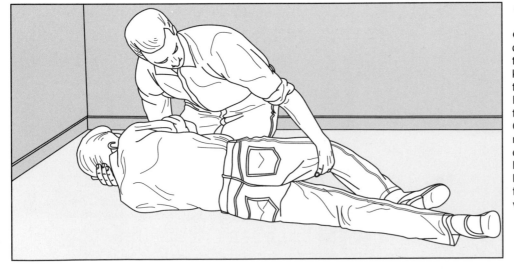

3 **Stabilizing the victim.** With one hand still under the victim's head, supporting it at the neck, use your other hand to pull the victim's upper leg toward you, bending it at the hip and the knee *(left)*; this position prevents the victim from rolling forward onto his chest. Raise the victim's head slightly and extend his lower arm straight out under it. Gently lower the victim's head until it rests comfortably on his extended arm, cushioned by the shoulder; reposition his extended arm, if necessary, to keep his head from falling off it. Then, carefully pull your knees away from the victim's chest and abdomen.

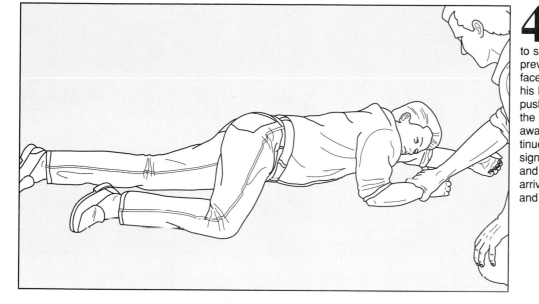

4 **Opening the victim's airway.**
Bend the victim's arm closest to you at the elbow *(left)*, allowing it to support his upper body; this position prevents the victim from rolling onto his face. Open the victim's airway by tilting his head back, gently lifting the chin and pushing the forehead; this action raises the lower jaw and draws the tongue away from the back of the throat. Continue monitoring the victim's vital life signs *(page 16)*, checking for breathing and taking a pulse until medical help arrives. Help the victim to stay calm and keep others away.

TREATING A VICTIM OF A FAINTING SPELL

Fainting spells. A fainting spell is a self-correcting form of mild shock that occurs when the blood supply to the brain drops, resulting in the victim's partial or complete loss of consciousness. A wide range of conditions can provoke a fainting spell—including overheating, fatigue, hunger and sudden emotional upset. Usually, the victim of a fainting spell recovers in a few moments when he is placed on his back with his head lower than his feet. Although a fainting spell is seldom serious, the victim can sustain an injury if he loses consciousness without notice. Often, the victim may exhibit signs of an impending fainting spell just prior to it; if they are detected, action can be taken quickly *(step right)* and the victim may not lose consciousness. Signs of an impending fainting spell include:

- Extreme pallor

- Sweating—beads of perspiration

- Cold or clammy skin

- Shallow or uneven breathing *(page 16)*

- Dizziness

- Numbness or tingling of the hands or feet

- Nausea

- Visual disturbances—images dark or blurry

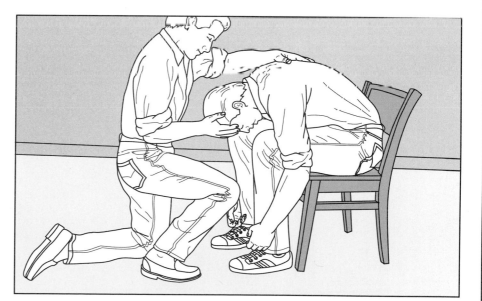

Treating a fainting-spell victim. If the victim exhibits signs of an impending fainting spell, take him to a well-ventilated area—outdoors, if possible. Have the victim sit and lower his head between his knees *(above)*. Loosen the victim's clothing at the neck, chest and waist. To keep the victim from falling forward, support his head with your hands or knees. If the victim suffers a fainting spell, place him on his back with his head lower than his feet; elevate his legs and feet with a pillow or blanket. Monitor the victim's vital life signs *(page 16)*, checking for breathing and taking a pulse; keep others away. Apply a cold cloth to the victim's face. If the victim does not recover within 2 minutes, seek medical help immediately.

TREATING A VICTIM OF SHOCK

Shock. Shock is the body's response to a failure of the circulatory system in providing sufficient blood and oxygen to the brain or other vital organ. Shock may be provoked by a loss of blood or other body fluid and can also result from a heart attack, nerve injury, fright, pain or an allergic reaction. Some degree of shock—immediate or delayed—may occur with any injury or illness; its effects can be lessened if its signs are detected and action is taken quickly *(step right)*. Signs of shock include:

• Restlessness and anxiety

• Pallor or bluish color of the skin

• Profuse sweating

• Cold or clammy skin

• Shallow, uneven or rapid breathing *(page 16)*

• Weak, irregular or rapid pulse *(page 16)*

• Extreme thirst

• Nausea or vomiting

• Unconsciousness *(page 16)*

• Glazed eyes with dilated pupils

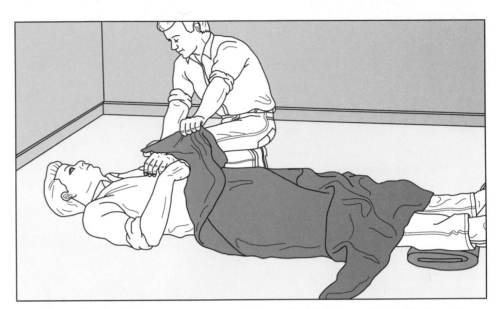

Treating a shock victim. Have someone call for medical help immediately. **Caution:** Do not move the victim if a spinal injury is suspected *(page 16)* or he is in pain. If the victim is unconscious *(page 16)*, place him in the recovery position *(page 20)*. If the victim is conscious, place him on his back with his head lower than his feet; elevate his legs and feet with a blanket or pillow. Loosen the victim's clothing at the neck, chest and waist. Monitor the victim's vital life signs *(page 16)*, checking for breathing and taking a pulse until medical help arrives. Keep the victim warm by covering him with a blanket *(above)*; keep others away. Do not apply a hot water bottle or heating pad or give the victim anything to eat or drink.

TREATING A VICTIM OF A FALL

Treating a fall victim. Have someone call for medical help immediately. **Caution:** Do not move the victim if a spinal injury is suspected *(page 16)* or he is in pain. Loosen the victim's clothing at the neck, chest and waist. Monitor the victim's vital life signs *(page 16)*, checking for breathing and taking a pulse until medical help arrives. Keep the victim warm, covering him with a blanket *(left)*; keep others away. Do not apply a hot water bottle or heating pad or give the victim anything to eat or drink.

TREATING A VICTIM OF A FALL (continued)

Preventing falls. Falls are a leading cause of injury in the home—especially for young children. To prevent falls on stairways, keep them well lit and free of clutter; discourage young children from playing on them. Install a specially-designed safety gate at the top and the bottom of each stairway to restrict the access of infants and young children to it; a gate held in place by pressure should only be used at the bottom of a stairway. Use only gates with openings smaller than a child's head and that are tall enough to prohibit a child from climbing over them. When installing a gate, position it low enough to the floor to keep a child from crawling under it *(left)*. To prevent falls from windows, do not rely on screens; keep unattended windows closed—an opening as small as 5 inches is enough for a young child to fit through. Discourage children from playing around windows by moving furniture away from them.

TREATING A CONSCIOUS CHOKING VICTIM (ADULTS AND CHILDREN)

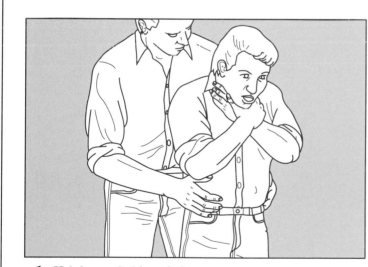

1 **Helping a choking victim.** Have someone call for medical help immediately. If the victim is an infant, treat him *(page 26)*. If you are the victim, help yourself *(page 26)*. Otherwise, encourage the victim to dislodge the obstruction by coughing *(above)*; any obstruction in his windpipe can cut off oxygen, giving him only minutes to live. If the victim does not dislodge the obstruction or cannot speak, act quickly to brace him *(step 2)*, preparing to deliver abdominal thrusts; if the victim is a child, place him on his back and deliver abdominal thrusts immediately *(step 4)*.

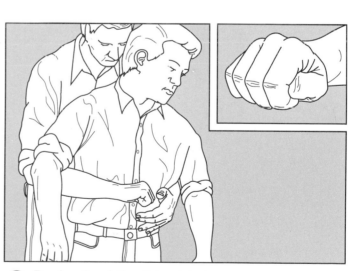

2 **Bracing the victim.** If the victim loses consciousness, treat him *(page 25)*. Otherwise, standing behind the victim, wrap your arms around his waist and under his arms. Make a fist with your hand, keeping your thumb tucked inside your fingers *(inset)*. Place your fist thumb-first against the victim's abdomen, just above the navel and below the rib cage *(above)*; if the victim is obese or pregnant, place your fist thumb-first against the midpoint of the breastbone just below the level of the armpits, using your fingers to locate and trace the curve of the rib cage to find it.

TREATING A CONSCIOUS CHOKING VICTIM (ADULTS AND CHILDREN) (continued)

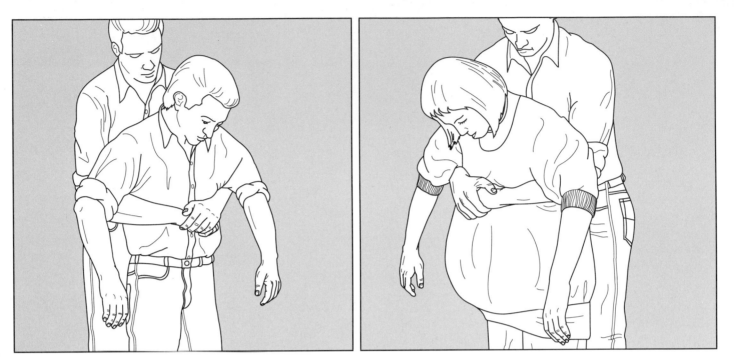

3 **Delivering abdominal thrusts to an adult.** If the victim is not obese or pregnant, grasp your fist with your other hand and press it into the abdomen, rolling it inward and upward in one short, quick thrust *(above, left)*; if the victim is obese or pregnant, grasp your fist with your other hand and press it straight into the chest cavity in one short, quick thrust *(above, right)*. Apply moderate pressure only with the thumb of your fist. Without opening your fist or shifting its position, repeat the procedure, continuing to deliver short, quick thrusts until the obstruction is removed. If the victim loses consciousness, treat him *(page 25)*. Otherwise, place the victim in the recovery position *(page 20)*.

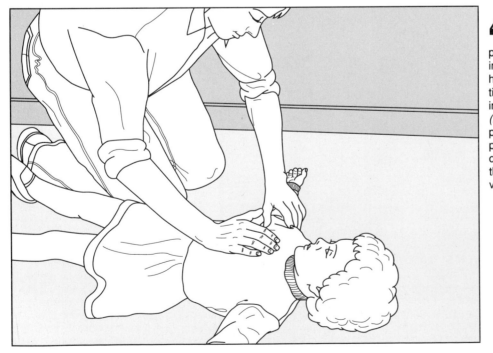

4 **Delivering abdominal thrusts to a child.** If the victim loses consciousness, treat him *(page 25)*. Otherwise, place the victim gently on his back, supporting his head in your hands, then kneel beside him. Place the palm of one hand on the victim's abdomen and press firmly on it, rolling inward and upward in one short, quick thrust *(left)*; apply light pressure only with your palm—not your fingers. Without shifting the position of your palm, repeat the procedure, continuing to deliver short, quick thrusts until the obstruction is removed. Then, place the victim in the recovery position *(page 20)*.

TREATING AN UNCONSCIOUS CHOKING VICTIM (ADULTS AND CHILDREN)

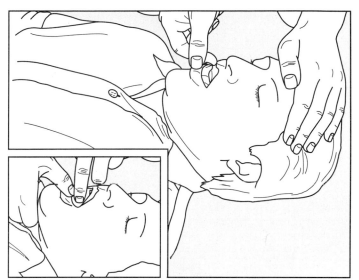

1 **Removing the obstruction.** Have someone call for medical help immediately. If the victim is an infant, treat him *(page 26)*. Otherwise, carefully lower the victim to the ground, placing him on his back; if necessary, have someone help you support the victim's weight, using your hands to set his head down gently *(above, left)*. Open the victim's mouth with the forefinger and thumb of one hand, then sweep the inside of his mouth for any obstruction using the forefinger of the other hand. Crossing your finger over your thumb, place your thumb against the victim's lower teeth and your finger against his upper teeth, then uncross your finger and thumb *(above, right)*, opening his mouth. Holding the victim's lower jaw and pressing down his tongue with your thumb to keep his mouth open, run your finger in along one cheek, across the throat and back along the other cheek *(inset)*, pulling out any obstruction. Monitor the victim's vital life signs *(page 16)*, checking for breathing and taking a pulse. If there is no breathing or the breathing is shallow or uneven, blow air into the victim's lungs *(step 2)*. Otherwise, place the victim in the recovery position *(page 20)*.

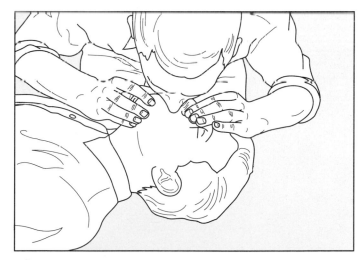

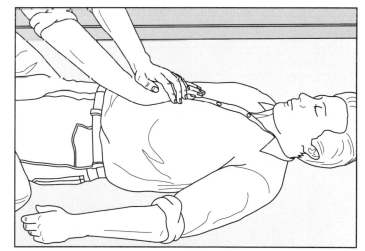

2 **Blowing air into the lungs.** Open the victim's airway by tilting his head back, gently lifting the chin and pushing down the forehead; this action raises the lower jaw and draws the tongue away from the back of the throat. Holding the victim's lower jaw to keep his mouth open, pinch his nostrils to close them. Take a deep breath, press your open mouth over the victim's mouth, forming a tight seal, and deliver the full breath slowly *(above)*; the victim's chest should rise. If the victim has a mouth injury or you cannot form a tight seal over his mouth, raise his lower jaw to close his mouth and deliver a full breath slowly through his nostrils. If the victim's chest does not rise, deliver abdominal thrusts immediately *(step 3)*. Otherwise, continue the procedure, checking for breathing response *(page 18)* until medical help arrives.

3 **Delivering abdominal thrusts.** If the victim is not obese or pregnant, place the palm of one hand against the abdomen; covering it with the other hand, press firmly, rolling inward and upward in one short, quick thrust *(above)*. If the victim is obese or pregnant, place the palm of one hand against the midpoint of the breastbone; covering it with the other hand, press firmly straight into the chest cavity in one short, quick thrust. Apply pressure only with your palm—not your fingers. Deliver 6 to 10 short, quick thrusts the same way, then sweep the victim's mouth again to remove any obstruction *(step 1)*. When the obstruction is removed, place the victim in the recovery position *(page 20)*. Otherwise, continue the procedure, monitoring the victim's life signs *(page 16)* until medical help arrives.

SELF-HELP FOR A CHOKING VICTIM

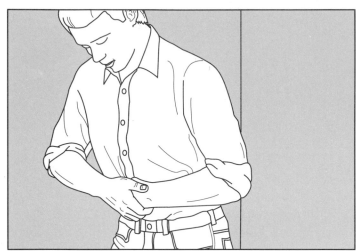

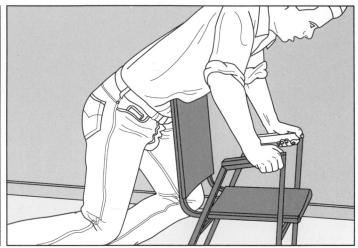

Self-delivering abdominal thrusts. Have someone call for medical help immediately. Make a fist with your non-dominant hand, keeping your thumb tucked inside your fingers *(inset, page 23)*. Place your fist thumb-first against your abdomen, just above your navel and below your rib cage. Grasp your fist with your other hand and press it into the abdomen, rolling it inward and upward in one short, quick thrust *(above, left)*; apply moderate pressure only with the thumb of your fist. Without opening your fist or shifting its position, repeat the procedure, continuing to self-deliver short, quick thrusts until the obstruction is removed. Or, the edge of a chair, table, sink, fence or other firm object can also serve well in a choking emergency. Gripping the object firmly with both hands, place your abdomen against its edge and press yourself into it, rolling inward and downward in one short, quick thrust *(above, right)*. Repeat the procedure, continuing to self-deliver short, quick thrusts until the obstruction is removed.

TREATING A CONSCIOUS CHOKING VICTIM (INFANTS)

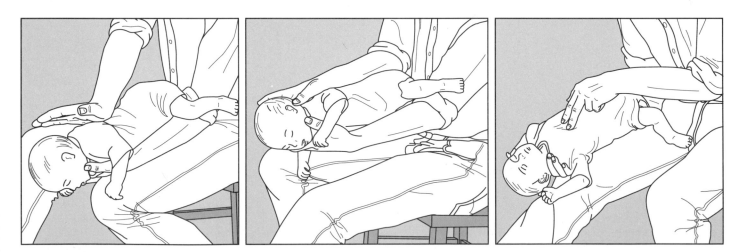

Removing the obstruction. Have someone call for medical help immediately. If the victim loses consciousness, treat him *(page 27)*. Otherwise, place the victim face down on your thigh, using one hand to support his head lower than his feet. Using the palm of your other hand, deliver 4 firm blows to the victim's back between his shoulder blades *(above, left)*. Then, supporting the victim between your arms and with your hands, roll him over *(above, center)* and place him face up on your other thigh, again with his head lower than his feet. If the obstruction is removed, place the victim in the recovery position *(page 20)*, keeping him from rolling onto his back. Otherwise, place 2 fingers against the midpoint of the victim's chest, about 1 inch below the nipples, and press straight into the chest cavity to a depth of 1/2 to 1 inch in one short, quick thrust *(above, right)*. Deliver 4 short, quick thrusts about 1 second apart the same way. When the obstruction is removed, place the victim in the recovery position. Otherwise, repeat the procedure, rolling the victim face down to deliver back blows and face up to deliver chest thrusts until medical help arrives.

TREATING AN UNCONSCIOUS CHOKING VICTIM (INFANTS)

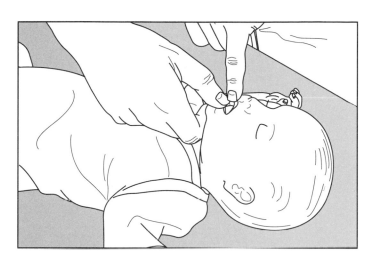

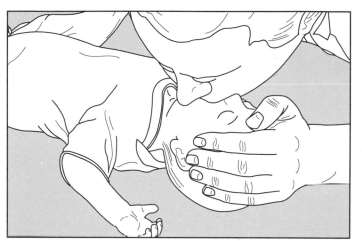

1 **Removing the obstruction.** Have someone call for medical help immediately. Gently open the victim's mouth using one hand, pressing down his tongue with your thumb and supporting his lower jaw with your forefinger. Looking into the victim's mouth, use the baby finger of your other hand to sweep in along one cheek, across the throat and back along the other cheek *(above)*, pulling out any obstruction. **Caution:** Do not make a blind finger sweep inside the mouth of an infant. Monitor the victim's vital life signs *(page 16)*, checking for breathing and taking a pulse. If there is no breathing or the breathing is shallow or uneven, blow air into the victim's lungs *(step 2)*. Otherwise, place the victim in the recovery position *(page 20)*, keeping him from rolling onto his back.

2 **Blowing air into the lungs.** Open the victim's airway by tilting his head back, gently lifting the chin and pushing down the forehead; this action raises the lower jaw and draws the tongue away from the back of the throat. Holding the victim's lower jaw to keep his mouth open, take a breath and press your open mouth over the victim's mouth and nose, forming a tight seal. Deliver the breath through the victim's mouth and nostrils slowly in 1 short blow *(above)*, without allowing air to flow from his lungs; his chest should rise. **Caution:** Do not deliver a full, deep breath to an infant; air may be forced into his stomach. If the victim's chest does not rise, deliver back blows and chest thrusts immediately *(step 3)*. Otherwise, continue the procedure, checking for breathing response *(page 19)* until medical help arrives.

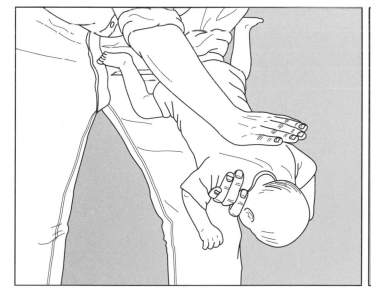

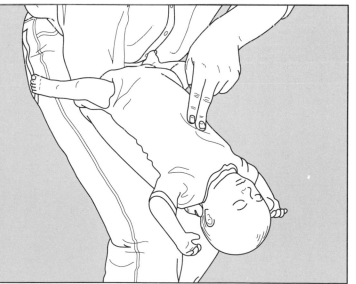

3 **Delivering back blows and chest thrusts.** Place the victim face down on your thigh, using one hand to support his head lower than his feet. Using the palm of your other hand, deliver 4 firm blows to the victim's back between his shoulder blades *(above, left)*. Then, supporting the victim between your arms and with your hands, roll him over and place him face up on your other thigh, again with his head lower than his feet. If the obstruction is removed, place the victim in the recovery position *(page 20)*, keeping him from rolling onto his back. Otherwise, place 2 fingers against the midpoint of the victim's chest, about 1 inch below the nipples, and press straight into the chest cavity to a depth of 1/2 to 1 inch in one short, quick thrust *(above, right)*. Deliver 4 short, quick thrusts about 1 second apart the same way, then sweep the victim's mouth again to remove any obstruction *(step 1)*. When the obstruction is removed, place the victim in the recovery position. Otherwise, continue the procedure, monitoring the victim's vital life signs *(page 16)* until medical help arrives.

CONTROLLING BLEEDING

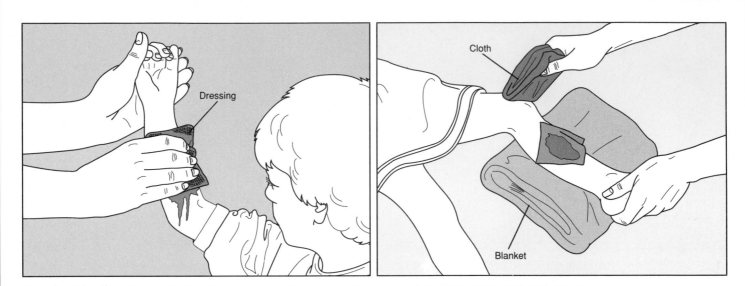

Stopping bleeding. To stop the bleeding, apply direct pressure with a gauze dressing or clean cloth and elevate the injury, raising the victim's arm above his head *(above, left)* or propping up the victim's leg with a blanket *(above, right)* or pillow. Direct pressure applied to the wound should stop the flow of blood and allow it to clot. If the dressing or cloth becomes blood-soaked, add another one over the first one; avoid lifting the dressing or cloth to inspect the wound. Continue applying direct pressure and keeping the injury elevated until the bleeding stops. If the wound is minor, wash it with soap and water, then bandage it: leg or arm *(step below)*; hand or foot *(page 29)*; head *(page 30)*. If the bleeding persists or the wound is deep or gaping, seek medical help immediately.

BANDAGING A LEG OR ARM INJURY

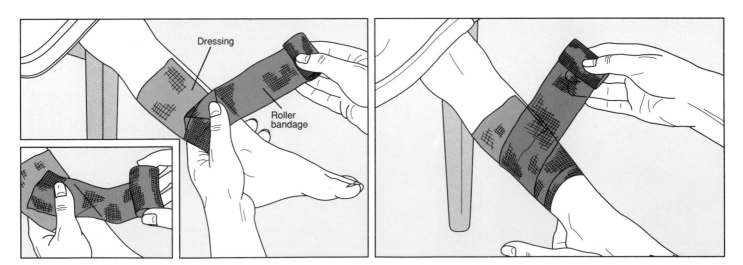

Bandaging a leg or arm wound. Apply direct pressure to stop the bleeding *(step above)*, then cover the wound with a clean gauze dressing. To hold the dressing in place on the limb, wrap it with a narrow gauze roller bandage—tight enough to hold it without restricting blood circulation. Starting at the narrowest part of the limb on one side of the dressing, hold the end of the roller bandage *(inset)* and wrap it once around the limb, allowing one corner to protrude. Fold the corner over the first turn, then secure it by wrapping the roller bandage around the limb *(above, left)* and over it. Continue wrapping the roller bandage around the limb until the dressing is covered, overlapping it by 1/3 to 1/2 its width each turn *(above, right)*. Wrap the roller bandage around the limb several extra turns, then hold it in place and use scissors to snip off the excess. To secure the end of the roller bandage, use medical tape or a safety pin; or, snip it along the center, then wrap the strands in opposite directions around the limb and tie them together.

BANDAGING A HAND OR FOOT INJURY

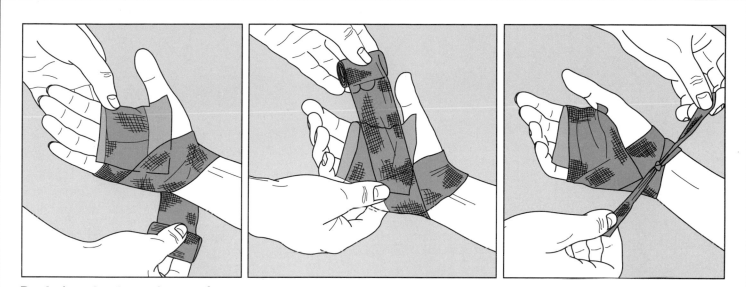

Bandaging a hand or wrist wound. Apply direct pressure to stop the bleeding *(page 28)*, then cover the wound with a clean gauze dressing. To hold the dressing in place on the wound, wrap the hand and wrist with a narrow gauze roller bandage—tight enough to hold it without restricting blood circulation. Start by wrapping the roller bandage several turns around the hand, then across it and around the wrist *(above, left)*. Cross the roller bandage over the turn around the wrist *(above, center)* and wrap it again around the hand, completing a figure-8 pattern. Continue wrapping the roller bandage around the hand and wrist following the same pattern until the dressing is held in place on the wound. Wrap the roller bandage around the wrist several extra turns, then hold it in place and use scissors to snip off the excess. To secure the end of the roller bandage, use medical tape or a safety pin; or, snip it along the center, then wrap the strands in opposite directions around the wrist and tie them together *(above, right)*.

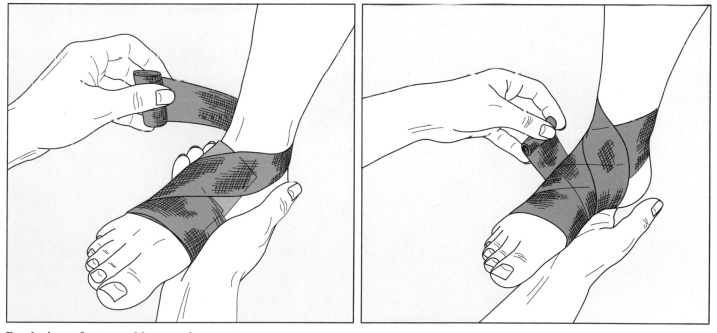

Bandaging a foot or ankle wound. Apply direct pressure to stop the bleeding *(page 28)*, then cover the wound with a clean gauze dressing. To hold the dressing in place, wrap the foot and ankle with a narrow gauze roller bandage—tight enough to hold it without restricting blood circulation. Start by wrapping the roller bandage several turns around the foot, then across it and around the ankle *(above, left)*. Cross the roller bandage over the turn around the ankle and wrap it again around the foot *(above, right)*, completing a figure-8 pattern. Continue wrapping the roller bandage around the foot and ankle following the same pattern until the dressing is held in place. Wrap the roller bandage around the foot several extra turns, then hold it in place and use scissors to snip off the excess. To secure the end of the roller bandage, use medical tape or a safety pin; or, snip it along the center, then wrap the strands in opposite directions around the ankle and tie them together.

BANDAGING A HEAD INJURY

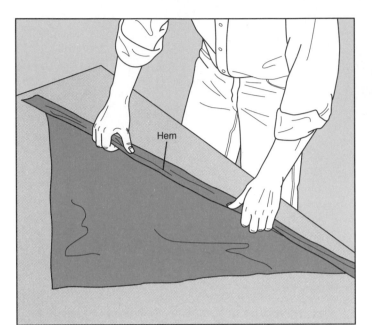

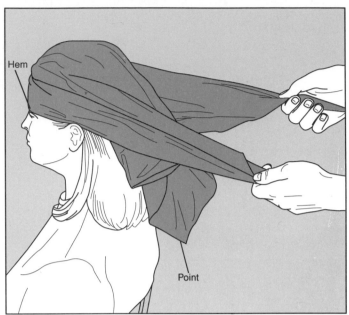

1 **Preparing the triangular bandage.** Have the victim sit upright on a chair, then apply direct pressure to stop the bleeding *(page 28)* and cover the wound with a clean gauze dressing. To hold the dressing in place, wrap the victim's head turban-style with a large triangular bandage. Lay the bandage on a clean, flat surface and fold a 2-inch hem along the base of it *(above)*. Standing behind the victim, hold the bandage hem-down to drape it over his head, covering the dressing.

2 **Draping the bandage.** Centering the point of the bandage with the nape of the victim's neck, drape it over his head and stretch the hem across his forehead, as low as possible to his eyebrows without covering them. Still holding the bandage by the hem, bring the ends of it around to the back of the victim's head *(above)*, as low as possible to his ears without covering them. Hold the ends of the bandage securely—it should be tight enough to hold the dressing without restricting blood circulation.

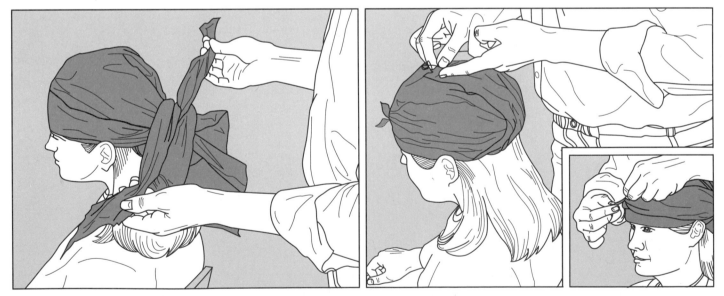

3 **Securing the bandage.** Cross the ends of the bandage at the back of the victim's head *(above, left)* and bring them around to the front of his head. To secure the bandage, tie the ends together across the victim's forehead *(inset)*, as low as possible to his eyebrows without covering them; or, use medical tape or a safety pin. Then, tug gently on the point of the bandage at the back of victim's head, putting light pressure on the dressing. To secure the point of the bandage, raise it over and tuck it behind the hem at the back of the victim's head; or, secure it to another part of the bandage using medical tape or a safety pin *(above, right)*, being careful not to prick the victim's head. Seek medical help following any head injury.

MAKING AN ARM SLING

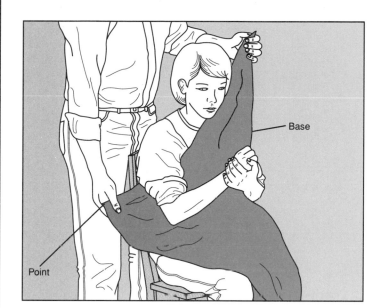

Base

Point

1 Draping the bandage. Have the victim stand or sit upright. Make an arm sling using a large triangular bandage; or, improvise using a scarf, necktie or belt or by supporting the injured arm between buttons on the victim's jacket or shirt. Having the victim or a helper support the injured arm diagonally across the chest, place the bandage under it, being careful not to apply pressure. Draw the bandage across the victim's chest, draping one end of its base over the shoulder of the uninjured arm and hanging its point below the elbow of the injured arm (above).

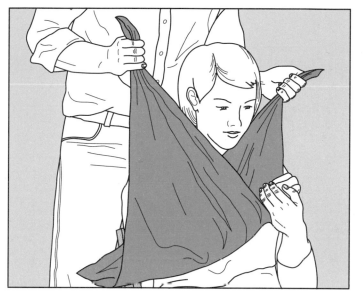

2 Folding the bandage around the arm. Fold the bandage carefully over the victim's injured arm, drawing the other end of its base up to the shoulder of the injured arm. Then, gently adjust the position of the bandage (above) until the ends of its base meet at the back of the victim's neck. If the victim complains of extreme pain, do not continue—stabilize the injured arm in a comfortable position and seek medical help immediately. Otherwise, adjust the bandage until the hand of the injured arm is supported about 4 inches above the elbow of the uninjured arm.

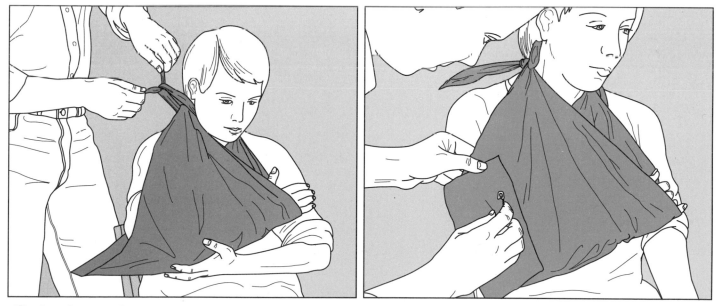

3 Securing the sling. With the victim or a helper still supporting the injured arm, secure the bandage at the side of the victim's neck, tying the ends of its base into a knot (above, left). Draw together the sides of the bandage at its point and fold them toward the victim's elbow, then gently fold the bandage over his upper arm and secure it with medical tape or a safety pin (above, right), being careful not to prick the victim's arm. Or, grip the bandage at its point and twist up the excess, then tie it into a knot at the victim's elbow.

MAKING AN ARM SLING (continued)

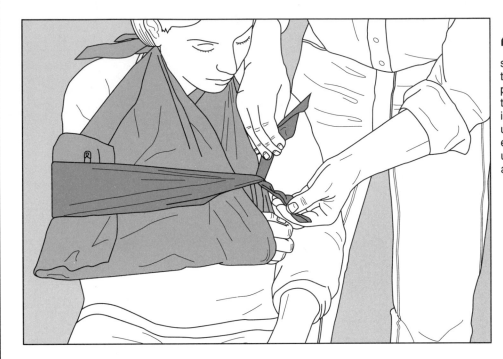

4 **Stabilizing the sling.** To immobilize the victim's arm and hold it against his chest for additional support, make a swathe about 4 inches wide using a large triangular bandage *(step below)*; or, improvise using a towel, blanket or shirt. Wrap the swathe around the victim just above the injured arm, passing over it and under the uninjured arm. To secure the swathe, tie its ends together into a knot on one side of the uninjured arm *(left)*. Seek medical help for any arm injury requiring a sling.

MAKING A SWATHE

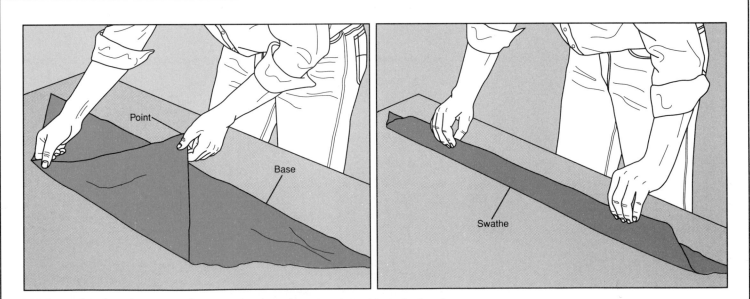

Folding a bandage into a swathe. To make a swathe, use a large triangular bandage. Lay the bandage on a clean, flat surface. First, fold the bandage in half, bringing its point over to its base *(above, left)*. Then, fold the bandage in half again, bringing its short edge over to its base. Continue folding the bandage in half the same way, making a swathe of the necessary width: about 4 inches wide to stabilize a sling *(step 4, above)* or secure a ring pad or other bandage; about 2 inches wide *(above, right)* to make a ring pad *(page 33)*. Make a number of swathes and keep them in your first-aid kit, preparing yourself to respond quickly in the event of a future medical emergency.

MAKING A RING PAD

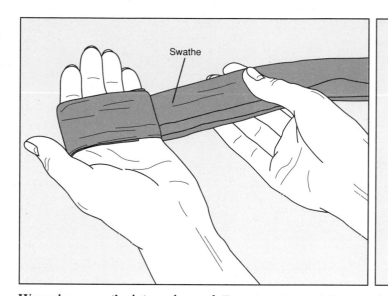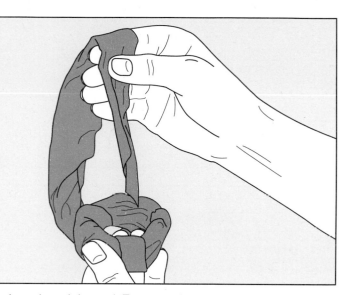

Swathe

Wrapping a swathe into a ring pad. To make a ring pad, first fold a large triangular bandage into a swathe about 2 inches wide *(page 32)*. Then, wrap the swathe twice around your hand *(above, left)*, forming a loop of the necessary diameter. Slide the loop off your hand and wrap the rest of the swathe length through and tightly around it in turns *(above, right)*, continuing until you form a

doughnut-shaped ring pad. To secure the end of the swathe, tuck it under a turn of the ring pad or use medical tape or a safety pin. To make a ring pad of a large diameter, tie together 2 swathes, if necessary, and use the same procedure. Make 1 or 2 swathes of different diameters and keep them in your first-aid kit, preparing yourself to respond quickly in the event of a future medical emergency.

SECURING A SHORT EMBEDDED OBJECT

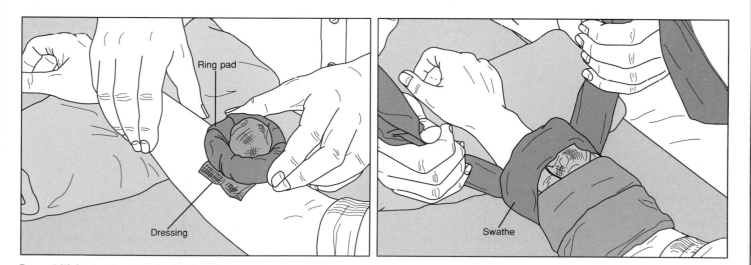

Ring pad

Dressing

Swathe

Immobilizing a short embedded object. Caution: Do not attempt to pull out the embedded object; seek medical help immediately. If the embedded object protrudes more than 2 inches from the skin, immobilize it *(page 34)*. Otherwise, elevate the injury, supporting it with a blanket or pillow, if necessary. Place a gauze dressing on the injury, covering the wound and the embedded object; do not apply any pressure to the embedded object. Make a ring pad of a diameter large enough to fit around the embedded object *(step above)* and position it on the injury *(above, left)*. To secure the ring pad, make 2 swathes about 4 inches wide *(page 32)*. Wrap each swathe around the injury over opposite sides of the ring pad *(above, right)* and tie its ends together into a knot.

STABILIZING A LONG EMBEDDED OBJECT

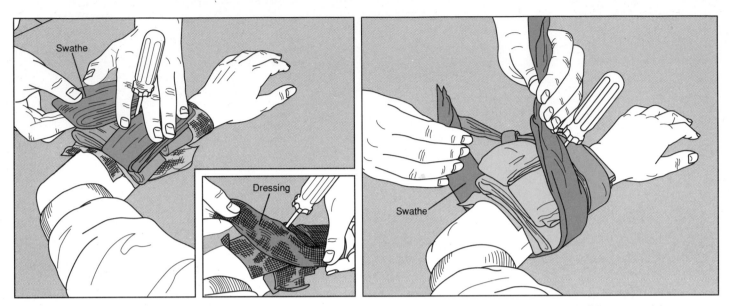

Immobilizing a long embedded object. Caution: Do not attempt to pull out the embedded object; seek medical help immediately. If the embedded object protrudes up to 2 inches from the skin, immobilize it *(page 33)*. Otherwise, elevate the injury, supporting it with a blanket or pillow, if necessary. Place gauze dressings on the injury, covering the wound around the embedded object *(inset)*; do not apply any pressure to the embedded object. Make enough swathes about 4 inches wide *(page 32)* to build up around the embedded object; fold the ends of each swathe into the center to double its thickness and position it on the injury *(above, left)*. Or, use feminine napkins the same way. To secure the swathes around the embedded object, make 2 swathes about 4 inches wide. Wrap each swathe around the injury on opposite sides of the embedded object *(above, right)* and tie its ends together into a knot.

PREVENTING EYE MOVEMENT

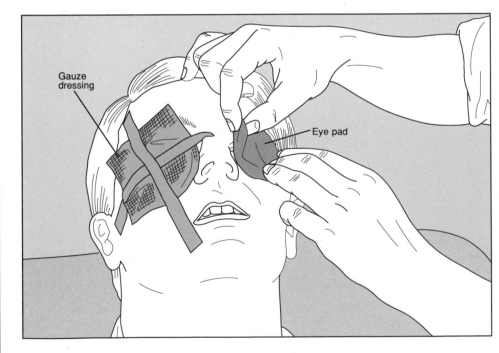

Applying eye pads. Flush any chemical or remove any foreign particle from the victim's eye *(page 35)*; seek medical help immediately for any eye injury involving a chemical or a foreign particle that cannot be removed. To prevent eye movement by the victim, cover both his eyes with eye pads. Have the victim close his eyes and lie down, verbally calming him. Gently place an eye pad on one eye, then cover it with a gauze dressing. Secure the dressing using medical tape, placing 2 strips in opposite directions across the eye without applying pressure on it. Repeat the procedure on the other eye *(left)*. Do not allow the victim to open or touch his eyes.

FLUSHING CHEMICALS FROM THE EYE

Flushing a chemical from the eye. Holding the eyelids of the injured eye apart with your fingers, position the injured eye under a gentle flow of cool water from a faucet *(above, left)* or pitcher; tilt the head to one side to prevent the chemical from washing into the uninjured eye. If you are outdoors, flush the injured eye the same way using a flow of water from a garden hose *(above,*

center). **Caution:** Remove any nozzle from the garden hose to prevent any eye injury from a strong jet of water. Do not allow a child to flush an injured eye on his own; hold his head with one hand and use the other hand to flush the injured eye for him *(above, right)*. Flush the injured eye for about 15 to 30 minutes, then prevent eye movement *(page 34)* and seek medical help immediately.

REMOVING FOREIGN PARTICLES FROM THE EYE

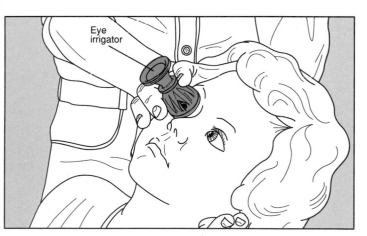

Eye irrigator

Removing a foreign particle from the eye. Hold the injured eye fully open using the forefinger and thumb of one hand. Inspect the eye closely for a foreign particle; if necessary, have the victim slowly rotate his eye to help expose it. **Caution:** Do not attempt to wipe away any foreign particle that is on the cornea, is embedded or adhered, or cannot be seen. Otherwise, gently wipe away the foreign particle using the twisted end of a tissue moistened with water *(above, left)*. Or, fill an eye irrigator with cool water and use it

to flush out the foreign particle. Have the victim lean forward with his eyes closed, then press the rim of the eye irrigator to the injured eye and tilt the victim's head back; some water may leak out. Have the victim open his eyes *(above, right)* and blink several times; the water inside the eye irrigator should flush out the foreign particle. Have the victim lean forward again to remove the eye irrigator. If the foreign particle cannot be removed, prevent eye movement *(page 34)* and seek medical help immediately.

TREATING A VICTIM OF A BURN

Treating burns. A burn is an injury to the skin tissue that may result from exposure to heat, a chemical, the sun, a hot liquid or steam, electrical current or lightning. The severity of a burn depends on the surface area and depth of the injury: a first-degree burn may cause reddening of the skin; a second-degree burn may cause the skin to turn red and blister; a third-degree burn may result in dry, pale white skin or brown, charred skin. By acting quickly *(step right)*, the pain and scarring of a burn can be lessened. Treat a burn following the precautions listed below:

• Seek medical help immediately for any burn larger in size than the victim's hand.

• Remove the victim's clothing, jewelry and footwear before any swelling begins.

• Leave clothing adhered to a burn; do not try to remove it.

• Do not apply any antiseptic spray or ointment; never apply butter, margarine or oil to a burn.

• Do not apply a chemical neutralizer such as vinegar, baking soda or alcohol to a chemical burn.

• Never break burn blisters.

• Do not breathe on or touch a burn.

• Do not touch a victim in contact with electrical current; push him away from the source using a wooden implement *(page 88)*.

Treating a burn victim. Gently remove the victim's clothing from the burn; do not attempt to remove any clothing adhered to it. Take off the victim's jewelry and footwear. If the burn is severe, gently cover it with a gauze dressing and seek medical help immediately. Otherwise, immerse the burn in cold water. Flush the burn with a gentle flow of water from a shower head *(above)* or garden hose or cover it lightly with a clean cloth soaked in water *(inset)*. Flush or soak the burn for at least 5 minutes, then bandage it: leg or arm *(page 28)*; hand or foot *(page 29)*; head *(page 30)*.

TREATING EXPOSURE TO LOW TEMPERATURE

Treating hypothermia. Hypothermia is caused by prolonged exposure to cold water or air; its victim can have a body temperature below 95 degrees Fahrenheit and not shiver, as well as slowed, shallow or uneven breathing and a slow, weak or irregular pulse. Move the victim indoors, remove any wet clothing and wrap him in dry blankets; focus on warming body areas where heat loss is greatest: the head, neck, chest, armpits and groin. Do not give the victim anything to eat or to drink. Call for medical help immediately and place the victim in the recovery position *(page 20)*. Monitor the victim's vital life signs *(page 16)*, checking for breathing, taking a pulse and taking his temperature until medical help arrives.

Treating frostbite. Unprotected skin exposed to extreme cold and high wind may become numb and white, symptoms of frostbite; the nose, ears, face, hands and feet are especially susceptible. Move the victim indoors and keep him warm *(step right)*, focusing on body areas where heat loss is greatest: the head, neck, chest, armpits and groin; allow the frostbitten skin to warm gradually. If you are outdoors, warm the frostbitten skin with heat from your hands or armpits. Frostbite is classified by degrees of severity; seek medical help immediately for severe frostbite.

• **First degree.** Reddish skin and prickly, burning sensations.

• **Second degree.** Blistered or mottled gray skin and prickly, burning sensations that lead to numbness.

• **Third degree.** Shiny-white, leathery skin and numbness.

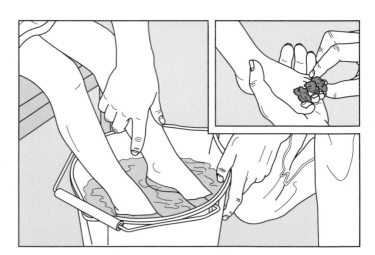

Treating a frostbite victim. Seek medical help immediately if the frostbite is severe. **Caution:** Do not rub or walk on frostbitten skin; crystallized moisture in it can cause severe injury. Gradually warm the frostbitten skin, using a bucket or basin filled with tepid water for feet *(above)* or hands. To help retain heat, roll up gauze dressings and place them between the toes *(inset)* or fingers. **Caution:** Do not immerse frostbitten skin in hot water or apply direct heat. After warming the frostbitten skin, apply a gauze dressing and secure it with medical tape.

HANDLING EXPOSURE TO HIGH TEMPERATURE

Treating heat-related illnesses. Heat-related illnesses are caused by the body's stress in trying to regulate its temperature during exposure to extreme heat. The sweating that cools the body can result in the depletion of important fluids and salts, causing muscular pains, spasms or cramps and exhaustion. Heat stroke is a serious heat-related illness resulting from the body's inability to regulate its temperature; the body's sweating mechanisms may not function and its temperature may rise rapidly. Quick action can reduce the seriousness of a heat-related illness *(step right)*. In the event of a heat wave or extremely high temperature, follow the precautions listed below:

• Consume plenty of liquids to help replenish the body fluids lost by sweating. In extreme heat conditions, drink about 10 ounces of water every 15 minutes.

• Avoid drinking alcohol.

• Do not eat hot foods or have heavy meals.

• Avoid strenuous exercise, outdoor activity and manual labor.

• Stay out of direct exposure to the sun; if possible, keep indoors in a well-ventilated, cool room.

• If you are outdoors, stay in the shade and wear a hat to protect your head against the sun.

• Dress properly for hot weather—do not wear heavy clothing. Wear light-colored clothing to help reflect heat and sunlight.

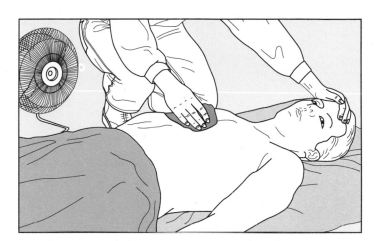

Treating a heat victim. Have the victim lie down in a cool place with his feet and legs elevated; support them with a pillow or blanket. Loosen the victim's clothing at the neck, chest and waist; remove excess clothing. Give the victim plenty of water to drink. Monitor the victim's vital life signs *(page 16)*, checking for breathing, taking a pulse and taking his temperature. To help lower the victim's temperature, give him a cool bath or shower, then have him lie down in a cool, air-conditioned room; direct a fan toward him, if possible. Gently rub the victim with a cloth soaked in cool water *(above)*; or, apply ice packs. If the victim loses consciousness or you cannot lower his temperature, call for medical help immediately.

TREATING POISONOUS PLANT IRRITATIONS

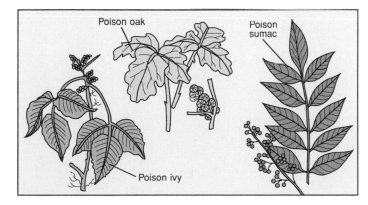

Identifying poisonous plants. A poisonous plant can grow as a bush, climbing vine, shrub or small tree. Poison ivy and poison oak can be identified by their leaves; only one leaf composed of three leaflets grows from each stem node, the center leaflet having the longest stem. Poison ivy leaflets are oval, tapered to a pointed tip *(above, left)*, and red in spring. Poison oak leaflets are rounder, lobed like oak leaves *(above, center)*, hairy on the top and velvety on the bottom. Poison ivy and poison oak may have greenish flowers in late spring and berries later; poison ivy berries remain all winter. Poison sumac *(above, right)* grows as a woody shrub or a small tree from 5 to 25 feet tall in the eastern U.S. and Canada.

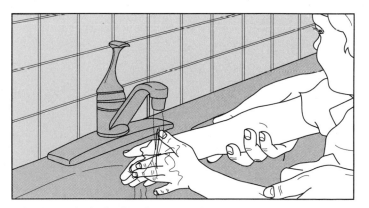

Treating skin irritation from a poisonous plant. Skin contact with a poisonous plant can cause an itchy rash, sometimes accompanied by headache and fever. Remove any clothing from the irritated skin and wash it with soap and water *(above)*; also wash any clothing in contact with the poisonous plant. To reduce itching, use a cotton ball to dab the irritated skin with hydrocortisone cream or calamine lotion; the itchiness should subside in 2 to 3 days. Do not scratch the skin; to help prevent a child from scratching himself, trim his fingernails. If the itchiness does not subside, seek medical help.

HANDLING SNAKEBITES

Treating a snakebite. Most snakes in the U.S. and Canada are not poisonous; the victim of a snakebite may experience no more than its initial pinch. A snakebite from a rattlesnake or a copperhead, water-moccasin or coral snake, however, can constitute a serious medical emergency; in 70 per cent of these snakebites, venom is injected—in an amount that depends on the size of the snake. Although a lethal amount of venom is seldom injected, treat any potentially poisonous snakebite as serious; call for medical help immediately. Blood is usually present around a snakebite and it may not clot if venom has been injected; to limit the poisoning effects of venom, restrict the flow of blood to the snakebite *(step right)*. If venom has not been injected with the snakebite, no symptoms should develop; otherwise, be alert to the following signs:

- Extreme pain and swelling around the snakebite

- Skin discoloration, swelling or blistering around the snakebite

- Shallow or uneven breathing *(page 16)*

- Slow, rapid or irregular pulse *(page 16)*

- Physical weakness

- Nausea or vomiting

- Visual disturbances

- Shock *(page 22)*

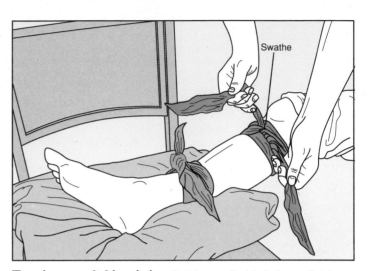

Treating a snakebite victim. Call for medical help immediately. Have the victim lie down and keep still, placing the injury on a pillow and keeping it level. To limit the poisoning effects of any venom, restrict the flow of blood to the snakebite by tying a swathe *(page 32)* about 4 inches from each side of it *(above)*; tie each swathe tight enough for a finger to fit under it and loosen it if any swelling occurs. **Caution:** Do not tie a swathe around the victim's neck, head or torso. Monitor the victim's vital life signs *(page 16)*, checking for breathing and taking a pulse until medical help arrives.

HANDLING INSECT BITES AND STINGS

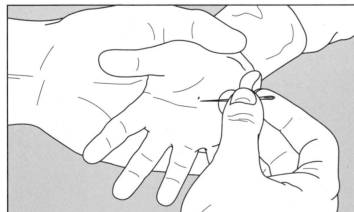

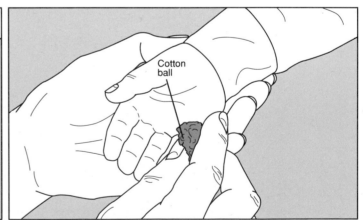

Treating an insect bite or sting. Remove any bee stinger and sac immediately. Sterilize a needle by holding it over a flame, then wipe it clean with a sterile piece of gauze; or, wipe it using a sterile piece of gauze dipped in rubbing alcohol or soak it in boiling water for 3 to 5 minutes. Use the tip of the needle to work out the stinger and sac *(above, left)*. Do not use tweezers; they can squeeze additional venom from the sac into the victim. Wash the skin with soap and water, then apply an ice pack to help relieve any pain or swelling. Monitor the victim's vital life signs *(page 16)*, checking for breathing; if he experiences difficulty breathing, physical weakness or extreme swelling, seek medical help immediately. To reduce itching, use a cotton ball to dab the skin with hydrocortizone cream or calamine lotion *(above, right)* or apply a paste of sodium bicarbonate and water; the itchiness should subside in 2 to 3 days. Do not scratch the skin; to help prevent a child from scratching himself, trim his fingernails. If the itchiness does not subside, seek medical help.

TREATING A VICTIM OF INGESTED POISON

Treating an ingested-poison victim. A child under 5 is the most likely victim of ingested poison; be alert to the following symptoms: breath odor; lip or mouth discoloration; dilated pupils; hot, dry skin; rapid, shallow or uneven breathing *(page 16)*; rapid, weak or irregular pulse *(page 16)*; lethargy or odd behavior; nausea, abdominal cramps or vomiting. If you suspect a child is the victim of ingested poison, ask him to show you the product he swallowed and call your local poison control center, hospital emergency room or physician immediately with the information; also provide the victim's age, his weight and the amount of the product he swallowed.

• Childproof your home *(step below)*, installing locks on the doors of all cupboards, cabinets and closets and all drawers containing medication or potentially harmful household products.

• Keep medication and household products out of the reach of children; remove them from under sinks and other accessible places.

• Keep medication and household products in their original containers and do not remove the labels or instructions. Never transfer a medication or household product to a food or drink container.

Open the victim's mouth and remove any foreign substance. If the victim vomits, place him in the recovery position *(page 20)*. **Caution:** Do not give the victim anything to eat or drink and do not induce vomiting unless you are advised by a medical professional. If you are advised to induce vomiting, give the victim syrup of ipecac or glasses of warm water; or, instruct him to tickle the back of his throat with his finger. Monitor the victim's vital life signs *(page 16)*, checking for breathing and taking a pulse. Seek medical help immediately and bring the container of the product ingested.

Follow precautions to prevent an accidental poisoning:

• Carefully read the label on a medication before administering it and follow the instructions exactly, paying close attention to warning and caution statements.

• Always replace the safety cap on a container. Put a medication or household product away safely as soon as you are finished with it; do not leave it out and unattended.

• Keep a bottle of syrup of ipecac on hand; use it to induce vomiting only when instructed by a medical professional.

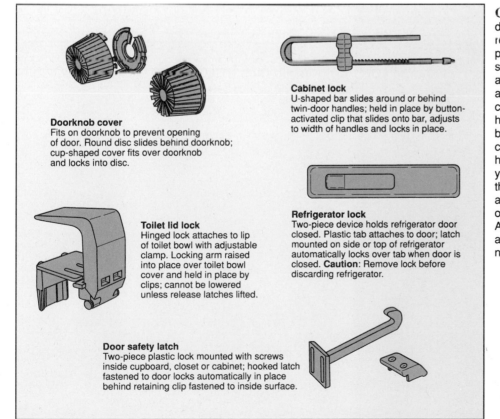

Doorknob cover
Fits on doorknob to prevent opening of door. Round disc slides behind doorknob; cup-shaped cover fits over doorknob and locks into disc.

Cabinet lock
U-shaped bar slides around or behind twin-door handles; held in place by button-activated clip that slides onto bar, adjusts to width of handles and locks in place.

Toilet lid lock
Hinged lock attaches to lip of toilet bowl with adjustable clamp. Locking arm raised into place over toilet bowl cover and held in place by clips; cannot be lowered unless release latches lifted.

Refrigerator lock
Two-piece device holds refrigerator door closed. Plastic tab attaches to door; latch mounted on side or top of refrigerator automatically locks over tab when door is closed. **Caution:** Remove lock before discarding refrigerator.

Door safety latch
Two-piece plastic lock mounted with screws inside cupboard, closet or cabinet; hooked latch fastened to door locks automatically in place behind retaining clip fastened to inside surface.

Childproofing your home. Provide an added measure of security for young children by restricting their access to potentially harmful products and areas in the house. Basic security devices for young children are available at child-product specialty stores as well as building supply centers and hardware centers. The locks at left include options for helping to keep young children out of cupboards, cabinets, closets and other places containing medication or potentially harmful household products. Other locks can hinder young children from climbing into and trapping themselves in a refrigerator or from playing around a toilet bowl and injuring themselves or damaging the plumbing system. **Caution:** A childproof lock is designed to deter children and is not a substitute for adult supervision; never leave a child unattended in the house.

PROVIDING MINOR FIRST AID

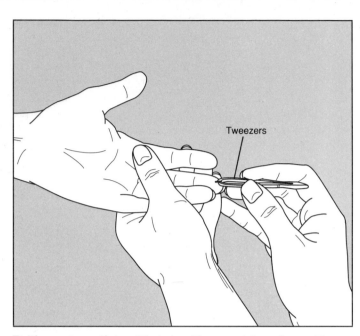

Pulling out a splinter. Wash the skin around the splinter with soap and water. A metal splinter may require treatment for tetanus; seek medical help. Otherwise, sterilize a needle and tweezers with rubbing alcohol or over a flame. Ease out the splinter from under the skin using the needle, then pull it out with tweezers *(above).* Wash the wound again with soap and water. If the splinter cannot be removed or the wound becomes infected, seek medical help.

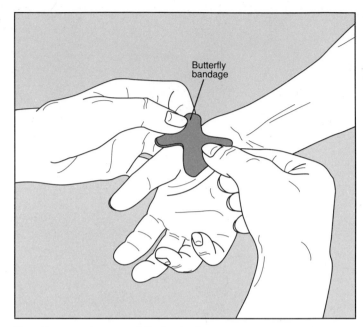

Treating a cut or scratch. Apply direct pressure to stop the bleeding *(page 28)*. If the wound is minor, wash it with soap and water, then bandage it: leg or arm *(page 28)*; hand or foot *(page 29)*; head *(page 30)*. For a narrow, shallow wound, draw its edges together and place one or more butterfly bandages along its length *(above)*; keep the wound bandaged until it heals completely. If the bleeding persists, the wound is deep or gaping, or the wound becomes infected, seek medical help immediately.

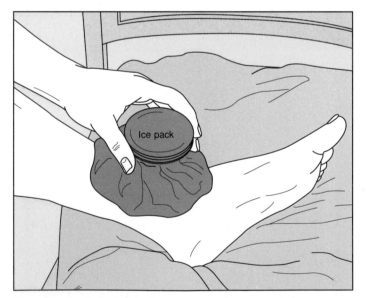

Treating a sprain or strain. Have the victim lie down or sit upright and remove any jewelry, clothing and footwear from the injury. Apply an ice pack or a plastic bag of ice cubes wrapped in a towel to soothe the injury and reduce any swelling *(above)*. After 48 hours, use a heating pad, a hot water bottle or a towel soaked in hot water to ease any pain and speed up the healing. If the pain does not subside after several days, seek medical help.

Stopping a nosebleed. Have the victim sit upright and lean slightly forward. To stop the bleeding, pinch the nostrils together just below the bone in the nose *(above)*; the bleeding should stop in 5 to 10 minutes. If the bleeding persists, wrap ice cubes in a towel or face cloth and hold it in turn against each side of the nose. If the bleeding still persists, seek medical help. Do not blow your nose for at least 2 hours after the bleeding stops.

PROVIDING MINOR FIRST AID (continued)

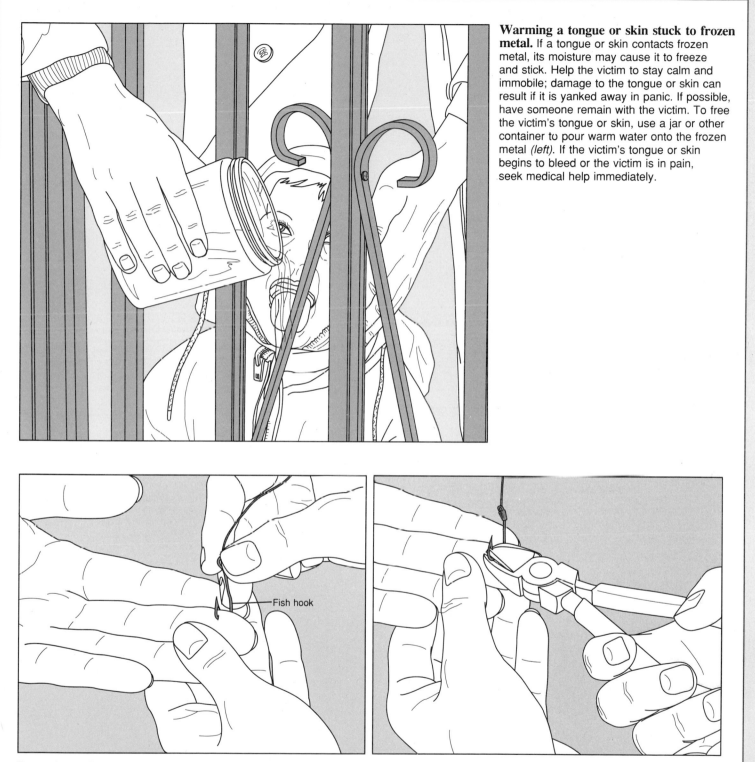

Warming a tongue or skin stuck to frozen metal. If a tongue or skin contacts frozen metal, its moisture may cause it to freeze and stick. Help the victim to stay calm and immobile; damage to the tongue or skin can result if it is yanked away in panic. If possible, have someone remain with the victim. To free the victim's tongue or skin, use a jar or other container to pour warm water onto the frozen metal *(left)*. If the victim's tongue or skin begins to bleed or the victim is in pain, seek medical help immediately.

Fish hook

Removing a fish hook. Most splinters can be removed from the skin with a sterilized needle and tweezers *(page 40)*. An embedded fish hook, however, usually must be cut off and carefully backed out of the skin. If the fish hook is deeply embedded in the skin or removing it is likely to result in additional injury, seek medical help immediately. Otherwise, gently push the fish hook through the skin until its barb is exposed *(above, left)*. Then, cut off the barb with wire cutters *(above, right)* and gently work the fish hook back out of the skin. Wash the wound with soap and water, then bandage it: leg or arm *(page 28)*; hand or foot *(page 29)*. Seek medical help for any tetanus treatment required.

HAZARDOUS MATERIALS

In addition to the known hazards of many household products, your home may also contain unknown sources of pollutants—materials releasing harmful gases or particles into the air you breathe or the water you drink. Many common household products and home repair materials contain chemicals that are poisonous if ingested; others that are caustic and can burn the eyes and skin or that emit toxic fumes and can cause dizziness, faintness or even loss of consciousness. As well, the walls and woodwork of a house built before 1960 may contain paint with a high lead content—hazardous if inhaled or ingested. And lead ions can leach into your water supply from lead pipes or lead solder used to join copper pipes. Protecting your family from hazardous materials requires a combination of preventive measures and safe work habits; consult the Troubleshooting Guide *(right)* for procedures to follow in a household emergency involving hazardous materials; it lists quick-action steps to take and refers you to information on pages 44 and 45.

If any family member suffers frequent or recurring illnesses that may be related to the air or water of your house, have your home professionally inspected and tested by a local or federal building authority or a certified house inspector as soon as possible. Refer to page 44 for information on identifying possible sources of indoor pollutants. For example, if you suspect a buildup of radon gas in the house, use a radon gas detection kit *(page 44)*. To prevent carbon monoxide poisoning, install at least one carbon monoxide gas detector in your home *(page 44)* and have any gas appliance, water heater and heating system professionally serviced at least once each year; have the gas company or your local fire department measure the level of carbon monoxide in the house. Make sure you and your family members are familiar with the distinctive odor of natural and propane gas; as an added precaution, install a gas detector near each gas appliance as well as any gas water heater and heating system *(page 44)*.

Take special precautions when using, storing and disposing of any household chemical product *(page 45)*; carefully read the label on its container and follow the manufacturer's instructions, heeding any hazard warning *(page 43)*. Protect yourself and the environment by obtaining information on the properties of the household chemical products in your home—and the harmful health effects associated with their use. If you are uncertain about the safety of any chemical product, ask your retailer or the manufacturer to provide you with its safety data sheet.

The list of Safety Tips *(right)* reviews basic precautions to follow in helping to prevent a household emergency involving a hazardous material. If you are ever in doubt about the safety of your home or your ability to handle an emergency involving a hazardous material, do not hesitate to call for help. Post the telephone numbers for your local hospital emergency room, poison control center, physician, and police and fire departments near the telephone; in most regions, dial 911 in the event of any life-threatening emergency.

SAFETY TIPS

1. If a member of your household suffers frequent or recurring illnesses that may be air- or water-borne, identify possible sources of indoor pollutants *(page 44)* and have your house professionally inspected and tested as soon as possible.

2. Use a radon gas detection kit to measure the level of radon gas in the house and install a carbon monoxide gas detector as well as natural gas and propane gas detectors *(page 44)*.

3. If your water has a peculiar taste, odor or color, or if members of your household suffer frequent illnesses that may be water-borne, have your water professionally tested *(page 107)*.

4. Carefully read the label on the container of any household product; follow the manufacturer's instructions for its use and pay special attention to hazard warnings *(page 43)*.

5. Never pour a chemical product down a house drain or into a septic system; it can harm the sewage system and may leach into the water supply. Call your local department of public works, the mayor's office or an environmental protection agency for the disposal regulations in your community.

6. Cloths soaked in paint, solvent, or adhesive or refinishing products can ignite spontaneously; hang them outdoors and allow them to dry thoroughly or store them in airtight metal or glass containers.

7. When using a flammable chemical product, have a fire extinguisher rated ABC or BC on hand *(page 55)* and know how to use it *(page 61)*. Do not pour water on a chemical fire. Install smoke detectors *(page 55)* throughout your home—including in your work area.

TROUBLESHOOTING GUIDE

SYMPTOM	PROCEDURE
Exposure to indoor pollutant suspected: family member suffers frequent illnesses	Identify sources of indoor pollutants *(p. 44)*
	Use radon gas detection kit *(p. 44)*
	Use carbon monoxide gas detector *(p. 44)*; have home tested for carbon monoxide
	Use natural and propane gas detectors *(p. 44)*; have gas appliances, water heater and heating system professionally serviced
Chemical product ingested	Treat ingested-poison victim *(p. 39)*
	Use chemical products safely *(p. 45)*
Chemical product in eye or on skin	Flush chemical from eye *(p. 35)*; treat chemical-burn victim *(p. 36)*
	Use chemical products safely *(p. 45)*
Dizziness, nausea, or blurred vision when using chemical product	Leave room immediately to get fresh air
	Read instructions on container label and seek medical help if necessary
	Use chemical products safely *(p. 45)*
Chemical product spilled	Clean up chemical spill *(p. 45)*
	Use chemical products safely *(p. 45)*

Safety goggles
Protect eyes from chemical splashes and foreign particles; should fit snugly.

Passive carbon monoxide gas detector
Sensor darkens in color in response to rising levels of carbon monoxide gas; replace detector annually or when it reaches its expiry date.

Dust mask
Disposable filter prevents inhalation of fine dust and fibers; works effectively up to 6 hours.

Chemical cartridge respirator
Interchangeable cartridges filter out toxic vapors; works effectively up to 8 hours. Follow manufacturer's instructions for use and store in sealed plastic bag.

Carbon monoxide gas detector
Battery-operated detector sounds alarm when dangerous levels of carbon monoxide gas present. Test batteries each month.

Radon gas detection kit
Activated-charcoal detector used for short-term testing of radon concentration levels in house; send detection kit to certified laboratory for analysis.

Rubber gloves
Heavy rubber gloves protect hands from caustic chemicals; can be made of rubber, neoprene or vinyl—recommended type usually specified on container label.

Natural gas and propane gas detector
Plug-in detector sounds alarm when concentrations of natural gas or propane gas present. Test detector once each month.

Flammable
A triangle with flames warns that product contains a flammable substance.

Explosive
A triangle with exploding object warns that container may explode if heated or punctured.

Poison
A triangle with skull and crossbones warns that product is poisonous if ingested or inhaled.

Caustic
A triangle with hand and test tube warns that product contains chemical which can burn skin and eyes.

CHECKING FOR INDOOR POLLUTANTS

Identifying indoor pollutants. Within your home there can be health-threatening pollutants. If any family member suffers frequent illnesses, have your house professionally inspected and tested; consult your local or federal environmental protection agency or department of health for a list of certified building inspectors and testing laboratories in your area.

To help you identify sources of indoor pollutants within your home, refer to the guidelines below:

• **Radon gas.** Radon gas, produced by uranium decay, is colorless and odorless; it can leach into a house through water from a private well, cracks in a foundation or a dirt floor. Prolonged exposure to radon gas increases the risk of lung cancer; use a radon gas detection kit to test for radon gas *(step below, left)*.

• **Asbestos.** Asbestos is a fire- and corrosion-resistant mineral product that may be in pipe coverings, insulation, floor or ceiling tiles, roofing materials, textured paints, and spackling or joint compounds; its use as a building material in the U.S. was outlawed in the 1970s. Asbestos is safe unless it is cut, flaking or damaged—then, it releases particles into the air. If you suspect your house contains asbestos, call an asbestos-removal professional; do not vacuum or sweep up the fibers.

• **Formaldehyde gas.** Plywood, particleboard, fiberboard and other manufactured products may contain formaldehyde, used as a binder and adhesive; urea formaldehyde foam insulation, used extensively in the 1970s, has formaldehyde in it. Formaldehyde leaches into the air in a process called "outgassing". To reduce the formaldehyde level in your home, use solid wood products or seal all unfinished wood products and have any urea formaldehyde foam insulation removed.

• **Lead.** Until the 1960s, lead was a major ingredient of house paints—dangerous only if chips of it are eaten or if dust from sanding or fumes from heat-stripping it are inhaled. To check the lead content of a paint, take a chip for professional testing. Lead ions from lead pipes or lead solder used to join copper pipes can leach into your water supply; check for lead pipes and lead solder *(page 107)*. Lead ions can leach into your food from lead-glazed crockery made in the U.S. before 1971; imported crockery is spot-checked by the Food and Drug Administration and may not be lead-free.

• **Carbon monoxide gas.** Carbon monoxide gas is colorless and odorless; it is produced when a gas burner has inadequate air supply for proper combustion and can build up in a fireplace if the flue damper is closed before a fire is completely extinguished. Install a carbon monoxide gas detector in your home *(step below, center)*; have any gas appliance, water heater and heating system professionally serviced at least once a year.

• **Natural and propane gas.** Natural and propane gas are treated with a sulphur-based chemical to give them a strong odor similar to rotten eggs, enabling a leak to be easily detected; as a precaution, install a natural gas and propane gas detector near any gas appliance, water heater and heating system *(step below, right)*.

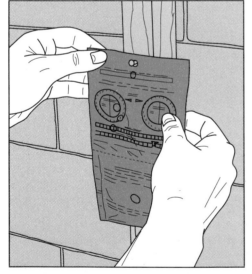

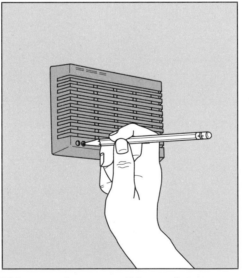

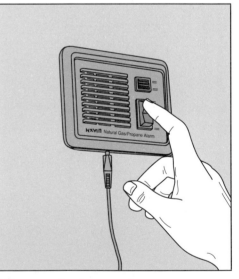

Using a radon gas detection kit. Set up a radon gas detection kit *(page 43)* following the manufacturer's instructions, placing it at the lowest level of your house about 20 inches above the floor and at least 4 inches from any object *(above)*; avoid placing it near any heat source or in any draft. Mark the kit identification number, set-up date and set-up site on the log sheet. When the test period elapses, remove the kit and seal it in its storage packet. Record the retrieval date on the log sheet and return it with the storage packet to the manufacturer for analysis.

Using a carbon monoxide gas detector. Following the manufacturer's instructions, install at least one battery-operated carbon monoxide gas detector *(page 43)* on the ceiling or at the top of a wall in your home—preferably more than 6 feet above the floor near a gas appliance, water heater or heating system or a fireplace. Test the detector once each month, depressing the test button *(above)* and holding it for 10 seconds. Replace the battery if the detector does not sound when it is tested—or if it emits a chirping sound, indicating the battery is wearing down.

Using a natural gas and propane gas detector. Following the manufacturer's instructions, install at least one natural gas and propane gas detector *(page 43)* on a wall near each gas appliance, water heater and heating system: 6 to 12 inches below the ceiling for natural gas; 3 to 4 inches above the floor for propane gas. Plug in the detector and test it once each month, depressing the test switch *(above)* and holding it for 10 seconds. If the detector does not sound, replace it or have it professionally serviced.

USING CHEMICAL PRODUCTS SAFELY

Preventing chemical emergencies. Special care is required when using any chemical product, including prescription medication—and proper use of chemical products includes safely storing and disposing of them. The chemicals contained in many common household products are poisonous if ingested; others are caustic and can burn the eyes and skin or emit toxic fumes that can cause dizziness, faintness or even loss of consciousness. Read the label on the container of any household product; follow the manufacturer's instructions and pay special attention to hazard warnings, usually identified by symbols *(page 43)*. If you are uncertain about the safety of a household product, ask your retailer or the manufacturer for its safety data sheet—which gives information on its physical, chemical and toxicological nature. Follow the guidelines listed below to help prevent a chemical emergency:

• Always wear the proper protective gear when working with chemical products *(page 43)*.

• If you transfer a chemical product or medication from its original container, label the new container and transfer as well any hazard warning and special instructions about its use. Never transfer a chemical product or medication to a food or drink container.

• Keep all chemical products and medication out of the reach of children. If a child contacts or ingests a poisonous material, call the poison control center immediately, then treat the victim *(page 39)*.

• Store chemical products in a cool, dry, locked cupboard; keep the containers capped tightly.

• Never mix ammonia with household bleach; the solution produces deadly fumes.

• Do not use an aerosol near any heat source or puncture the can.

• When using a chemical product that emits toxic fumes, ventilate the work area well; if you feel faint or sick, leave the room and get fresh air, then improve ventilation before continuing to use it.

• Do not eat food or drink alcoholic beverages while using chemical products that emit toxic fumes—the combination can cause illness. Do not smoke while using a flammable chemical product.

• Keep a fire extinguisher rated ABC or BC *(page 55)* around flammable chemical products; know how to use it *(page 61)*.

• Do not pour any chemical product down a house drain or into a septic system. Call your local department of public works, the mayor's office or an environmental protection agency for the disposal regulations in effect for your community

CLEANING UP A CHEMICAL SPILL

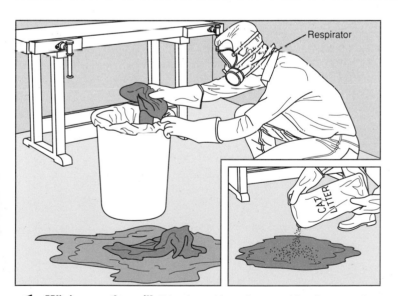

1 **Wiping up the spill.** Wearing rubber gloves, rubber boots, safety goggles and a respirator, clean up any spill of a toxic chemical immediately; extinguish any flame and keep people and pets away. Open all the windows and doors of the room to the outdoors. If the spill is small, soak it up with cloths or paper towels, then place them in a plastic garbage bag for disposal *(above)*. For a large spill, pour an absorbent material such as cat litter or vermiculite on it *(inset)*; when the spill is soaked up, scoop up the absorbent material with a shovel or a broom and dust pan, then bag it for disposal.

2 **Washing the spill site.** Wearing rubber gloves, rubber boots, safety goggles and a respirator, remove remaining traces of the spill using a clean cloth or stiff-bristled brush dipped in an appropriate solvent—usually marked on the label of the chemical container. Then, scrub the area thoroughly with a solution of mild household detergent and warm water *(above)*, rinse it and wipe it dry with clean cloths or paper towels. Dispose of chemical-soaked cloths, paper towels and absorbent material following the regulations of your community. Change out of your clothes and launder them separately.

HOUSEHOLD SECURITY

A break-in can rob you of valuable possessions in minutes and leave you with psychological scars for years. Take precautions to ensure your home is not an easy target for an intruder. Check your house regularly for vulnerable spots and undertake remedial action as soon as possible; see page 47 for typical security locks and devices, most of which are readily available at a building supply center or hardware store. Remember that home security also includes the house surrounds—locking the front door on your way out is rarely enough of a deterrent for a motivated burglar.

The Safety Tips listed at right cover basic guidelines to follow in helping to maintain household security. Specific measures to take in securing the windows and doors of your home—the openings most vulnerable to forced entry by an intruder—are presented within the chapter. For example, secure a sliding window or patio door using a bar lock or temporarily with a broom handle or other length of wood *(page 49)*. Or, install nails to secure a double-hung window *(page 50)*. When installing security locks and devices, keep in mind your need for unobstructed primary *(page 63)* and secondary *(page 64)* fire escape routes; call your local police or fire department for assistance in determining the security measures best suited to your home.

Homeowner insurance policies typically provide basic protection against burglary and other types of theft. Update your insurance policy regularly, making sure your house and its contents are insured for an appropriate amount; usually, contents are covered for up to 50 per cent of the amount for the house. Consider adding special endorsements to your insurance policy for valuable artwork, jewelry and heirlooms. Notify your insurance agent of any upgrading in the security system of your home; in some instances, you may qualify for a discount in your insurance premium.

Consult the Troubleshooting Guide *(page 48)* for procedures on preventing and handling household security emergencies; it provides you with quick-action steps to take and refers you to pages 49 to 53 for detailed information. After a break-in, for instance, temporarily secure any damaged or broken door *(page 51)* or window *(page 52)* until a permanent repair can be undertaken. Or, in the event of a break-in while you are at home, avoid confronting the intruder, if possible; leave the house immediately and call the police department from the home of a neighbor. And in the event someone locked in a room requires assistance, you may have to force open a door to rescue him *(page 53)*.

Post the telephone numbers for your local police and fire departments and your insurance agent near the telephone. In most regions, dial 911 in the event of any life-threatening emergency. If you are ever in doubt about the security of your home or neighborhood, do not hesitate to call for help; even in non-emergency situations, your local police can answer questions about the security of your home and respond to concerns about suspicious activity or noises in your neighborhood.

SAFETY TIPS

1. Keep a hidden list of your valuable items and their serial numbers, as well as your credit cards and their account numbers. Open a safety deposit box for storing valuable items. Do not keep large sums of cash at home.

2. Engrave the valuable items in your home with the number of your driver's license; post stickers in the doors and windows of the house warning burglars your valuable items are stamped for identification. Photograph valuable items that cannot be engraved and keep the photographs in a safe place.

3. Form a neighborhood watch group to help prevent crime. For information on how to start up a group, contact your local police department or law enforcement agency.

4. Install security locks and devices *(page 47)* judiciously throughout your home. Consult a security professional about installing an alarm system; if necessary, call your local police department to have one recommended.

5. Do not hide any key to an exterior door of your house under a door mat or in any other outdoor location. When you are leaving the house, even for a short period of time, make sure all the windows and doors are closed and locked.

6. Do not keep a key in any lock; do keep a key near each lock to ensure it can be opened quickly in the event of a fire.

7. Keep the area around each entry to your home visible from the street and well lit at night. Trim the trees and shrubs in your yard away from the windows and doors, and install outdoor lighting fixtures around the perimeter of the house.

8. Do not leave a ladder unattended in your yard. Relocate any trellis, drainpipe or other outdoor fixture that can be climbed to gain access to an upper-story window.

9. Ensure each wooden exterior door is of solid wood. Replace any exterior door hinges with non-removable pins.

10. Keep selected lights and a radio on when you are away from home for a long period of time; use timer-extensions to turn them on and off automatically at preset times. Give a neighbor the telephone number where you can be reached.

11. Ask a reliable neighbor to check your house daily while you are away on vacation; have him park his car in your driveway. Arrange to have your lawn mowed or your driveway cleared of snow. Stop newspaper and milk deliveries and have someone collect your mail. Call your insurance agent for information on the security measures required by your homeowner insurance policy while you are absent; in some instances, failing to fulfill them may void the policy.

12. Ask your local police department to help you conduct a thorough security check of your home, identifying vulnerable spots and the best remedial actions to take.

13. Never leave a note on an exterior door when you leave the house; it can alert a burglar to your unoccupied home.

14. If you move to a new house, have each keyed lock of the doors and windows changed as soon as possible.

15. Have your house number prominently displayed and light it at night; in the event of a household security emergency, you will want the police to be able to find your house quickly.

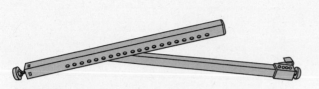

Security bar
For securing sliding window or patio door; hinged, adjustable metal bar fits between inside and outside frames.

Keyed security bolt
For securing sliding window or patio door; tempered metal bolt fits into predrilled hole and locked in place. Key nearby to unlock window or door in the event of an emergency.

Wide-angle door viewer
Special wide-angle lens allows view of exterior area around door or solid wood; available in 135-, 180- and 200-degree views.

Alarm systems
Many types available: most emit loud noise from a bell, siren or tone generator; some have strobe light that flashes when alarm activated and may have also built-in fire sensor.

Hasp lock
For temporarily securing door that sits flush with jamb when closed; secured with padlock.

Door guard
Strong zinc-alloy door guard allows door to be opened slightly while resisting forced entry.

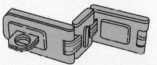

Flexible hasp lock
For temporarily securing door that does not sit flush with jamb when closed; secured with padlock.

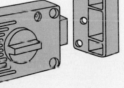

Deadbolt lock with alarmed rim
Battery-powered unit sounds alarm when force applied to locked door.

Padlock
To secure hasp locks; use rustproof type outdoors.

Outdoor lighting fixture
Incandescent floodlights shed narrow cone of light; low-pressure sodium lights cast bright circle of light. Choose fixture with light-sensitive photoelectric cell that automatically turns lights on and off.

Keyed sash-type window lock
For securing double-hung window with wooden frame; keyed section installed on top rail of lower window, stile section installed on bottom rail of upper window. Keep key nearby to unlock window in the event of an emergency.

Window guard
Adjustable to fit across most windows; choose type easy to remove from interior. Keep key nearby to unlock guard in the event of an emergency.

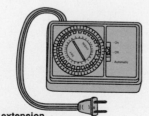

Timer extension
Can be programmed to turn lights on and off automatically at preset times.

TROUBLESHOOTING GUIDE

SYMPTOM	PROCEDURE
Break-in of your home suspected: door or window of house forced open	Do not enter house
	Call police department immediately from home of neighbor
	Enter house only when advised by police and begin insurance file: list valuables stolen and record any damage by taking photographs or using video camera
	Notify insurance agent of break-in as soon as police report completed
	Ask neighbors about any suspicious activity or noises and inform police of findings
	If necessary, temporarily secure any damaged or broken door (p. 51) or window (p. 52)
	Have any permanent repair required undertaken as soon as possible
Break-in of neighbor's home suspected: door or window of house forced open	Do not enter house
	Call police department immediately from your home; provide full address of neighbor's house
	Notify neighbor of break-in as soon as possible
	Ask neighbors about any suspicious activity or noises and inform police of findings
	If necessary, temporarily secure any damaged or broken door (p. 51) or window (p. 52)
Break-in attempt of your home suspected: suspicious activity or noises outside house	Avoid confronting any intruder
	Leave house immediately and call police department from home of neighbor
	Re-enter house only when advised by police and begin insurance file: record any damage by taking photographs or using video camera
	Notify insurance agent of break-in as soon as police report completed
	If necessary, temporarily secure any damaged or broken door (p. 51) or window (p. 52)
	Have any permanent repair required undertaken as soon as possible
Break-in attempt of neighbor's home suspected: suspicious activity or noises outside house	Call police department immediately from your home; provide full address of neighbor's house
	Stay on telephone and inform police of any further developments
	Notify neighbor of break-in as soon as possible
	If necessary, temporarily secure any damaged or broken door (p. 51) or window (p. 52)
House vulnerable to break-in	Follow basic safety tips (p. 46) to help prevent break-in
	Install security locks and devices (p. 47) judiciously; secure windows and doors (p. 49)
	Have alarm system professionally installed
	Have police department conduct security check of house
Exterior door lock broken	Temporarily secure door (p. 51)
	Have permanent repair undertaken as soon as possible
Window broken	Temporarily secure window (p. 52)
	Have permanent repair undertaken as soon as possible
Locked out of house	If exterior door lock frozen, chip any ice off lockset; heat key with match or lighter, or spray lock with commercial lock de-icer
	Call locksmith
Locked out of room; person in room requires assistance	Open locked interior door (p. 53) to rescue person
	If necessary, have someone call for medical help immediately; monitor victim's vital life signs (p. 16)
Locked out of room	Open locked interior door (p. 53)
	Fit credit card between latch and strike plate to work door open
	If door hinges accessible, remove them and pry door out of frame
	Call locksmith

SECURING WINDOWS AND DOORS

Installing security locks and devices. To help ensure your home is not an easy target for intruders, equip the windows and doors with security locks and devices *(page 47)*. Keep in mind your emergency escape routes *(page 63)*; a barred window, for example, may keep out an intruder but can obstruct your route to safety in the event of a fire. Call your local police or fire department for assistance in determining the security measures best suited to your needs and follow the guidelines below:

• On each double-hung window, install a sash-mounted window lock; for greatest security, use a keyed type *(page 47)*. Or, secure double-hung windows with nails *(page 50)*.

• To secure a sliding window or patio door, install a keyed security bolt *(page 47)* or an adjustable bar lock *(step right)*; as a temporary measure, use a broom handle or a length of wood *(step below)*.

• An adjustable window guard *(page 47)* can be used to secure a window at ground level; be sure any primary *(page 63)* or secondary *(page 64)* escape route is not obstructed.

• Ensure each wooden exterior door is of solid wood; equip it with a deadbolt lock, using heavy-duty screws to fix the strike plate. As an added security measure, install an alarmed-rim type of deadbolt lock *(page 47)*.

• Install a wide-angle door viewer in each solid exterior door *(page 50)*; as an added security measure, also install a door guard *(page 47)*.

• Always lock the windows and doors of your house before you leave it. Do not keep the key in any security lock or device—even if it cannot be seen from outdoors. Lock any interior door to the basement, garage or utility room, for example, isolating the area from other rooms of the house.

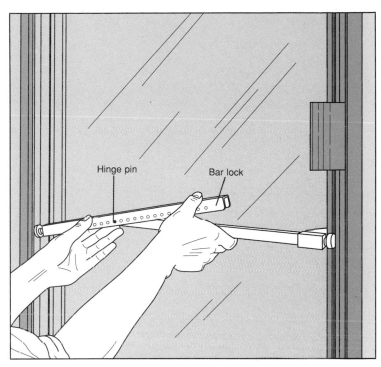

Securing a sliding window or patio door. To secure a sliding window or patio door, install an adjustable bar lock or a keyed security bolt *(page 47)*; as a temporary measure, use a broom handle or a length of wood *(step below)*. To adjust the length of a bar lock, depress the hinge pins and separate the bar sections. Close the window or patio door and align the bar sections across it parallel to each other, one end against the inside frame and one end against the outside frame; then, depress and fit in the hinge pins. For a small adjustment to the length of the bar lock, rotate the pad at each end of it. To install the bar lock, position it against the inside and outside frames, then press down *(above)* until it snaps snugly into place.

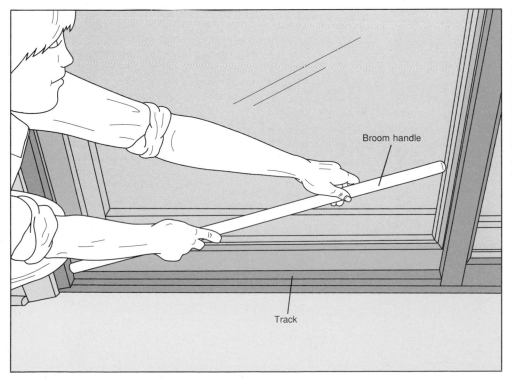

Temporarily securing a sliding window or patio door. To temporarily secure a sliding window or patio door, use a broom handle or a length of wood; for greatest security, install an adjustable bar lock *(step above)* or a keyed security bolt *(page 47)*. To determine the length of the broom handle or wood needed, close the window or patio door and measure the distance along the bottom track between the inside and outside frames. Cut the broom handle or wood to length using a saw, then wedge it into place along the bottom track between the inside and outside frames, angling it into position *(left)*.

SECURING WINDOWS AND DOORS (continued)

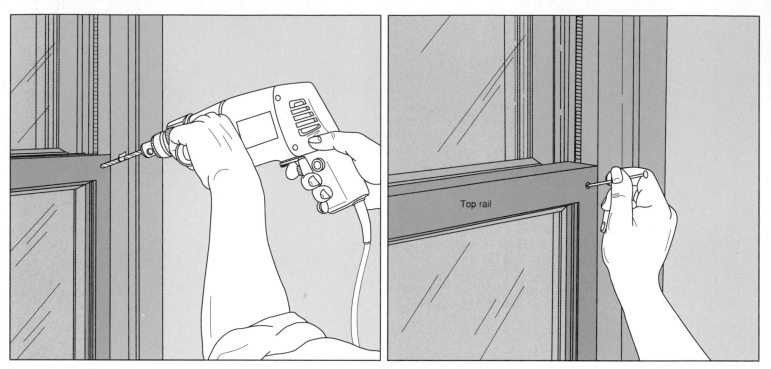

Securing a double-hung window. Secure a double-hung window using a sash-mounted window lock *(page 47)* or with nails. To install nails, close the window and bore a hole at each end of the top rail on the lower window about 1/2 inch from the edge. Using a drill fitted with a bit of a diameter slightly larger than a nail, bore each hole at a slight downward angle through the top rail of the lower window and about halfway into the bottom rail of the upper window *(above, left)*; wrap tape around the bit to know when to stop drilling. Fit a nail into each hole *(above, right)*, letting its head protrude slightly for easiest removal; or, take out the nail using a magnet. To disguise each nail, paint it to match the color of the window frame.

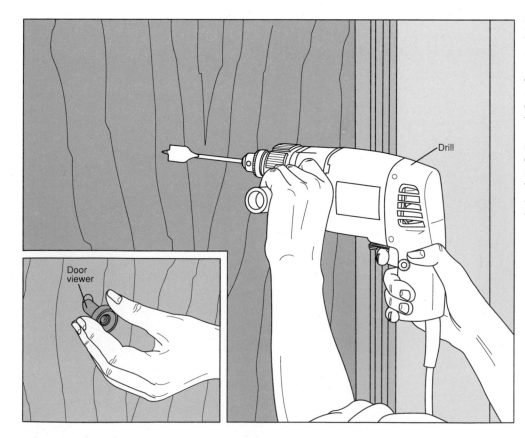

Installing a wide-angle door viewer. To permit you to see a caller without opening the door to him, install a wide-angle door viewer *(page 47)*. Mark the position for the door viewer at the center of the door at a height that all family members can reach. Using a drill fitted with a bit of the same diameter as the shank of the door viewer, bore through the door at the mark *(left)*. Unscrew the door viewer and fit each section into the hole from the appropriate side of the door, then screw the sections together *(inset)*; if necessary, use a screwdriver or a coin to tighten the door viewer. As an added security measure against the forced entry of a caller, also install a door guard *(page 47)*.

TEMPORARILY SECURING A DOOR

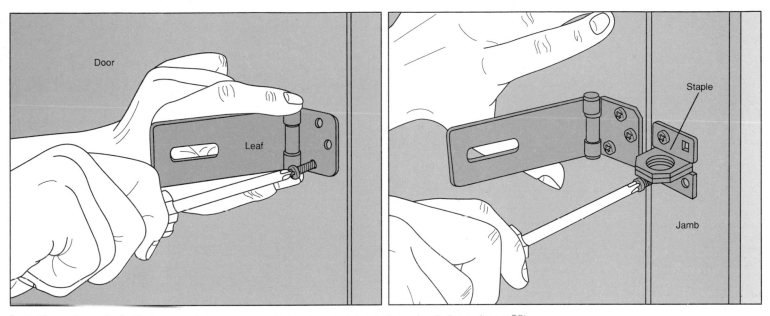

Installing a hasp lock. To temporarily secure an exterior door, install a buttress bar indoors *(page 52)*. Or, secure the door with a hasp lock *(page 47)*; if the door is not flush with the jamb when it is closed, use a flexible hasp lock *(step below)*. Close the door and position the hasp lock: the leaf section on the door and the staple section on the jamb; mark the edges of each section with a pencil. Holding the leaf section in position, mark each screw hole. Bore a hole for a screw at each mark using a drill fitted with a bit slightly smaller in diameter than the screw; mark the length of the screw on the bit with tape. Reposition the leaf section and drive in each screw with a screwdriver *(above, left)*. Holding the staple section in position, mark its screw holes, then bore holes and drive in its screws the same way *(above, right)*. Close the hasp lock and secure it with a padlock. Have a permanent repair undertaken as soon as possible.

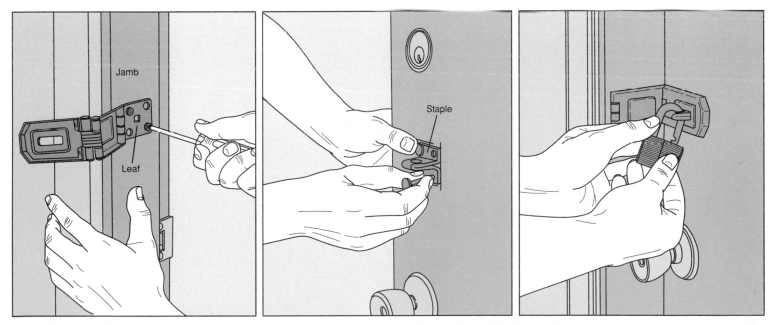

Installing a flexible hasp lock. To temporarily secure an exterior door, install a buttress bar indoors *(page 52)*. Or, secure the door with a flexible hasp lock *(page 47)*; if the door is flush with the jamb when it is closed, use a standard hasp lock *(step above)*. Close the door and position the flexible hasp lock: the leaf section on the jamb and the staple section on the door; if the door has a stop, follow the same procedure using a flexible hasp lock with an additional hinged plate. Mark the edges of each section with a pencil. Holding the leaf section in position, mark each screw hole. Bore a hole for a screw at each mark using a drill fitted with a bit slightly smaller in diameter than the screw; mark the length of the screw on the bit with tape. Reposition the leaf section and drive in each screw with a screwdriver *(above, left)*. Holding the staple section in position, mark each bolt hole, then bore a hole for a bolt at each mark using a drill fitted with a bit of the same diameter as the bolt. Reposition the staple section, fit a bolt into each hole *(above, center)*, and install a washer and a nut on each bolt; tighten the nuts with a wrench. Close the hasp lock and secure it with a padlock *(above, right)*. Have a permanent repair undertaken as soon as possible.

TEMPORARILY SECURING A DOOR (continued)

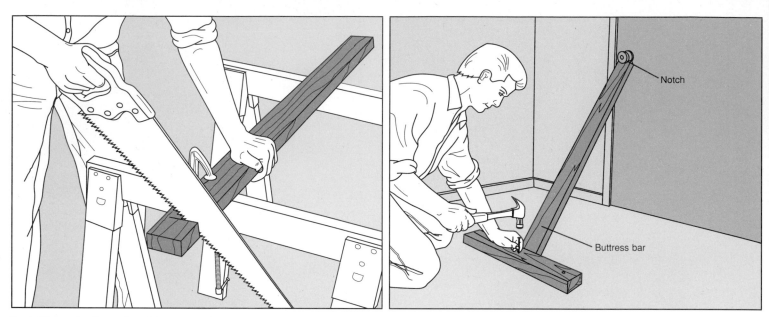

Installing a buttress bar. To temporarily secure an exterior door, use a hasp lock *(page 51)* or install a buttress bar indoors. To determine the length of the buttress bar needed, close the door and measure the distance between the doorknob and the floor, then add 12 inches. Mark a 2-by-4 to the length needed for the buttress bar and use a saw to cut it to length *(above, left)*; then, mark and cut a V-shaped notch at one end of it. Position the buttress bar against the door with its notch wedged snugly under the doorknob. Then, cut another 2-by-4 to use as a stopper perpendicular to the buttress bar. Position the stopper on the floor against the base of the buttress bar and secure it in place with nails *(above, right)*. Have a permanent repair undertaken as soon as possible.

TEMPORARILY SECURING A WINDOW

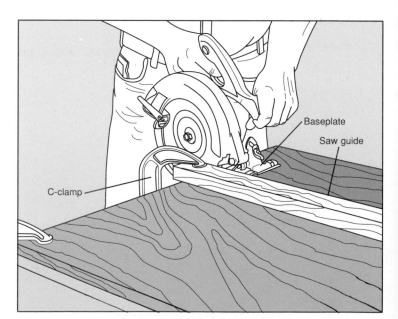

1 **Removing glass fragments.** To temporarily secure a broken window, install a plywood panel indoors across the opening. Wearing work gloves and safety goggles, first remove any shards of glass protruding from the window frame. Working from the top to the bottom of the window, carefully pull each shard straight out of the frame *(above)*; gently wiggle any stubborn shard free. Place the shards in a cardboard box or another unbreakable container for safe disposal.

2 **Preparing the plywood panel.** To determine the size of the plywood panel needed, measure the length and width of the opening, then add 8 to 12 inches to each dimension. Mark a 1-inch plywood panel to the length and width needed, then cut it to size using a circular saw. To direct the saw, use a straight 2-by-4 or other board as a guide, clamping or nailing it in place along the outer edge of the baseplate. Push the saw slowly along the cutting mark, keeping the baseplate against the guide *(above)*.

TEMPORARILY SECURING A WINDOW (continued)

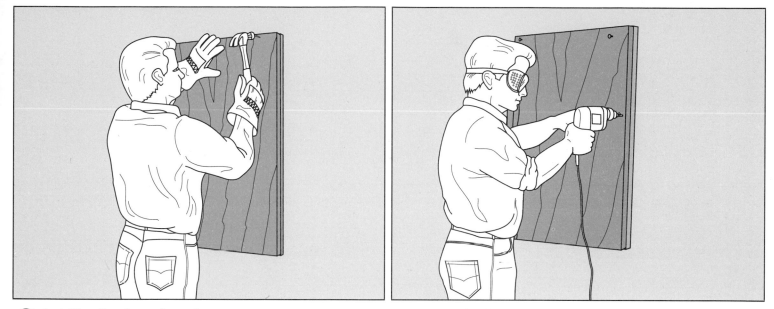

3 **Installing the plywood panel.** Position the plywood panel across the opening, overlapping it by 4 to 6 inches on each side; if necessary, work with a helper to support the plywood panel. To hold the plywood panel in position, drive nails through it and partway into the trim behind it *(above, left)*. Then, install the plywood panel with screws. Using a drill fitted with a bit of a diameter slightly smaller than a screw, bore a hole every 18 to 24 inches along each side of the plywood panel at least 1/2 inch from the edge *(above, right)*; mark the length of a screw on the bit with tape. Secure the plywood panel in place by driving a screw into each hole with a screwdriver. Have a permanent repair undertaken as soon as possible.

FREEING SOMEONE FROM A LOCKED ROOM

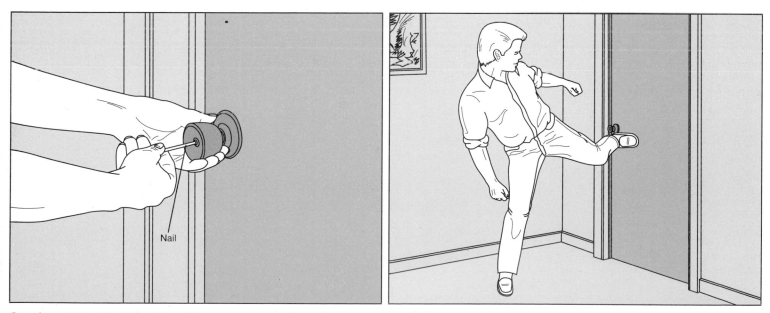

Nail

Opening a locked interior door. To rescue a person locked in a room, first check the doorknob for an access hole to the locking mechanism. If there is an access hole in the doorknob, push a nail, awl, baking pin, knitting needle or other long, thin implement straight into it and turn the doorknob back and forth *(above, left)* until the spring-loaded pin of the locking mechanism releases and the door opens. If there is no access hole in the doorknob, use force to break open the door as a last resort in an emergency situation. Using the flat of one foot, kick the door sharply just below the doorknob *(above, right)* until it opens; or, sit on the floor and kick the door the same way with both feet.

FIRE

Fire can strike anywhere in the house at any time without warning; knowing how to respond can save lives. While many fires can be contained in their early stages, flames can quickly spread out of control. The ability to control a fire can be important; evacuating at the right time, however, is crucial. Prepare a fire escape plan *(page 63)* and conduct fire drills with your family. If any escape route calls for a fire ladder *(page 55)*, have each family member practice using it. Have only one person climb down the fire ladder at a time; then, have him hold the bottom of it steady for the next person. To carry a small child, have him wrap his arms and legs securely around you, then climb down the fire ladder face to face with him. Place an infant in an infant carrier and climb down the fire ladder the same way.

Smoke detectors *(page 55)* are your first line of defense against a fire, providing valuable time for you to control it or evacuate; about 75 per cent of household fires start off as slow and smoldering ones. Install smoke detectors judiciously throughout your home *(page 58)*; regularly test and service them *(page 59)*. Install fire extinguishers *(page 55)* in strategic areas throughout the house *(page 58)*; practice using a fire extinguisher *(page 59)* outdoors on a calm day, protecting the ground from any residue with plastic sheeting or old bed linens. **Caution:** If a fire is not small and contained or you doubt your ability to use a fire extinguisher, evacuate the house immediately and call the fire department from the home of a neighbor. Keep in mind that a typical household fire extinguisher holds a pressurized cargo of 2 1/2 to 7 pounds that lasts for only 8 to 20 seconds. Always have the fire department check the house after any fire—even if you have already extinguished it.

The Troubleshooting Guide on pages 56 and 57 places emergency procedures at your fingertips, listing quick-action steps to take and referring you to pages 58 to 65 for more detailed information; read the instructions before you need them. Familiarize yourself with the procedure for putting out a small cooking fire *(page 60)*, electrical fire *(page 61)*, chemical fire *(page 61)* and upholstery fire *(page 62)*. If a person's clothing catches on fire, smother the flames, wrestling the victim to the ground and rolling him over on it, if necessary *(page 62)*. Refer to the list of Safety Tips *(right)* for guidelines in preventing a household fire emergency.

Post the telephone numbers for your local fire department, hospital emergency room, ambulance service and physician near the telephone and do not hesitate to call for help; even in non-emergency situations, qualified professionals can answer questions concerning the safety and protection of your home. If you are ever in doubt about the fire safety and protection of your home, have it checked as soon as possible by the fire department, a local or federal building authority, or a certified home inspector. In most areas, dial 911 in the event of any life-threatening emergency.

SAFETY TIPS

1. Prepare a fire evacuation plan *(page 63)*, mapping a primary and secondary escape route from each room of the house. Post the plan at strategic locations throughout the house; in the event of a fire emergency, you will want anyone to be able to find and use it.

2. Install smoke detectors judiciously throughout your home *(page 58)*. Keep at least one fire extinguisher rated ABC *(page 55)* on hand and know how to use it *(page 59)*.

3. Conduct fire drills with your family; every member should know how to evacuate from each room of the house in the event of a fire.

4. Keep your escape routes clear and unobstructed at all times. Keep your basement, garage, utility room and attic free of accumulated clutter.

5. Store paint thinners, solvents and other flammable chemicals in airtight containers away from sources of heat; do not store gasoline near other flammables. Hang rags soaked in flammable chemicals outdoors or store them in airtight metal or glass containers.

6. Keep matches and lighters out of the reach of children. Make sure smoking materials are completely extinguished before discarding them. Never smoke in bed or if you feel drowsy.

7. Follow all precautions for the safe use of each system in your home that is a potential fire hazard: electricity *(page 78)*; gas *(page 90)*; heating and cooling *(page 108)*.

8. Use only electrical units that bear a recognized seal of approval; look for the UL (Underwriters Laboratories) or CSA (Canadian Standards Association) stamp.

9. Do not use a light bulb of a wattage higher than stamped on the fixture; avoid using high-wattage bulbs in closets.

10. Maintain your fireplace and use it safely *(page 65)*; have the chimney flue professionally cleaned at least once a year.

11. Place any portable space heater at least 3 feet away from curtains and other flammables, and away from other sources of heat—including fireplaces, radiators, appliances and entertainment units.

12. Do not wear loose clothing when cooking. Keep curtains, towels and other flammables away from the range and other kitchen appliances that supply heat. Keep the handles of pots on the stove turned inward and do not leave cooking oil, fat or grease unattended on a hot burner. Regularly clean your range and any hood fan.

13. Never thaw a frozen water pipe with a propane torch; the pipe can conduct heat and ignite the wall or ceiling.

14. Keep fire hydrants near your home free of snow and other obstructions. Have your house number displayed prominently and light it at night.

15. Purchase nightclothes, mattresses, linens and draperies of fabrics that meet current safety standards for inflammability.

16. If you keep a natural evergreen tree indoors at Christmas time, give it plenty of water; it may soak up more than 1 gallon of water each day.

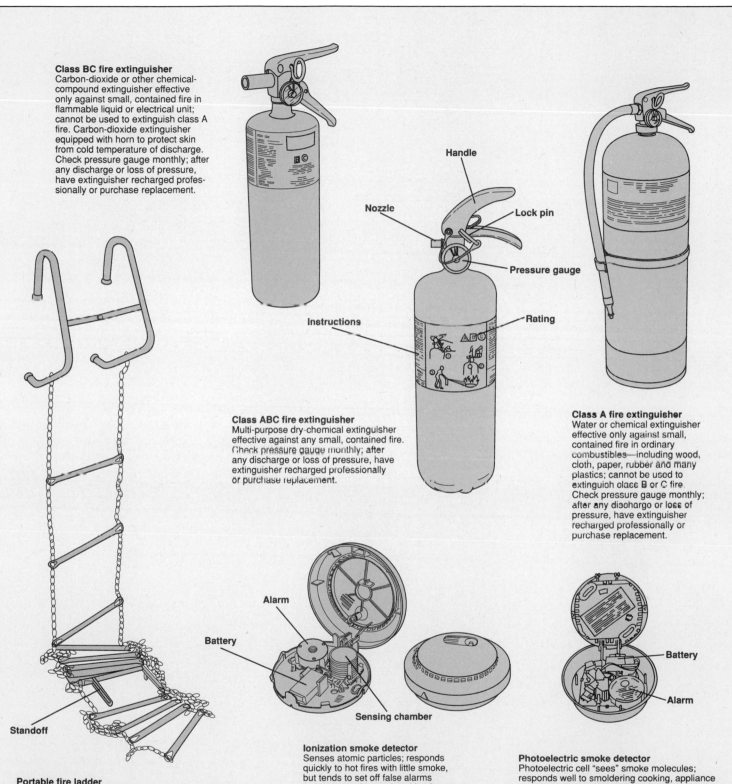

Class BC fire extinguisher
Carbon-dioxide or other chemical-compound extinguisher effective only against small, contained fire in flammable liquid or electrical unit; cannot be used to extinguish class A fire. Carbon-dioxide extinguisher equipped with horn to protect skin from cold temperature of discharge. Check pressure gauge monthly; after any discharge or loss of pressure, have extinguisher recharged professionally or purchase replacement.

Handle

Nozzle

Lock pin

Pressure gauge

Instructions

Rating

Class ABC fire extinguisher
Multi-purpose dry-chemical extinguisher effective against any small, contained fire. Check pressure gauge monthly; after any discharge or loss of pressure, have extinguisher recharged professionally or purchase replacement.

Class A fire extinguisher
Water or chemical extinguisher effective only against small, contained fire in ordinary combustibles—including wood, cloth, paper, rubber and many plastics; cannot be used to extinguish class B or C fire. Check pressure gauge monthly; after any discharge or loss of pressure, have extinguisher recharged professionally or purchase replacement.

Alarm

Battery

Sensing chamber

Battery

Alarm

Standoff

Portable fire ladder
Made of metal tubing and chain links, and available in lengths of 15 or 25 feet; fits inside small box for convenient storage near window. Standoffs hold ladder away from exterior wall.

Ionization smoke detector
Senses atomic particles; responds quickly to hot fires with little smoke, but tends to set off false alarms in presence of normal cooking fumes. Some detectors have built-in light to illuminate escape route when detector sounds. Test batteries once each week and clean detector regularly *(page 59).*

Photoelectric smoke detector
Photoelectric cell "sees" smoke molecules; responds well to smoldering cooking, appliance or upholstery fire and not prone to false alarms. Some detectors have built-in light to illuminate escape route when detector sounds. Test batteries once each week and clean detector regularly *(page 59).*

TROUBLESHOOTING GUIDE

SYMPTOM	PROCEDURE
House on fire or filling with smoke	Evacuate house immediately using primary *(p. 63)* or secondary *(p. 64)* escape route
	Call fire department from home of neighbor
	After fire extinguished, re-enter house safely and clean up *(p. 132)*
Room on fire or filling with smoke	Have someone call fire department immediately
	Control fire using ABC fire extinguisher *(p. 59)*
	If fire not small and contained or if flames or smoke come from wall or ceiling, evacuate house immediately using primary *(p. 63)* or secondary *(p. 64)* escape route and call fire department from home of neighbor
	Have fire department check house—even if fire out
	Clean up *(p. 132)*
Chimney on fire: loud, roaring noise from chimney; smoke entering room from chimney	Evacuate house immediately using primary *(p. 63)* or secondary *(p. 64)* escape route
	Call fire department from home of neighbor
	After fire extinguished, re-enter house safely and clean up *(p. 132)*
	Have fireplace inspected and repaired
	Use fireplace safely *(p. 65)*
Clothing on fire	Rescue victim on fire *(p. 62)*
	Have someone call for medical help immediately; treat burn victim *(p. 36)*
	Monitor victim's vital life signs *(p. 16)*
Cooking fire: flames from pan or pot	Control cooking fire by smothering flames *(p. 60)*
	If fire not small and contained, evacuate house immediately using primary *(p. 63)* or secondary *(p. 64)* escape route and call fire department from home of neighbor
Cooking fire: flames from stove	Have someone call fire department immediately
	Control cooking fire using baking soda *(p. 60)*
	If fire not small and contained, evacuate house immediately using primary *(p. 63)* or secondary *(p. 64)* escape route and call fire department from home of neighbor
	Have fire department check house—even if fire out
	Clean up *(p. 132)*
Cooking fire: flames from range	Have someone call fire department immediately
	Control cooking fire using ABC or BC fire extinguisher *(p. 60)*
	If fire not small and contained, evacuate house immediately using primary *(p. 63)* or secondary *(p. 64)* escape route and call fire department from home of neighbor
	Have fire department check house—even if fire out
	Clean up *(p. 132)*
Electrical fire: flames or smoke from outlet, switch or fixture	Have someone call fire department immediately
	Control electrical fire using ABC or BC fire extinguisher *(p. 61)*
	If fire not small and contained or if flames or smoke come from wall or ceiling, evacuate house immediately using primary *(p. 63)* or secondary *(p. 64)* escape route and call fire department from home of neighbor
	Have fire department check house—even if fire out
	Clean up *(p. 132)*
	Have electrical system inspected and repaired
	Use electricity safely *(p. 78)*
Electrical fire: flames or smoke from appliance, entertainment unit, power tool, extension cord or other electrical unit	Have someone call fire department immediately
	Immediately shut off electricity to system *(p. 82)*
	Control electrical fire using ABC or BC fire extinguisher *(p. 61)*

SYMPTOM	PROCEDURE
	If fire not small and contained or if flames or smoke come from wall or ceiling, evacuate house immediately using primary *(p. 63)* or secondary *(p. 64)* escape route and call fire department from home of neighbor
	Have fire department check house—even if fire out
	Clean up *(p. 132)*
	Have electrical unit and electrical system inspected and repaired
	Use electricity safely *(p. 78)*
Sparks or burning odor from outlet, switch, fixture, appliance, entertainment unit, power tool or other electrical unit	Do not touch electrical unit
	Immediately shut off electricity to circuit *(p. 83)* or system *(p. 82)*
	If electricity to circuit or system cannot be shut off immediately, unplug or switch off source *(p. 87)*
	If flames or smoke come from electrical unit, have someone call fire department immediately
	Control electrical fire using ABC or BC fire extinguisher *(p. 61)*
	If fire not small and contained or if flames or smoke come from wall or ceiling, evacuate house immediately using primary *(p. 63)* or secondary *(p. 64)* escape route and call fire department from home of neighbor
	Have fire department check house—even If fire out
	Clean up *(p. 132)*
	Have electrical unit and electrical system inspected and repaired
	Use electricity safely *(p. 78)*
Chemical fire: flames or smoke from paint, solvent or other chemical	Have someone call fire department immediately
	Control chemical fire using ABC or BC fire extinguisher *(p. 61)*
	If fire not small and contained, evacuate house immediately using primary *(p. 63)* or secondary *(p. 64)* escape route and call fire department from home of neighbor
	Have fire department check house—even if fire out
	Clean up *(p. 132)*
Upholstery fire: flames or smoke from chair, sofa or mattress	Have someone call fire department immediately
	Control upholstery fire using ABC or A fire extinguisher *(p. 62)*
	If fire not small and contained, evacuate house immediately using primary *(p. 63)* or secondary *(p. 64)* escape route and call fire department from home of neighbor
	Have fire department check house—even if fire out
	Clean up *(p. 132)*
Garbage fire: flames or smoke from garbage can or pail	Have someone call fire department immediately
	Control garbage fire using ABC or A fire extinguisher *(p. 59)* or water from garden hose
	If fire not small and contained, evacuate house immediately using primary *(p. 63)* or secondary *(p. 64)* escape route and call fire department from home of neighbor
	Have fire department check house—even if fire out
	Clean up *(p. 132)*
Smoke detectors missing or not installed judiciously	Install smoke detectors judiciously throughout house *(p. 58)*
Smoke detector emits chirping sound	Replace batteries *(p. 59)*
Smoke detector sets off false alarms	Relocate smoke detector *(p. 58)*
Fire extinguishers missing or not installed judiciously	Install fire extinguishers judiciously throughout house *(p. 58)*
Fire extinguisher gauge shows pressure loss	Replace fire extinguisher or have it recharged professionally
Fire extinguisher nozzle blocked	Clear fire extinguisher nozzle using wire
Fire extinguisher corroded or damaged	Replace fire extinguisher

INSTALLING A FIRE EXTINGUISHER

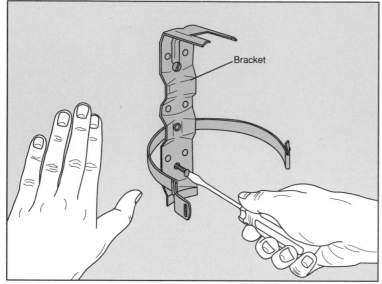

Bracket

Collar

Strap

Mounting a fire extinguisher. Install a fire extinguisher *(page 55)* in each potentially hazardous location of the house: the kitchen, the garage, the utility room and the basement, for example. Mount each fire extinguisher at a stud about 5 feet above the floor near a doorway. If necessary, locate the stud by tapping along the wall and listening for a change from a hollow to a solid sound; or, use a stud finder or a density sensor. Position the bracket of the fire extinguisher on the wall at the stud and mark the screw holes using a pencil. Bore a pilot hole for each screw using a drill fitted with a bit of a diameter slightly smaller than the screw; mark the screw length on the bit by wrapping masking tape around it. Reposition the bracket on the wall and drive in each screw with a screwdriver *(above, left)*. Fit the handle of the fire extinguisher on the collar of the bracket *(above, right)*, then wrap the strap around the canister and fasten the clip.

INSTALLING A SMOKE DETECTOR

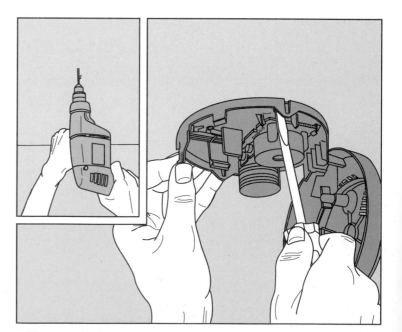

1 Marking holes for the anchors and screws. Install at least one battery-operated smoke detector *(page 55)* on the ceiling or at the top of a wall of each story in the house: in the hallway near the bedrooms, in the kitchen and living room, and at the top of the stairs, for example. Hold the base of the smoke detector in one hand and open the cover by releasing its locking clip, gently pulling the tab or at the arrow marked on it. With the cover of the smoke detector open, position the base on the ceiling or wall and use a pencil to mark the holes for anchors and screws *(above)*.

2 Mounting the smoke detector. Wearing safety goggles, bore a hole for each anchor using a drill fitted with a bit of the same diameter *(inset)*; mark the anchor length on the bit by wrapping masking tape around it. Use a hammer to tap each anchor into place until it is flush with the surface. Drive a screw into each anchor with a screwdriver until its head protrudes about 1/8 inch. Position the base of the smoke detector on the screws and turn it to lock it in place, then tighten the screws *(above)*. Install a battery and close the cover of the smoke detector. Test the smoke detector *(page 59)*.

SERVICING A SMOKE DETECTOR

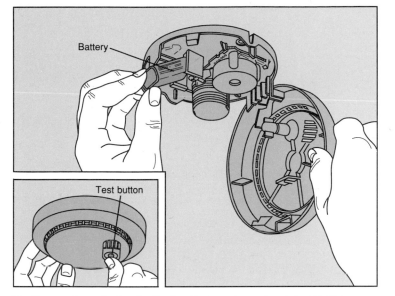

Battery

Test button

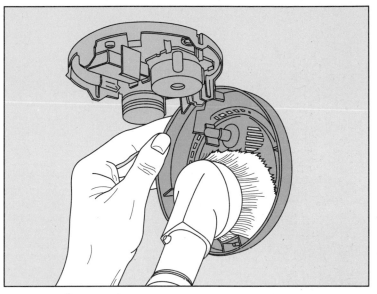

Testing and replacing batteries. Test each smoke detector once a week. Press the test button *(inset)* or buy a can of smoke-detector tester aerosol at a hardware store and spray it toward the vents. Replace the battery if the smoke detector does not sound when it is tested—or if it emits a chirping sound, indicating the battery is wearing down. Open the cover of the smoke detector, gently pulling the tab or at the arrow marked on it. Remove the battery and install an exact duplicate *(above)*, making sure its terminals contact properly; the smoke detector may sound for 1 or 2 seconds, indicating it works. Close the cover of the smoke detector and test it again.

Cleaning off a smoke detector. Clean off each smoke detector at least once every 6 months; a buildup of cobwebs, dirt, grease or other debris can cause a smoke detector to sound false alarms or otherwise malfunction. Keep the vents of the smoke detector clear using a vacuum, opening the cover and cleaning them off with a round, soft bristled brush attachment *(above)*; if necessary, use a cloth dipped in a solution of mild household detergent and water to wipe off the interior and exterior surfaces of the cover. After cleaning off the smoke detector, close the cover, then test the battery *(stop left)*.

USING A FIRE EXTINGUISHER

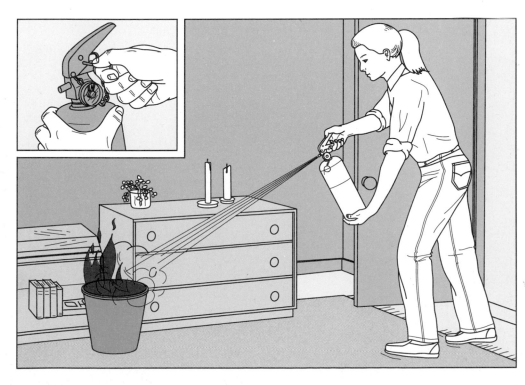

Controlling a fire. Have someone call the fire department immediately. Lift the fire extinguisher out of its bracket and set it upright on the ground. Steadying the fire extinguisher with one hand, pull the lock pin out of the handle with the other hand *(inset)*. Keeping the fire extinguisher upright, lift it up and aim the nozzle or hose at the base of the fire, positioning yourself 6 to 10 feet away and with your back to an accessible exit. Squeeze the two levers of the handle together *(left)* and spray in a quick side-to-side motion. Keep spraying until the fire is completely extinguished. Watch carefully for flashback, or rekindling of the fire, and be prepared to spray again. If the flames spread, or the fire extinguisher empties before the fire is extinguished, evacuate the house immediately *(page 63)*. Replace the fire extinguisher or have it professionally recharged after each use.

CONTROLLING A COOKING FIRE

Smothering a cooking fire in a pan or pot. Caution: Do not move any pan or pot on the stove or open the oven door. If the flames do not block access to the controls, turn off the burners and any hood fan. Protecting your hand with an oven mitt or a pot holder, cover the pan or pot with a fitted lid, angling it into place *(above)*. **Caution:** Do not clamp the lid straight down; the rush of air can spread the flames. If there is no fitted lid on hand, use a plate or platter slightly larger than the pan or pot. Let the pan or pot cool before removing the lid. If the flames spread, have someone call the fire department immediately, then control the fire with baking soda *(step right)* or a fire extinguisher *(step below)*.

Controlling a cooking fire with baking soda. Caution: Do not move any pan or pot on the stove or open the oven door. If the fire is small and contained in a pan or pot, smother it *(step left)*. If the fire is not small and contained, evacuate the house immediately *(page 63)* and call the fire department from the home of a neighbor. Otherwise, have someone call the fire department, then control the fire with a fire extinguisher *(step below)* or baking soda. If the flames do not block access to the controls, turn off the burners and any hood fan. Protecting your hand with an oven mitt or a pot holder, pour baking soda on the fire until it is extinguished *(above)*. **Caution:** Do not apply salt, water, baking powder or flour; they can spread the flames. Allow the range to cool before cleaning up.

Class ABC or BC
fire extinguisher

Controlling a cooking fire with a fire extinguisher. Caution: Do not move any pan or pot on the stove or open the oven door. If the fire is small and contained in a pan or pot, smother it *(step above, left)*. If the fire is not small and contained, evacuate the house immediately *(page 63)* and call the fire department from the home of a neighbor. Otherwise, have someone call the fire department, then control the fire with baking soda *(step above, right)* or a fire extinguisher rated ABC or BC *(page 55)*. If the flames do not block access to the controls, turn off the burners and any hood fan. Positioning yourself 6 to 10 feet away from the fire, spray it with the fire extinguisher *(page 59)* in a quick side-to-side motion until it is extinguished *(left)*. **Caution:** The fire may flare and appear to grow at first; be prepared to move back. Allow the range to cool before cleaning up *(page 138)*. Replace the fire extinguisher or have it professionally recharged.

CONTROLLING AN ELECTRICAL FIRE

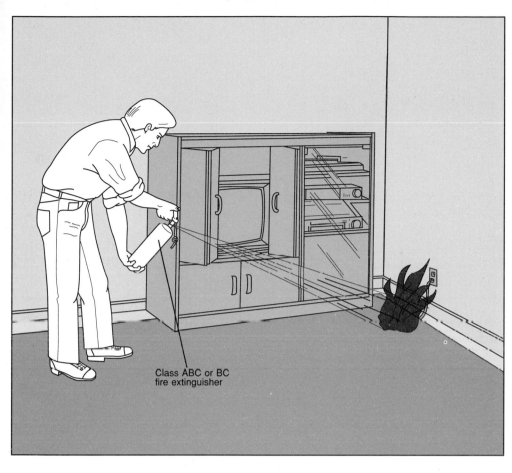

Extinguishing an electrical fire. Have someone call the fire department immediately; if the fire is not small and contained or there are flames or smoke coming from the walls or ceilings, evacuate the house *(page 63)* and call the fire department from the home of a neighbor. To control a small, contained fire in an electrical unit or at an outlet or switch, use a fire extinguisher rated ABC or BC *(page 55)*. **Caution:** Do not use water on an electrical fire. Positioning yourself 6 to 10 feet away from the fire, spray it with the fire extinguisher *(page 59)* in a quick side-to-side motion until it is extinguished *(left)*. When the fire is extinguished, unplug or switch off the electrical hazard *(page 87)* or shut off electricity at the service panel *(page 82)*. Have the electrical unit and your electrical system professionally inspected. Clean up *(page 138)* and replace the fire extinguisher or have it professionally recharged.

Class ABC or BC
fire extinguisher

CONTROLLING A CHEMICAL FIRE

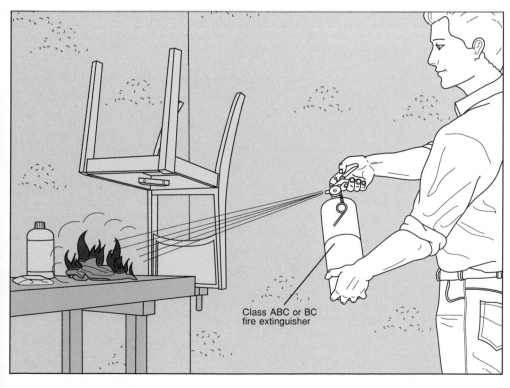

Extinguishing a chemical fire. Have someone call the fire department immediately; if the fire is not small and contained, evacuate the house *(page 63)* and call the fire department from the home of a neighbor. To control a small, contained fire in paints, fuels, solvents or other flammable chemicals, use a fire extinguisher rated ABC or BC *(page 55)*. **Caution:** Do not use water on a chemical fire. Positioning yourself 6 to 10 feet away from the fire, spray it with the fire extinguisher *(page 59)* in a quick side-to-side motion until it is extinguished *(left)*. Clean up *(page 138)*, disposing of the burned chemical according to the instructions of the fire department. Replace the fire extinguisher or have it professionally recharged.

Class ABC or BC
fire extinguisher

CONTROLLING AN UPHOLSTERY FIRE

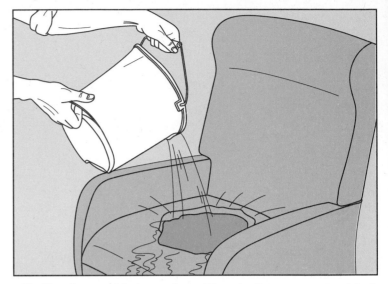

1 **Extinguishing the fire.** Have someone call the fire department immediately; if the fire is not small and contained, evacuate the house *(page 63)* and call the fire department from the home of a neighbor. To control a small, contained fire in upholstery, use a fire extinguisher rated ABC or A *(page 55)*. Positioning yourself 6 to 10 feet away from the fire, spray it with the fire extinguisher *(page 59)* in a quick side-to-side motion until it is extinguished *(above)*.

2 **Dousing smoldering embers.** When the flames are extinguished, douse any smoldering embers with water, using a bucket to pour it onto the upholstery *(above)*. Continue the procedure until the embers are put out and the area around the fire is thoroughly soaked, then take the chair or other upholstered furnishing outdoors. Clean up *(page 138)*, disposing of the burned upholstery according to the instructions of the fire department. Replace the fire extinguisher or have it professionally recharged.

RESCUING A VICTIM ON FIRE

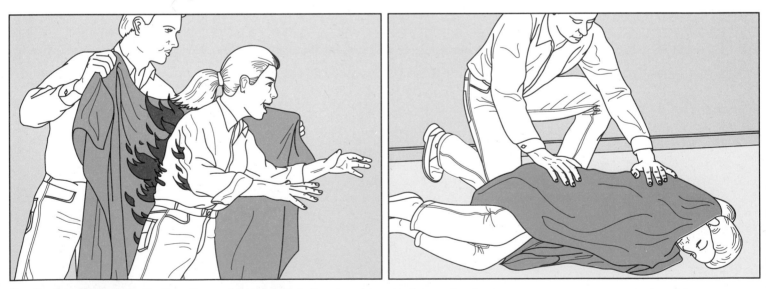

Smothering the flames. Caution: If your clothes catch on fire, do not run; moving can fan the flames. Immediately drop to the ground and roll on it to smother the flames, keeping your hands over your face to protect your mouth and nose. Shout the same procedure at any victim if his clothes catch on fire; if necessary, grab a blanket, rug or coat and wrestle him to the ground *(above, left)*, wrapping him tightly in it and rolling him over to smother the flames *(above, right)*.
Caution: Do not use a fire extinguisher rated ABC to extinguish the flames; the gas produced can be toxic. Have someone call for medical help immediately, then treat the burn victim *(page 36)*, monitoring his vital life signs *(page 16)*.

PREPARING A FIRE EVACUATION PLAN

Planning an escape route. Fire can strike any part of the house at any time with little or no warning; knowing how to respond in advance can save lives. Prepare a fire evacuation plan and conduct fire drills with all family members; from each room, especially on an upper story, there should be 2 possible escape routes: a door and a window. Ensure each family member knows how to evacuate quickly and safely in the event of a fire—no matter where he may be. Use the following guidelines to prepare for a fire emergency:

• Prepare a fire-escape floor plan, mapping a primary escape route from each room of the house; also map a secondary escape route for use in the event the primary route is blocked by fire or smoke.

• Post your fire-escape floor plan in convenient, central areas of the house where guests and babysitters can see it; make sure it specifies a family meeting spot outside the house.

• Keep your primary and secondary escape routes accessible.

• Have family members practice any escape route involving the use of a portable fire ladder; to build their confidence, practice at a ground-floor window.

• Conduct family fire drills regularly to avoid any panic or confusion in the event of a fire. End each fire drill at the predetermined meeting spot outside the house.

• Post the telephone number of your local fire department at each telephone in the house; note that in most areas, you can dial 911 in the event of a life-threatening emergency.

• Install smoke detectors *(page 58)* and service them regularly *(page 59)*; they are your first line of defence against a fire.

• Install fire extinguishers *(page 58)* and know how to use them *(page 59)*; practice outdoors on a calm day, using plastic sheeting or old bedsheets to protect the ground from any residue.

• Keep bedroom doors closed and unlocked when sleeping; in the event of a fire, a closed, unlocked door can provide extra time for your escape. Do not allow children to sleep in isolated areas of the house where they can be trapped by flames or smoke.

• If a fire is not small and contained, do not attempt to extinguish it; evacuate the house immediately *(step below)* and call the fire department from the home of a neighbor.

• Never waste valuable time trying to save personal possessions during a fire; it could cost you your life.

• Do not attempt to re-enter a burning house for any reason; inform firefighters of any trapped victim or pet.

ESCAPING A FIRE (PRIMARY ROUTE)

Using a primary escape route. If the room is filled with smoke, immediately drop to the floor; the gas produced by a fire can be fatal and the freshest air is at ground level. To minimize smoke inhalation, tie a rag, towel, pillowcase or article of clothing around your head, covering your nose and mouth. Crawl across the floor to the door of your primary escape route, staying as low to the floor as possible. If the door is closed, check it for heat by lightly touching the doorknob *(above, left),* the top of the door and the door trim. If you do not detect heat, brace the door with your shoulder and open it slightly, checking for flames and smoke. If you detect heat, flames or smoke, close the door and use your secondary escape route *(page 64)*. Otherwise, crawl out of the room *(above, right)*, close the door behind you and follow your primary escape route to safety.

ESCAPING A FIRE (SECONDARY ROUTE)

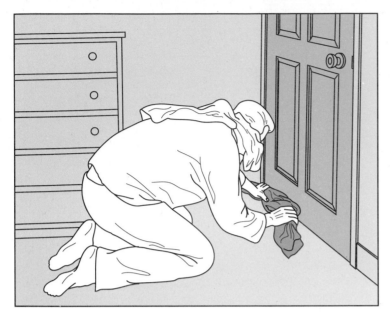

1 **Sealing off the door.** If heat, flames or smoke obstruct your primary escape route *(page 63)*, close each door of the room immediately. With your nose and mouth covered to minimize the inhalation of smoke, seal around each door and any vent using rags, towels, bed linens or articles of clothing *(above)*; if possible, soak them with water. If heat, flames and smoke do not obstruct your secondary escape route through a window, open it and climb out to safety; break it only if necessary *(step 2)* and if you are above the ground floor, use a portable fire ladder *(step 3)*. Otherwise, stay in the room and wait for help. Open a window only enough to shout for help and to hang a light-colored marker, indicating your location, then close it. If possible, call the fire department from the room and give your exact location—even if firemen have already arrived.

2 **Breaking the window.** If your secondary escape route is through a window you cannot open, break it. **Caution:** If your secondary escape route is obstructed by heat, flames or smoke, do not break the window; the air let in can fan the fire. Otherwise, stand to one side of the window with your face turned away from it and use a chair or other heavy object to break it *(above)*. Repeat the procedure, if necessary, to break the window enough to climb out of it. Protecting your hand by wrapping a rag, towel, pillowcase or article of clothing around it, pick out or snap off any jagged shards of glass from the window frame *(inset)*. Place a folded blanket on any remaining shards of glass along the bottom of the window frame, then climb out of the window and follow your secondary escape route to safety; if you are above the ground floor, use a portable fire ladder *(step 3)*.

3 **Setting up the fire ladder.** If your secondary escape route is through a window above the ground floor, use a portable fire ladder *(page 55)* to climb to safety. If heat, flames or smoke obstruct your secondary escape route, stay in the room and wait for help *(step 1)*, keeping each window closed. Otherwise, holding the fire ladder firmly by the sill hooks, drop the rungs and chain out of the window *(above, left)*; if any rung tangles in the chain, raise the ladder back up, untangle it and lower it again. When the ladder is fully extended, pull the sill hooks apart until they snap in place perpendicular to the crossbrace, then position each one over the window sill and securely under the window frame *(above, right)*.

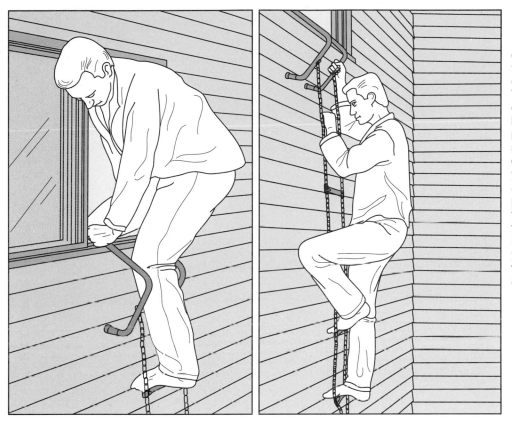

4 **Climbing down the fire ladder to safety.** Carefully climb out of the window, first thrusting one foot outdoors and straddling the window sill sideways. Holding onto the fire ladder by the sill hooks, reach your head out of the window far enough to see the rungs. Then, slowly lower your foot to the nearest rung of the fire ladder, shifting your weight to it, and bring the other foot out of the window *(far left)*; place both feet together on the same rung. As soon as you feel stable on the fire ladder, climb down it one rung at a time *(near left)*, keeping your weight as centered as possible on it to avoid swaying from side to side. Have only one person climb down the fire ladder at a time; then, have him hold the bottom of it steady for the next person. To carry a small child, have him wrap his arms and legs securely around you, then climb down the fire ladder face to face with him. Place an infant in an infant carrier and climb down the fire ladder the same way.

PREVENTING FIREPLACE AND CHIMNEY FIRES

Using a fireplace safely. A fireplace can be a safe source of warmth and enjoyment in your home—if it is properly maintained. Soot and creosote, natural products of wood combustion, can cause a fire if they are allowed to build up. Maintain your fireplace *(step right)* and follow the precautions listed below:

• Store firewood at least 3 feet from the fireplace and burn only dry firewood. Do not use flammable liquids to ignite firewood and use as little paper as possible to start a fire.

• Always use a metal fire screen or heat-resistant glass fire doors in front of the fireplace; a fire screen should cover each side of the fireplace opening.

• Never burn plastic or garbage in the fireplace; plastic can emit toxic fumes and garbage can burn out of control. Do not burn painted or pressure-treated wood; the wood can emit toxic fumes.

• Never leave a fire unattended in a fireplace.

• Do not close the flue damper until a fire is completely extinguished; a buildup of fatal carbon monoxide fumes can result.

• To prevent sparks and burning particles from flying onto nearby rooftops and to keep animals and leaves from entering, install a wire-mesh spark arrester on the top of the chimney.

• If your house is an older one, the chimney may not be lined with rectangular or square fireclay tiles or round glazed tiles; this can be a fire hazard and should be remedied by a professional.

Maintaining a fireplace. Regularly clean accumulated ashes out of the fireplace; do not allow them to build up. Use a fireplace broom to sweep the ashes onto a metal shovel *(above)*, then empty them into a metal container. Store the ashes outdoors in a covered metal container for disposal. Have the chimney flue cleaned at least once each year; if necessary, call your local fire department or building authority to have a qualified chimney sweep recommended. Age and temperature extremes can cause firebricks and mortar joints to loosen, crack or crumble. Periodically inspect your fireplace and have any damaged firebrick or mortar joint repaired as soon as possible.

WATER

A household water emergency can vary as much in degree as in origin; but whether it is due to a natural or environmental disaster, the aftermath of a fire, a faulty plumbing system, a leaking or overflowing appliance, or a hole in the roofing, siding or foundation, the damage to the structure of your home can be extensive. Refer to Cleaning Up *(page 132)* following a major water disaster and to Plumbing *(page 96)* in the event of a water emergency with a toilet, sink, bathtub, water pipe or other component of your plumbing system. Often, however, the source of a water emergency is difficult to trace; the water you detect running down a wall or dripping from a ceiling may have traveled a long, circuitous and hidden route. Fortunately, there are ways to minimize the damage of most water emergencies until the source can be located and repaired.

The Troubleshooting Guide on pages 67 and 68 places procedures for handling a water emergency at your fingertips and refers you to pages 69 to 77 for quick-action steps you can take. Know where the main water shutoff valve for your home is located *(page 99)* as well as the shutoff valve or valves for each fixture *(page 100)*. To contain a leak in the basement, plug any crack in a masonry wall *(page 69)*. If water leaks into the attic or from a ceiling, install a temporary water barrier in the attic *(page 69)* or pierce any water-laden ceiling *(page 70)*. Act quickly to cope with a leaking or overflowing appliance *(page 70)* or a leaking water heater *(page 71)*.

Ventilate your house *(page 137)* as soon as possible after a water emergency. To remove any standing water, use a submersible pump, a wet-dry vacuum or a mop *(page 72)*; for more than 18 inches of standing water, use a trash pump *(page 136)*. Air out any wet electrical box *(page 73)*. Ventilate each inside *(page 73)* and outside *(page 75)* interior wall that water has penetrated or remove any damaged section of plaster *(page 74)*, drywall *(page 76)* or wood panels *(page 77)*.

The list of Safety Tips at right covers basic guidelines for preventing and handling a water emergency; refer to page 67 for tools and supplies you may need. A water emergency can turn electricity into a deadly hazard by making your body a convenient path for current; in wet or damp conditions, do not touch any electrical unit—even a switch or power cord. Before coping with a leaking or overflowing appliance or leaking water heater, airing out an electrical box, or ventilating any wall or removing a damaged section of it, shut off power to the circuit of the appliance or water heater, the circuits of the room *(page 83)* or the system *(page 82)*.

When in doubt about your ability to handle an emergency, do not hesitate to call for help. Post the telephone numbers for your water utility, your electricity utility, a 24-hour plumber and your insurance agent near the telephone. Also seek technical help when you need it; if you are ever in doubt about the structural soundness of your roofing or siding, for example, have it inspected by a professional. Even in non-emergency situations, a certified home inspector or other qualified building authority can answer questions concerning the condition of your home.

SAFETY TIPS

1. Locate and label or tag the main shutoff valve for your home's water supply *(page 99)* as well as the shutoff valve or valves for each fixture *(page 100)*; in the event of an emergency, you will want anyone to be able to find them quickly.

2. Label the main circuit breaker, the main fuse block or the service disconnect breaker for your electrical system; also map the circuits of your home and label them at the service panel *(page 84)*. In the event of an emergency, you will want anyone to be able to shut off the power quickly.

3. Before entering a flooded room, shut off power to it *(page 83)* or the system *(page 82)*; if the service panel is wet or the area around it is flooded, call your electricity utility to have power to your house shut off.

4. Do not touch a leaking or overflowing appliance or a leaking water heater; shut off power to the circuit of the appliance or water heater, the circuits of the room *(page 83)* or the system *(page 82)*.

5. Never work with electricity in wet or damp conditions and do not use any electrical appliance, tool or extension cord if it is wet or damp. If an appliance falls into a sink, bathtub or toilet, do not reach in to retrieve it.

6. Before removing the cover plate for an electrical box, turn off power to the circuits of the room *(page 83)* or the system *(page 82)*. Leave a note on the service panel to keep anyone from restoring power while you are working.

7. Before ventilating a wall or removing any damaged section of it, make careful exploratory holes with a hand drill to check for hidden electrical wires, pipes and insulation; work carefully around any obstruction.

8. After a major water disaster, re-enter your house safely *(page 135)*. Check the ceiling for bulges and other signs of damage, and release any trapped water.

9. Do not attempt a repair to your roofing or siding when it is wet or windy. Never work on the roof if it is wet or laden with snow or ice. Never undertake a repair on the roofing or siding near an overhead utility line.

10. Keep a roll of heavy-duty plastic sheeting on hand for use as a temporary water barrier in the event of an emergency.

11. Each spring and fall, check the roofing and siding system of your home—the attic, the vents, the siding material, the roofing material, the gutters and downspouts, the flashing, and the fascia boards. Have any repairs required undertaken as soon as possible.

12. Have your plumbing system inspected periodically and have any problem you detect remedied as soon as possible. Regularly check that any sump pump installed in your home is in good working order.

13. Wear the proper protective gear for the job: safety goggles when working above your head; work gloves when handling fiberglass insulation; rubber gloves when working with hydraulic cement; a hard hat to protect your head against falling debris.

14. To avoid inhaling plaster dust and mineral or glass fibers, wear a dust mask when breaking out drywall or plaster and when removing fiberglass insulation.

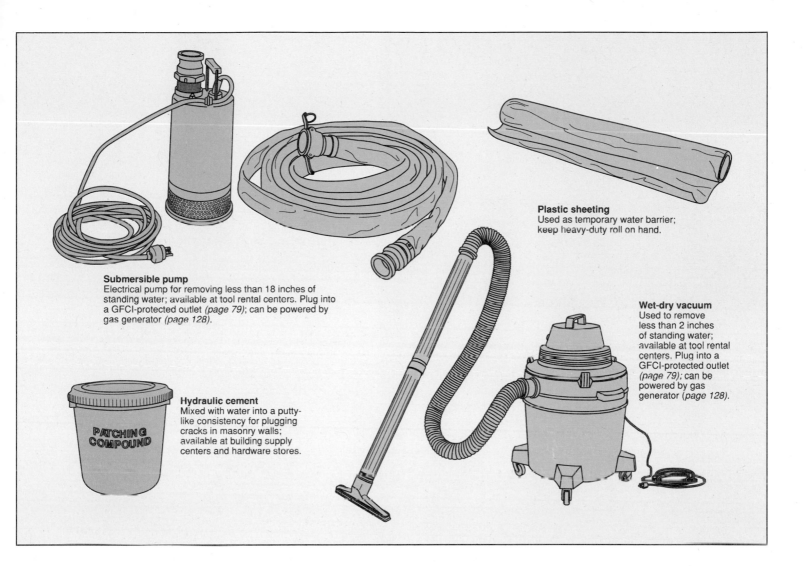

Submersible pump
Electrical pump for removing less than 18 inches of standing water; available at tool rental centers. Plug into a GFCI-protected outlet *(page 79)*; can be powered by gas generator *(page 128)*.

Hydraulic cement
Mixed with water into a putty-like consistency for plugging cracks in masonry walls; available at building supply centers and hardware stores.

Plastic sheeting
Used as temporary water barrier; keep heavy-duty roll on hand.

Wet-dry vacuum
Used to remove less than 2 inches of standing water; available at tool rental centers. Plug into a GFCI-protected outlet *(page 79);* can be powered by gas generator *(page 128).*

TROUBLESHOOTING GUIDE continued▶

SYMPTOM	PROCEDURE
Room flooded	Do not enter room
	Shut off electricity to circuits of room *(p. 83)* or system *(p. 82)*; if service panel wet or area around it flooded, call electricity utility to shut off system
	Remove standing water with trash pump *(p. 136)*; submersible pump, wet-dry vacuum, mop *(p. 72)*
	Air out electrical boxes *(p. 73)*
	Ventilate inside *(p. 73)* and outside *(p. 75)* interior walls; remove damaged wall sections of plaster *(p. 74)*, drywall *(p. 76)* or wood panels *(p. 77)*
	Ventilate house *(p. 137)*
Basement flooded	Do not enter basement
	Shut off electricity to circuits of basement *(p. 83)* or system *(p. 82)*; if service panel wet or area around it flooded, call electricity utility to shut off system
	Remove standing water with trash pump *(p. 136)*; submersible pump, wet-dry vacuum, mop *(p. 72)*
	Air out electrical boxes *(p. 73)*
	Ventilate house *(p. 137)*

TROUBLESHOOTING GUIDE (continued)

SYMPTOM	PROCEDURE
Wall wet; water running down it	If plumbing system problem suspected, shut off main water supply *(p. 99)*
	Shut off electricity to circuits of room *(p. 83)* or system *(p. 82)*
	Contain water in attic *(p. 69)* or release water from ceiling *(p. 70)*; plug leak in masonry wall *(p. 69)*
	Remove standing water with wet-dry vacuum or mop *(p. 72)*
	Air out electrical boxes *(p. 73)*
	Ventilate inside *(p. 73)* and outside *(p. 75)* interior walls; remove damaged wall sections of plaster *(p. 74)*, drywall *(p. 76)* or wood panels *(p. 77)*
	Ventilate house *(p. 137)*
Ceiling wet; water dripping from it	Do not stand under wet ceiling
	If plumbing system problem suspected, shut off main water supply *(p. 99)*
	Shut off electricity to circuits of room *(p. 83)* or system *(p. 82)*
	Contain water in attic *(p. 69)* or release water from ceiling *(p. 70)*
	Remove standing water with wet-dry vacuum or mop *(p. 72)*
	Air out electrical boxes *(p. 73)*
	Ventilate house *(p. 137)*
Appliance leaking or overflowing; water pooling on floor around it	Do not touch appliance
	Shut off electricity to circuit of appliance *(p. 83)* or system *(p. 82)*
	Cope with leaking or overflowing appliance *(p. 70)*
	Remove standing water with wet-dry vacuum or mop *(p. 72)*
Water heater leaking; water pooling on floor around it	Do not touch water heater
	Shut off electricity to circuit of water heater *(p. 83)* or system *(p. 82)*
	Cope with leaking water heater *(p. 71)*
	Remove standing water with wet-dry vacuum or mop *(p. 72)*
Service panel wet	Do not touch service panel
	Call electricity utility to shut off system
Appliance, water heater, outlet, switch or other electrical unit wet	Do not touch appliance, water heater, outlet, switch or other electrical unit
	Shut off electricity to circuit of appliance or water heater, circuits of room *(p. 83)* or system *(p. 82)*
	Air out electrical boxes *(p. 73)*
Inside interior wall water-damaged	Shut off electricity to circuits of room *(p. 83)* or system *(p. 82)*
	Air out electrical boxes *(p. 73)*
	Ventilate inside interior walls *(p. 73)*; remove damaged wall sections of plaster *(p. 74)*, drywall *(p. 76)* or wood panels *(p. 77)*
	Ventilate house *(p. 137)*
Outside interior wall water-damaged	Shut off electricity to circuits of room *(p. 83)* or system *(p. 82)*
	Air out electrical boxes *(p. 73)*
	Ventilate outside interior walls *(p. 75)*; remove damaged wall sections of plaster *(p. 74)*, drywall *(p. 76)* or wood panels *(p. 77)*
	Ventilate house *(p. 137)*

MINIMIZING LEAK DAMAGE

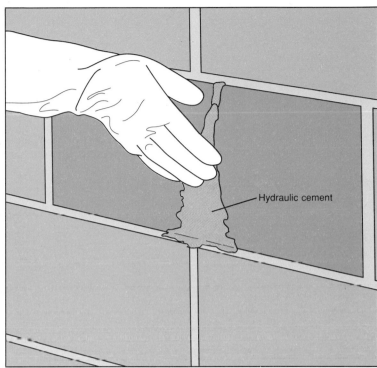

Hydraulic cement

Containing a leak in the basement. If water collects in the basement from a crack in a masonry wall, plug the crack with hydraulic cement. Wearing work gloves and safety goggles, use a cold chisel and a small sledgehammer *(above, left)* or ball-peen hammer to prepare the crack for plugging, undercutting it in a dovetail shape *(inset)*. Brush out loose particles with a stiff fiber brush and flush the crack with clean water. Wearing rubber gloves, prepare the cement according to the label

instructions, mixing only as much as you can use in 3 minutes. Work the cement into a plug with your hands, adding just enough water to give it the consistency of putty. Starting at the top of the crack, press in the cement with your fingers *(above, right)* and hold it in place until it sets—about 3 minutes. Continue the procedure until the entire length of the crack is plugged. Then, remove any standing water *(page 72)*.

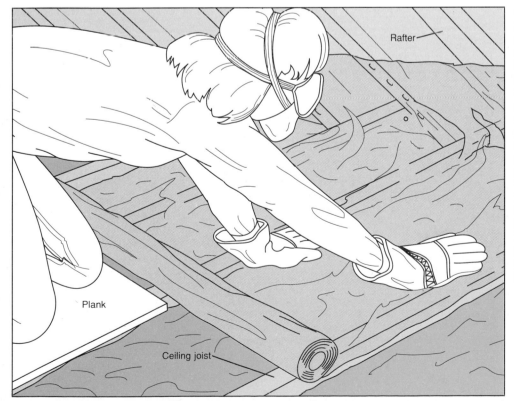

Rafter

Plank

Ceiling joist

Containing a leak in the attic. If water collects in the attic from a leak in the roofing or siding, contain it with plastic sheeting; if there is a large amount of water above a ceiling, release it *(page 70)* . If there is no floor in the attic, position planks across the ceiling joists to use as a walkway. Wearing work gloves, safety goggles and a dust mask, remove any water-laden insulation between the joists and bag it for disposal; if there is little headroom in the attic, wear a hard hat. Working across the attic, lay the sheeting across the ceiling joists *(left)* or on the floor; overlap parallel lengths of sheeting by 12 to 18 inches and seal the seams with duct tape. To minimize water runoff, use a staple gun to staple the outside edges of the sheeting to the rafters and studs along the attic perimeter. Remove standing water as it collects on the sheeting using a mop *(page 72)*. When repairs are made, take out the sheeting and replace any insulation you removed.

MINIMIZING LEAK DAMAGE (continued)

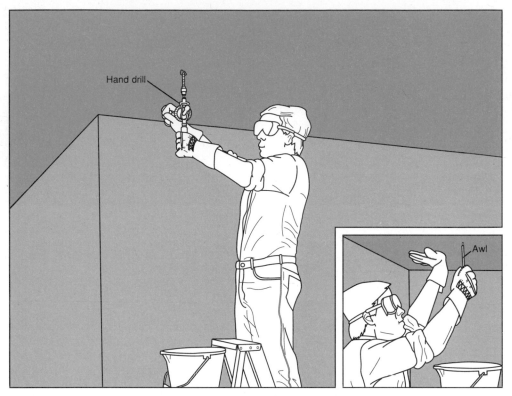

Releasing water from a ceiling. Caution: To prevent electrical shock, turn off power to the circuits of the room *(page 83)* or the system *(page 82)*; if you suspect water is leaking from a plumbing pipe, also shut off the main water supply *(page 99)*. Before entering the room, check the ceiling for bulges and other signs of damage; if necessary, release trapped water at the doorway *(page 135)*. If there is water trickling through the ceiling and it cannot be contained in the attic *(page 69)*, pierce the ceiling and collect the water in a bucket. Set up a stepladder under the wet ceiling with the bucket on it. Wearing safety goggles, pierce a drywall ceiling with an awl *(inset)* or an ice pick, twisting it to enlarge the hole. Pierce a plaster ceiling using a hand drill *(left)* or a long nail and a hammer. **Caution:** Do not use an electric drill. Pierce the ceiling in as many places as necessary to release the water. Then, remove any standing water *(page 72)*.

COPING WITH A LEAKING OR OVERFLOWING APPLIANCE

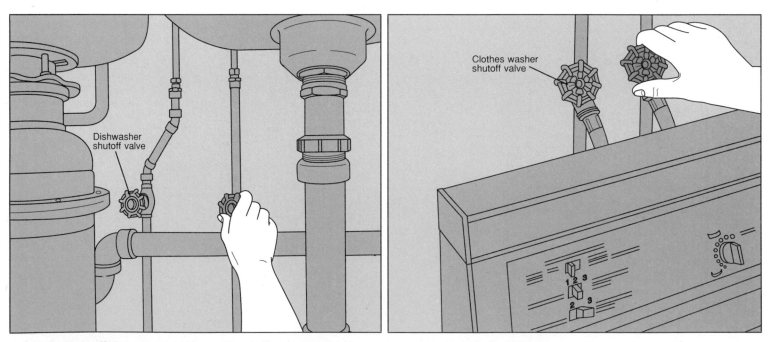

1 **Shutting off the water supply to the appliance. Caution:** To prevent electrical shock, do not touch the appliance; turn off power to its circuit *(page 83)* or the system *(page 82)*. Then, turn off and unplug the appliance. Locate each shutoff valve for the water supply to the appliance and turn the handle fully clockwise: for a dishwasher, usually one valve under the sink *(above, left)*; for a clothes washer, usually two valves behind it *(above, right)*. For a portable appliance, turn off the sink faucets. If a valve leaks or there is no valve, turn off the main water supply *(page 99)*.

COPING WITH A LEAKING OR OVERFLOWING APPLIANCE (continued)

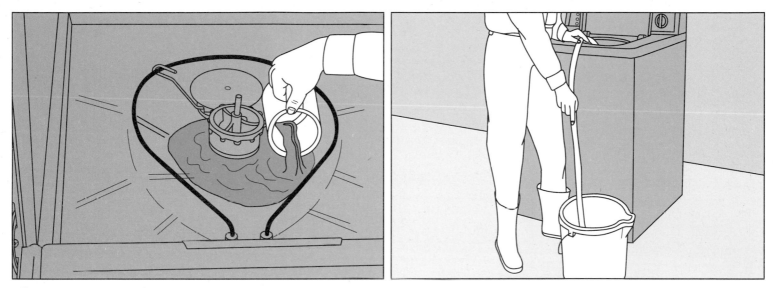

2 **Emptying water from the appliance.** Allow the water in the appliance to cool. Before opening the door of a dishwasher, place rags, towels, newspapers or plastic sheeting on the floor around it and set up a large, shallow container to collect any water that gushes out. Open the door of the appliance and use a container to bail out the water *(above, left)*. Or, use a length of hose to siphon out the water into a bucket set on the floor. Place one end of the hose in the water and suck on the other end of it to start the water flowing, then set the end in the bucket *(above, right)*; the water will continue flowing as long as the end of the hose is lower than the level of the water in the appliance. Bail or siphon most of the water out of the appliance, then use a sponge or towel to soak up the remaining water. Remove any standing water on the floor *(page 72)*.

DRAINING A LEAKING WATER HEATER

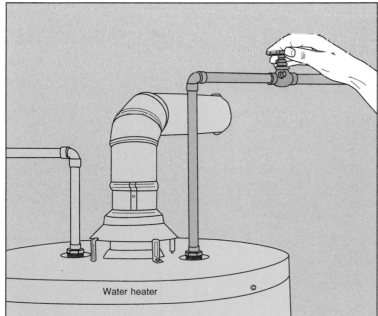

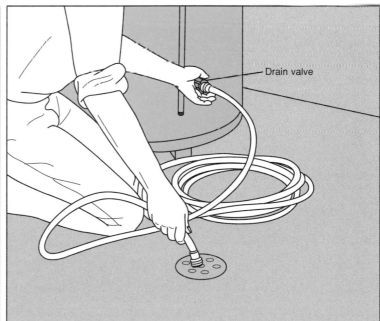

Turning off and draining a water heater. Caution: To prevent electrical shock, do not touch the water heater; turn off power to its circuit *(page 83)* or the system *(page 82)*. With a gas water heater, also turn off the gas supply to it *(page 92)*. Locate the shutoff valve for the water supply to the water heater, usually found near and above it, and turn the handle fully clockwise *(above, left)*. If the valve leaks or there is no valve, turn off the main water supply *(page 99)*. To drain the water from the water heater, connect a garden hose to the drain valve and run it to a floor drain *(above, right)*; or, set up a bucket under the drain valve. Then, open the drain valve, turning the handle fully counterclockwise. Allow the water to drain from the water heater; to speed up the draining, open the hot water faucet of a sink. If you are draining the water into a bucket, close the drain valve when the bucket is full, then empty the bucket and repeat the procedure until the water heater is empty. Remove any standing water on the floor *(page 72)*.

71

REMOVING STANDING WATER

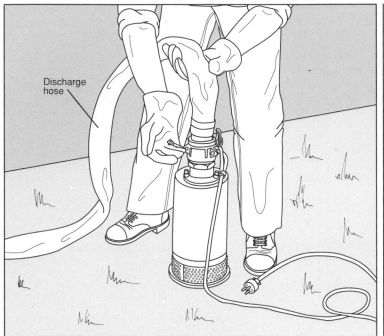

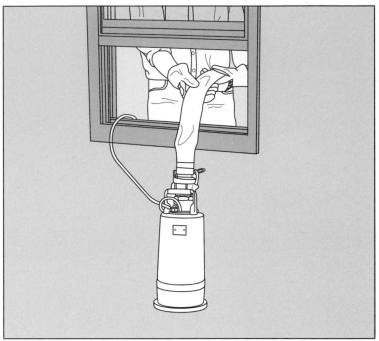

Using a submersible pump. To remove 18 inches or more of standing water, use a trash pump *(page 136)*; for less than 2 inches of standing water, use a wet-dry vacuum *(step below, left)* or a mop *(step below, right)*. Otherwise, use a submersible pump, available at a tool rental center; rent a discharge hose long enough to reach to an outdoor municipal storm drain. Push the discharge hose onto the discharge pipe, then close the clamp *(above, left)*. Holding the pump by the discharge hose, lower it into the water through an open window *(above, right)* until it sits level on the floor. Position the discharge hose at the storm drain, then plug the pump into a dry GFCI-protected outlet *(page 79)* and turn it on; if necessary, set up a gas-powered generator *(page 128)* to run it. Turn off the pump when it no longer sucks up water. Remove any remaining standing water with a wet-dry vacuum or a mop.

Using a wet-dry vacuum. To remove 2 inches or more of standing water, use a submersible pump *(step above)* or a trash pump *(page 136)*. Otherwise, use a mop *(step right)* or a wet-dry vacuum, available at a tool rental center. Wearing rubber boots and rubber gloves, push the intake hose onto the intake fitting, then plug the vacuum into a dry GFCI-protected outlet *(page 79)* and turn it on; if necessary, set up a gas-powered generator *(page 128)* to run it. Work the vacuum back and forth across the floor *(above)* until the water is removed. If necessary, turn off and unplug the vacuum to empty the tank.

Using a mop. To remove 2 inches or more of standing water, use a submersible pump *(step above)* or a trash pump *(page 136)*. Otherwise, use a wet-dry vacuum *(step left)* or a mop. Wearing rubber boots and rubber gloves, roll up rags, towels or newspapers and place them on the floor around the water to contain it. Work the mop back and forth across the floor *(above)*, soaking up the water. Wring the water out of the mop into a bucket and repeat the procedure, continuing until the water is removed. Dispose of the material used to contain the water or hang it up to dry.

VENTILATING ELECTRICAL BOXES

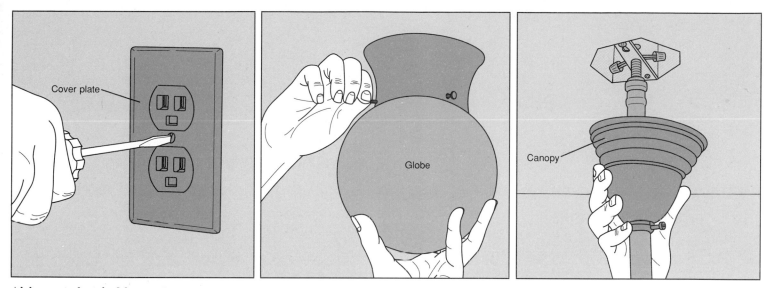

Airing out electrical boxes. Shut off power to the circuits of the room *(page 83)* or the system *(page 82)*. To release trapped water from an outlet or switch box, unscrew the cover plate *(above, left)* and lift it off the wall. To release trapped water from a fixture box covered by a globe, loosen any retaining screws holding the globe *(above, center)* and take it off; keep a bucket on hand to collect water. Unscrew the light bulb, then remove the mounting screws or locknut holding the fixture and pull it away from the ceiling or wall. **Caution:** Do not touch any bare wire ends. To release trapped water from a fixture box covered by a canopy or plate, remove any screws and loosen any retaining screw, locknut or cap holding the canopy or plate and pull it away from the ceiling *(above, right)* or wall. Before restoring power, have the wiring professionally inspected.

VENTILATING AN INSIDE INTERIOR WALL

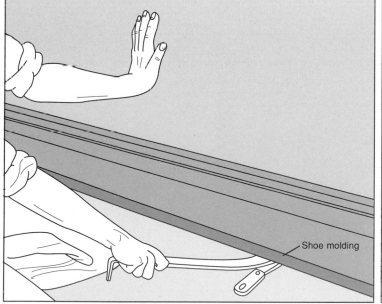

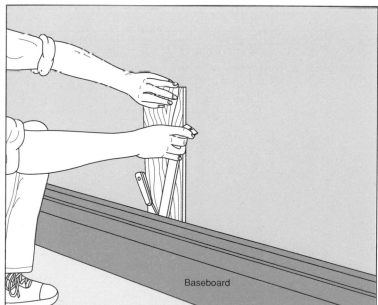

1 **Removing the shoe molding and baseboard.** Shut off power to the circuits of the room *(page 83)* or the system *(page 82)* and air out any wet electrical boxes *(step above)*. To ventilate a wall of plaster or remove a damaged section of it, break away as much plaster as necessary *(page 74)*. To ventilate an interior wall of drywall or wood panels or remove a damaged section at the bottom of it, take off the shoe molding and baseboard. Remove any obstructing cable and jack for the telephone or cover plate for an outlet box. Starting at one end of the wall, work a putty knife between the molding and the floor, then gently insert a pry bar and ease up the molding *(above, left)*. If the molding is nailed to the baseboard, leave it in place and take it off with the baseboard. Otherwise, continue along the wall the same way until the molding is removed. To take off the baseboard, start at one end of the wall and work the putty knife between the top of the baseboard and the wall, then insert a wood shim. Gently fit the pry bar between the putty knife and the shim, then ease out the baseboard *(above, right)*. Continue along the wall the same way until the baseboard is removed.

73

VENTILATING AN INSIDE INTERIOR WALL (continued)

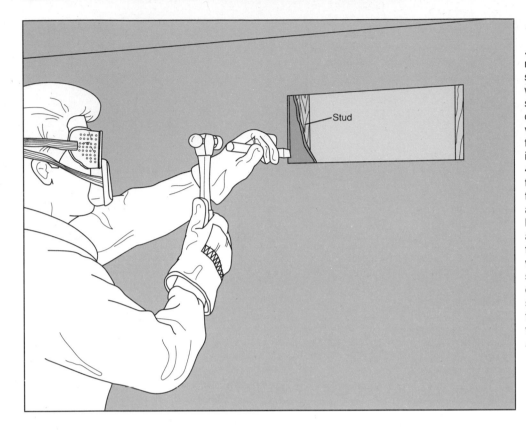

Stud

2 **Cutting ventilation holes.** To ventilate a wall of wood panels or remove a damaged section of it, take off as many panels as necessary *(page 77)*. To remove a damaged section of drywall, break away as much of the wall as necessary *(page 76)*. To ventilate an outside interior wall of drywall, break away enough of it to remove any wet insulation *(page 75)*. To ventilate an inside interior wall of drywall, protect the floor with a dropcloth and cut holes about 6 inches high in the wall between studs: at the top 4 to 6 inches below the ceiling; at the bottom 2 to 4 inches above the floor. If necessary, locate the studs—usually 16 inches apart—by tapping along the wall and listening for a change from a hollow to a solid sound; or, use a stud finder or a density sensor. Mark each hole on the wall, then wear work gloves to score along the marks with a utility knife and a straightedge. Wearing safety goggles and a dust mask, use a cold chisel and a ball-peen hammer *(left)* or small sledgehammer to break away the drywall. Use the same procedure to cut as many holes in the wall between studs as necessary to ventilate it. Also air out the house *(page 137)*.

REMOVING DAMAGED PLASTER

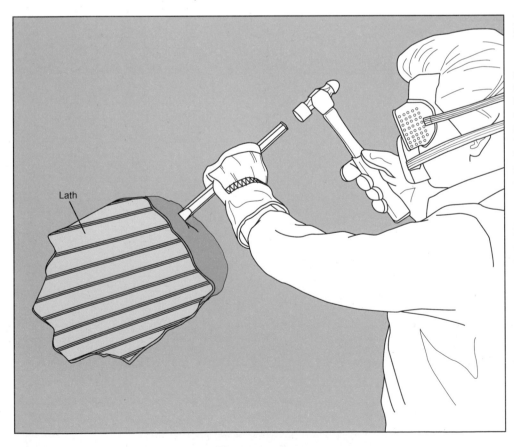

Lath

Breaking away the plaster. Shut off power to the circuits of the room *(page 83)* or the system *(page 82)* and air out any wet electrical boxes *(page 73)*. To ventilate the wall or remove a damaged section of it, protect the floor with a dropcloth and break away as much plaster as necessary; holes about 6 inches high at the top of the wall 4 to 6 inches below the ceiling and at the bottom of the wall 2 to 4 inches above the floor are usually sufficient to ventilate the wall between studs. Wearing work gloves, safety goggles and a dust mask, use a cold chisel and a ball-peen hammer *(left)* or small sledgehammer to break away the plaster, exposing the lath strips behind it. Knock out loose pieces of plaster from between the lath strips. If the wall can be replastered, work carefully to avoid damaging any lath strip; if the wall is repaired or replaced with drywall, the shoe molding and baseboard may have to be removed *(page 73)* along with the lath strips. Continue the procedure until the hole is large enough to ventilate the wall or the damaged plaster is removed. Also air out the house *(page 137)*.

VENTILATING AN OUTSIDE INTERIOR WALL

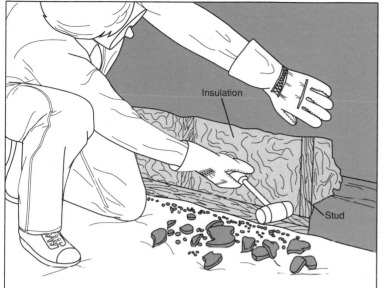

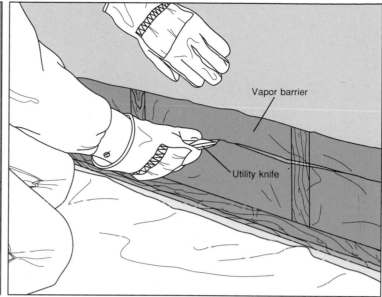

1 **Breaking away the wall.** Shut off power to the circuits of the room *(page 83)* or the system *(page 82)* and air out any wet electrical boxes *(page 73)*. To ventilate a wall of plaster or wood panels or remove a damaged section of it, break away as much plaster *(page 74)* or remove as many panels *(page 77)* as necessary. To remove a damaged section of drywall, break away as much of it as necessary *(page 76)*. To ventilate an inside interior wall of drywall, cut ventilation holes *(page 74)*. To ventilate an outside interior wall of drywall, remove the shoe molding and baseboard *(page 73)*, protect the floor with a dropcloth and break away enough drywall to remove any wet insulation. Wearing work gloves, use a utility knife and a straightedge to score along the wall about 4 inches above the damaged section. Wearing safety goggles and a dust mask, break away the drywall using a mallet *(above, left)* or small sledgehammer; if necessary, also use a cold chisel and a ball-peen hammer. Then, use the utility knife to cut away any plastic, foil or paper vapor barrier about 3 inches below the bottom edge of the remaining drywall *(above, right)*—leaving enough of it exposed to overlap comfortably with a new section of vapor barrier.

2 **Removing the wet insulation.** Wearing work gloves, safety goggles and a dust mask, use a board to compress the insulation and as a straightedge for cutting it with a utility knife; remove fiberglass batt insulation or plastic foam insulation the same way. Position the board between two studs just above the wet insulation and use the utility knife to slice along it through the insulation *(above, left)*; if necessary, hold up the bottom edge of the remaining vapor barrier to avoid damaging it. Pull the wet insulation out of the wall cavity and bag it for disposal. Continue along the wall the same way until all the wet insulation is pulled out. Remove any loose dirt and debris from the wall cavity using a putty knife *(above, right)* or a stiff-bristled brush, then clean and disinfect it *(page 138)*. Also air out the house *(page 137)*.

REMOVING DAMAGED DRYWALL

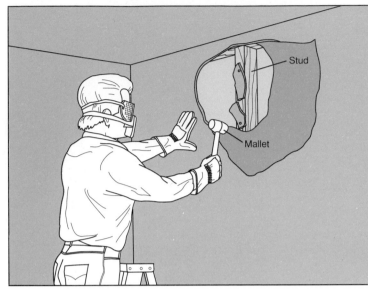

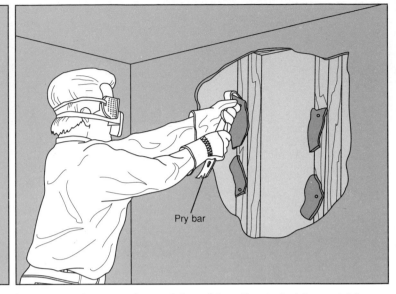

1 **Breaking away the drywall.** Shut off power to the circuits of the room *(page 83)* or the system *(page 82)* and air out any wet electrical boxes *(page 73)*; if the bottom of the wall is damaged, also remove the shoe molding and baseboard *(page 73)*. To remove a damaged section of the wall, protect the floor with a dropcloth and break away the drywall between studs. Wearing work gloves, safety goggles and a dust mask, start at the top of the damaged section at least 4 inches below the ceiling and break away the drywall using a mallet *(above, left)* or small sledgehammer. Use a pry bar to pull out

fasteners and remove pieces of drywall from the studs *(above, right)*. To break away the drywall along the top of the wall at the ceiling, use a cold chisel and a ball-peen hammer or small sledgehammer. Continue the procedure, working down and across the wall until the damaged drywall is removed. To check if the remaining drywall is dry and can be left in place, use a hand drill to drill small holes in it at several locations—the drywall dust should be chalky and powdery. If the drywall dust is chalky and powdery, snap off the remaining drywall cleanly along studs *(step 2)*; otherwise, continue breaking away the drywall.

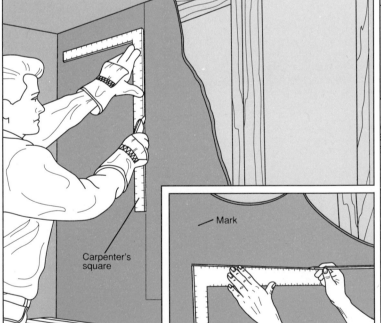

2 **Snapping off the drywall along studs.** If the remaining drywall is dry and can be left in place, snap it off vertically along the nearest stud on each side of the damaged section; if the damaged section does not extend the full height of the wall, also snap off the remaining drywall horizontally between the studs. Using a pencil and a carpenter's square, mark the wall vertically along the midpoint of each stud and, if necessary, horizontally between the studs *(inset)*.

Then, wear work gloves to score the wall along the marks with a utility knife and the straightedge *(above, left)*. Wearing safety goggles and a dust mask, grasp an edge of the remaining drywall and pull it out sharply *(above, right)*, snapping it off cleanly along the scored line. Continue the procedure until the remaining drywall is snapped off cleanly along each scored line. Remove any wet insulation *(page 75)*, using the utility knife to cut away any vapor barrier. Also air out the house *(page 137)*.

REMOVING DAMAGED WALL PANELS

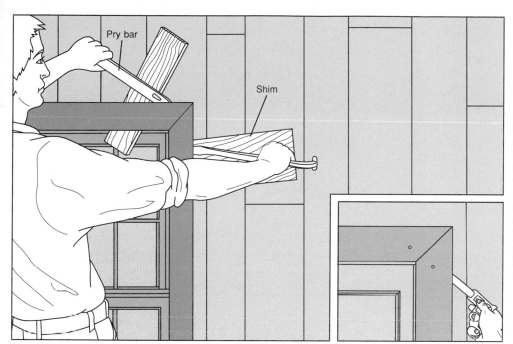

1 Removing the trim. Shut off power to the circuits of the room *(page 83)* or the system *(page 82)* and air out any wet electrical boxes *(page 73)*. Then, remove the shoe molding and baseboard along the bottom of the wall *(page 73)*. To ventilate the wall or remove a damaged section of it, take off any obstructing cover plate for an outlet or switch box or fixture. To remove the trim around a window or door, work a putty knife between the trim on the side and the wall, then insert a wood shim. Gently fit a pry bar between the putty knife and the shim, then ease out the trim. Continue along the trim the same way. At a corner joint, the trim on each side may be nailed together; use a nail set and a hammer to drive the nails through the trim or ease out the trim on each side of the corner together *(left)*. If the trim starts to split, fit a keyhole saw or hacksaw blade behind it and saw through the nails *(inset)*.

2 Prying off panels. Check the grooves of the panel for nail heads; if they are small, drive them through the panel with a nail set and a hammer. Starting at the bottom of the panel at a joint, work a putty knife under one side of it and insert a wood block to wedge it open. Fit a pry bar under the panel and ease it out *(above, left)*. Continue along the panel the same way until the side is loosened, then repeat the procedure along the other side of it. If the panel resists being loosened, it may be glued in place and have to be taken off in sections. When each side of the panel is loosened, pull it off *(above, right)*; if necessary, have a helper support one side of it. Take off as many panels as necessary the same way. Remove any wet insulation *(page 75)*, using the utility knife to cut away any vapor barrier. Also air out the house *(page 137)*.

ELECTRICITY

The electrical system of your home plays a major role in setting the level of comfort and convenience in your daily life. Electricity provides the power for lighting fixtures and lamps, major appliances such as refrigerators, ranges and dishwashers, small appliances such as toaster ovens, microwave ovens and hair dryers, entertainment units such as televisions, videocassette recorders and stereos, and electrical heating systems. Know how to live safely with electricity, both indoors and outdoors, and take measures to protect your children *(page 89)*. Keep a well-stocked electrical emergency kit on hand and be sure to install electrical safety devices judiciously throughout your home *(page 79)*.

Electricity brings with it the potential for great danger—more than any other system in your home, it is strictly regulated by codes and standards to protect you from fire and electrical shock. Before an emergency situation arises, consult the Troubleshooting Guide on pages 80 and 81 to have emergency procedures at your fingertips; quick-action steps to take are listed and references are given to more detailed procedures on pages 82 to 89. Know how to shut off your electrical system *(page 82)*. **Caution:** Work safely at the service panel *(page 82)* to avoid the possibility of electrical shock; always keep one hand free. If the circuits of your electrical system are not clearly and correctly labeled at the service panel, label them *(page 84)*.

The list of Safety Tips *(right)* reviews basic precautions to follow in preventing an electrical emergency in your home. Any switch, outlet, lighting fixture or lamp, appliance, entertainment unit or electrical tool can be vulnerable to wear and tear; fortunately, a cracked plug, a frayed power cord or extension cord and other advance warnings of a possible life- and property-threatening hazard can be detected. Periodically inspect the plugs, power cords and extension cords of your home for signs of damage *(page 85)*; replace any worn or damaged part before reusing the electrical unit. If an electrical fire should occur, know what to do and treat it with extra caution *(page 61)*. Water can turn a small electrical fault into a deadly hazard; do not handle any electrical unit, even a switch or an outlet, in damp or wet conditions. If you must rescue someone immobilized by a live current, do not touch the victim or the electrical unit; immediately shut off power at the service panel or use a wooden broom handle or chair to knock the victim free *(page 88)*.

If you are ever in doubt about the safety of your electrical system or your ability to handle an emergency, do not hesitate to call for help. Post the telephone numbers for your local electricity utility, fire department, police and hospital near your telephone; even in non-emergency situations, qualified professionals can answer questions concerning your electrical system. In most regions, you can dial 911 in the event of a life-threatening emergency.

SAFETY TIPS

1. Label the main circuit breaker, the main fuse block or the service disconnect breaker for your electrical system; also map the circuits of your home and label them at the service panel *(page 84)*. In the event of an emergency, you will want anyone to be able to shut off the power quickly.

2. Install electrical safety devices such as surge suppressors, ground-fault circuit interrupters (GFCIs) and cord shorteners judiciously throughout your home *(page 79)*.

3. Never work on the wiring of the service panel; entrance wires may remain live even when power is shut off at the main circuit breaker, main fuse block or service disconnect breaker.

4. Do not remove the cover of the service panel.

5. Never work with electricity in damp or wet conditions and do not use any electrical appliance, tool or extension cord if it is damp or wet.

6. Do not touch a metal faucet, pipe, appliance or other object when working with electricity.

7. Never splice a power cord or an extension cord or remove the grounding prong from a three-prong plug.

8. Do not plug a three-prong plug into a two-slot outlet.

9. Use an extension cord to supply electricity to an area only temporarily—not as permanent wiring. Never run a power cord or an extension cord under a rug or carpet or fasten it using tacks, pins or staples.

10. Keep children away from electrical units, power cords and extension cords. Cover any unused outlet with safety caps; install a plug cover at each used outlet.

11. Turn off each circuit breaker at least once a year to prevent the sticking or failing of any mechanical component.

12. Test each built-in ground-fault circuit interrupter (GFCI) monthly and each portable GFCI before using it.

13. Keep electrical appliances such as hair dryers, radios and shavers away from sinks, bathtubs and toilets.

14. Do not pull a power cord out of an outlet by the cord; hold and pull only the plug.

15. Never replace a blown fuse with one of higher amperage; do not use a penny, a washer or foil as a substitute for a fuse.

16 Do not poke a fork or other metal implement inside a toaster, hair dryer or other electrical appliance while it is plugged into an outlet—even if it is turned off.

17. Never use an extension cord with an amperage rating lower than the amperage rating of the electrical appliance or tool.

18. Use only electrical units, extension cords and safety devices that bear a recognized seal of approval; look for the UL (Underwriters Laboratories) or CSA (Canadian Standards Association) stamp.

19. Keep at least one fire extinguisher rated ABC *(page 55)* in your home and know how to use it in the event of a fire.

20. If your plumbing system is of metal, it may provide the electrical grounding for your home; if you replace a metal pipe with a plastic pipe or otherwise interrupt the integrity of any electrical grounding through a plumbing system of metal, install an electrical jumper wire *(page 103)*.

Type-S fuse
Fuse fits adapter screwed into service panel; adapter accepts only type-S fuse of matching amperage, guarding against accidental installation of fuse with higher amperage.

Standard plug fuse
Available in 15-, 20-, and 30-ampere ratings; amperage must match gauge of wire in circuit. Never replace fuse with one of higher amperage.

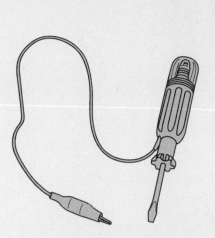

Knife-blade cartridge fuse
Used to protect electrical system; rated over 60 amperes.

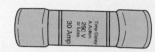

Ferrule-type cartridge fuse
Protects dedicated circuit for large appliance; available in ratings up to 60 amperes.

Continuity tester
Battery-powered, sends a small electrical current through circuit being tested; bulb glows if electrical current passes through circuit (continuity).

Fuse puller
Used to remove cartridge fuses; must be made of plastic or other nonconductive material.

Portable surge suppressor
Protects electrical units against power surges that can damage solid-state components; reset button reactivates internal circuit breaker.

Receptacle analyzer
Fits into slots of grounded outlet; three small display lights indicate: whether there is electrical current to outlet; whether hot and neutral wires are reversed; and whether outlet is grounded. If analyzer reveals wiring fault, have outlet connections serviced.

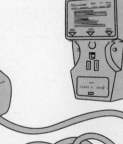

Portable ground-fault circuit interrupter (GFCI)
Plugs into grounded outlet to provide protection against electrical shock *(near left)*. Extension cord with built-in GFCI *(far left)* equipped with snap-shut cover to protect GFCI when not in use.

Fused extension cord
Heavy-duty extension cord coils back into its case after use; fuse protects circuit from being overloaded. If used outdoors, should be plugged into GFCI-protected outlet.

Safety caps
Fit into unused outlet slots to protect children from electrical shock.

Outdoor extension cord
Heavy-duty, three-prong extension cord rated for outdoor use.

Power cord shortener
Conceals up to 8 feet of excess power cord, preventing it from being played with by children or tripped over. Turn shortener until openings align, then rotate handle until center divider disappears; bend cord and insert it into opening, then rotate handle until cord desired length.

Plug cover
Fits onto post screwed to cover plate of duplex outlet, concealing plug and its prongs; prevents children from tampering with plug. To release plug cover, spread its tabs and pull it off post.

TROUBLESHOOTING GUIDE

SYMPTOM	PROCEDURE
Fire in electrical outlet, switch, fixture or appliance	Call fire department immediately
	If fire not small and contained, leave house and call fire department from home of neighbor
	If fire small and contained, shut off electricity to system *(p. 82)* and use fire extinguisher rated ABC or BC *(p. 61)*
	Have fire department check house—even if fire out
	Have system professionally inspected
Electrical shock	If victim immobilized by live current, do not touch victim or electrical source
	Immediately shut off electricity to system *(p. 82)*
	If electricity to system cannot be shut off immediately, unplug or switch off electrical source *(p. 87)* or knock victim free of electrical source *(p. 88)*
	Call for medical help and monitor vital life signs *(p. 16)*, checking for breathing and pulse
	If no breathing, administer artificial respiration *(p. 17)*
	If no pulse, administer cardiopulmonary resuscitation (CPR) only if qualified
	If breathing and no back or neck injury, place in recovery position *(p. 20)*
Service panel sparks, shocks or hot to touch	Do not touch service panel
	Call electricity utility immediately to shut off power
	Do not touch any switch, outlet or other electrical unit
	Have system professionally inspected
Switch sparks, shocks or hot to touch	Do not touch switch
	Immediately shut off electricity to circuit *(p. 83)* or system *(p. 82)*
	If electricity to circuit or system cannot be shut off immediately, switch off electrical source *(p. 87)*
	Have circuit and switch professionally inspected
Lighting fixture sparks, shocks or hot to touch	Do not touch lighting fixture or switch
	Immediately shut off electricity to circuit *(p. 83)* or system *(p. 82)*
	If electricity to circuit or system cannot be shut off immediately, switch off electrical source *(p. 87)*
	Have circuit, switch and lighting fixture professionally inspected
Outlet sparks, shocks or hot to touch	Do not touch outlet or extension cord, power cord or electrical unit plugged into outlet
	Immediately shut off electricity to circuit *(p. 83)* or system *(p. 82)*
	If electricity to circuit or system cannot be shut off immediately, unplug electrical source *(p. 87)*
	Have circuit, outlet, extension cord, power cord and electrical unit professionally inspected
Lamp, appliance, tool or other electrical unit sparks, shocks or hot to touch	Do not touch electrical unit, power cord, extension cord or outlet
	Immediately shut off electricity to circuit *(p. 83)* or system *(p. 82)*
	If electricity to circuit or system cannot be shut off immediately, unplug electrical source *(p. 87)*
	Have electrical unit, power cord, extension cord, outlet and circuit professionally inspected
Power cord or extension cord sparks, shocks or hot to touch	Do not touch power cord, extension cord, electrical unit or outlet
	Immediately shut off electricity to circuit *(p. 83)* or system *(p. 82)*
	If electricity to circuit or system cannot be shut off immediately, unplug electrical source *(p. 87)*
	Have power cord, extension cord, electrical unit, outlet and circuit professionally inspected
Electrical burn	Do not apply ointment or butter
	Soak injury in cold water; if necessary, cover with sterile gauze *(p. 36)*
	Seek medical attention immediately
Circuit breaker trips repeatedly or fuse blows repeatedly	Check for overloaded circuit; if necessary, lessen load on circuit *(p. 85)*
	Check for short circuit *(p. 85)*; if necessary, have circuit or electrical unit professionally inspected
Circuit unlabeled or labeled incorrectly	Map and label circuits *(p. 84)*

SYMPTOM	PROCEDURE
House, basement or room flooded	Do not enter house, basement or room
	Leave house and call electricity utility to shut off power
	Do not touch any switch, outlet or other electrical unit
	When electricity shut off, use trash pump *(p. 136)*; remove remaining standing water *(p. 72)*
	Have system and any flooded electrical unit professionally inspected
Major appliance or other electrical unit flooded or wet	Do not enter room
	If conditions around service panel wet, leave house and call electricity utility to shut off power
	If conditions around service panel dry, shut off electricity to system *(p. 82)*
	When electricity shut off, remove standing water *(p. 72)*
	Have system and major appliance or electrical unit professionally inspected
Small appliance or other electrical unit falls into filled sink, bathtub or toilet	Do not touch appliance or any plumbing fixture or pipe
	If you, outlet or plug wet, dry yourself and shut off electricity to circuit *(p. 83)* or system *(p. 82)*
	If you, outlet and plug dry, retrieve small appliance or other electrical unit *(p. 87)*
	Have small appliance or other electrical unit professionally inspected
No electricity	To prevent overloading of system or damaging of appliances and other electrical units when electricity restored, turn off or unplug appliances and other electrical units—including furnace, heater, air conditioner, refrigerator, freezer, clothes washer and dryer, dishwasher, microwave oven, computer, television, stereo and other entertainment units
	To know when electricity restored, turn on lamp or lighting fixture
	If neighbors have no power, call electricity utility to report power outage
	If neighbors have power, restore electricity to system *(p. 82)*; if electricity cannot be restored, have system professionally inspected
	Have emergency heating and light sources on hand; use portable gas-powered generator *(p. 128)*
	Keep refrigerator and freezer doors closed as much as possible
	When power restored, plug in and turn on only essential appliances; wait at least 30 minutes before plugging in and turning on other appliances and electrical units
Lightning storm	To guard against power surges, turn off electrical units with electronic components—including computer, television, stereo and other entertainment units; use surge suppressors *(p. 79)*
	Stay away from windows, doors, fireplaces, radiators, electrical units, plumbing fixtures and pipes
Underground power line broken during excavation	Do not touch power line; do not stand in any water near power line
	Call electricity utility, fire department or police immediately
	Treat power line as if live with electricity: stay far away from it and anything it touches, and warn others to stay away
Overhead power line down	Do not touch power line; do not stand in any water near power line
	Call electricity utility, fire department or police immediately
	Treat fallen power line as if live with electricity: stay far away from it and anything it touches, and warn others to stay away
Antenna fallen against power line	Do not touch any electrical unit linked to antenna—including television or other entertainment unit
	Do not attempt to dislodge antenna
	Call electricity utility, fire department or police immediately
	Treat power line and antenna as if live with electricity: stay far away from them and anything they touch, and warn others to stay away
Person trapped under downed power line	Do not touch victim or power line; do not stand in any water near power line
	Call for medical help and call electricity utility, fire department or police immediately
	Treat power line as if live with electricity: stay far away from it and anything it touches, and warn others to stay away
Power line fallen on car	If trapped in car, do not attempt to jump clear of car and do not touch any metal part
	Have someone call electricity utility, fire department or police immediately
	Treat power line as if live with electricity: keep feet on rubber mat and warn others to stay away

SAFETY AT THE SERVICE PANEL

Working safely at the service panel. Take basic safety precautions when working at the service panel, even to reset a circuit breaker or change a fuse. Keep a non-metallic flashlight on hand to avoid having to find the service panel in the dark. **Caution:** If the area around the service panel is flooded, stay away from it—call your electricity utility to shut off power to your house. If the area around the service panel is damp, stand on a dry board or wear dry rubber boots to work at the service panel. To prevent your body from becoming a route for electricity, wear heavy rubber gloves and work only with one hand; keep your other hand in your pocket or behind your back and avoid touching anything metal *(left)*. As an added precaution when shutting off a circuit breaker, use your knuckle; any shock will jerk your hand away from the service panel. **Caution:** Never remove the cover of the service panel; even if you have shut off electricity to the system, parts of the service panel may still be charged with voltage.

As a routine preventive measure, inspect the service panel of your home regularly. The main circuit breaker, main fuse block or service disconnect breaker and each individual circuit should be correctly labeled on the service panel; if the individual circuits are not identified, map them before an emergency situation occurs *(page 84)*. Once every year, turn off and back on the main circuit breaker *(step below)* or service disconnect breaker and each other circuit breaker *(page 83)* to prevent the sticking or failure of any mechanical component. Or, every 6 months, check that the main fuse block *(page 83)* and each other fuse *(page 84)* is installed tightly.

SHUTTING OFF ELECTRICITY TO THE SYSTEM

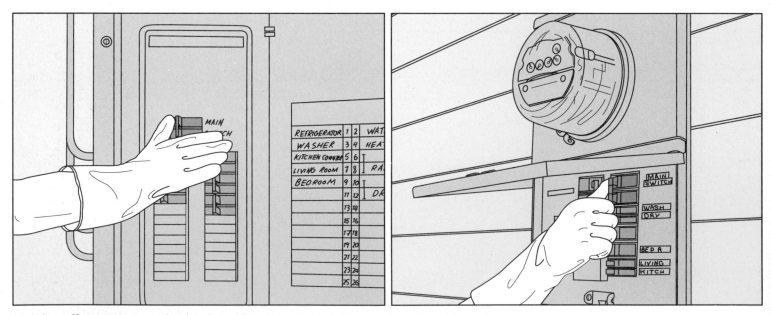

Shutting off power at a main circuit breaker. If your electrical system is protected by a service disconnect breaker or main fuse block, shut off electricity at it *(page 83)*. Otherwise, work in safe conditions *(step above)* to locate the main circuit breaker, a linked, double circuit breaker at the service panel; wearing a rubber glove, flip it to OFF, shutting off electricity. Usually, the main circuit breaker is isolated above *(above, left)* or at the top of *(above, right)* the individual circuit breakers and labeled MAIN. To restore electricity, flip the main circuit breaker to ON. If the main circuit breaker is not labeled, label it for easy identification in the event of a future emergency.

SHUTTING OFF ELECTRICITY TO THE SYSTEM (continued)

Shutting off power at a main fuse block. If your electrical system is protected by a main circuit breaker, shut off electricity at it *(page 82)*. If your electrical system is protected by a service disconnect breaker, shut off electricity at it *(step right)*. Otherwise, work in safe conditions *(page 82)* to locate the main fuse block, a large pull-out block usually at the top of the service panel; wearing a rubber glove, grip its handle and pull it straight out *(above)*, shutting off electricity; if there is more than one main fuse block, pull out each one the same way. If the service panel has a shutoff lever instead of a main fuse block, pull it down to shut off electricity. To restore electricity, push the main fuse block back until it snaps into place or push the shutoff lever up. If the main fuse block or shutoff lever is not labeled, label it for easy identification in the event of a future emergency.

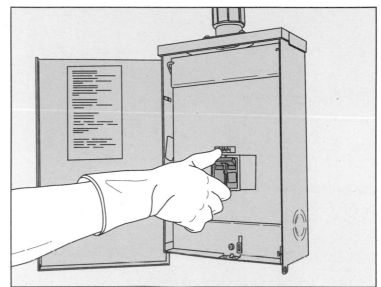

Shutting off power at a service disconnect breaker. If your electrical system is protected by a main circuit breaker, shut off electricity at it *(page 82)*. If your electrical system is protected by a main fuse block, shut off electricity at it *(step left)*. Otherwise, work in safe conditions *(page 82)* to locate the service disconnect breaker, housed in its own box outdoors near the electricity meter or indoors near the service panel; wearing a rubber glove, flip the service disconnect breaker to OFF *(above)*, shutting off electricity. To restore electricity, flip the service disconnect breaker to ON. If the service disconnect breaker is not labeled, label it for easy identification in the event of a future emergency.

SHUTTING OFF ELECTRICITY TO A CIRCUIT

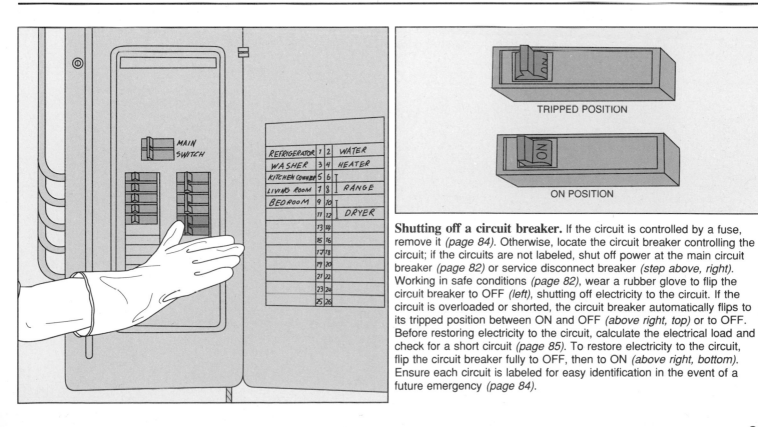

REFRIGERATOR	1	2	WATER
WASHER	3	4	HEATER
KITCHEN COUNTER	5	6	
LIVING ROOM	7	8	RANGE
BEDROOM	9	10	
	11	12	DRYER
	13	14	
	15	16	
	17	18	
	19	20	
	21	22	
	23	24	
	25	26	

TRIPPED POSITION

ON POSITION

Shutting off a circuit breaker. If the circuit is controlled by a fuse, remove it *(page 84)*. Otherwise, locate the circuit breaker controlling the circuit; if the circuits are not labeled, shut off power at the main circuit breaker *(page 82)* or service disconnect breaker *(step above, right)*. Working in safe conditions *(page 82)*, wear a rubber glove to flip the circuit breaker to OFF *(left)*, shutting off electricity to the circuit. If the circuit is overloaded or shorted, the circuit breaker automatically flips to its tripped position between ON and OFF *(above right, top)* or to OFF. Before restoring electricity to the circuit, calculate the electrical load and check for a short circuit *(page 85)*. To restore electricity to the circuit, flip the circuit breaker fully to OFF, then to ON *(above right, bottom)*. Ensure each circuit is labeled for easy identification in the event of a future emergency *(page 84)*.

SHUTTING OFF ELECTRICITY TO A CIRCUIT (continued)

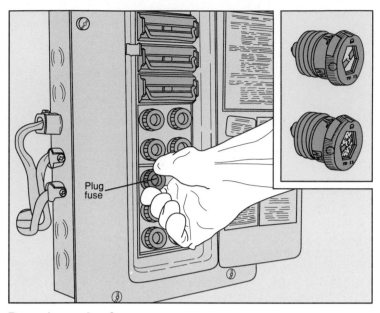

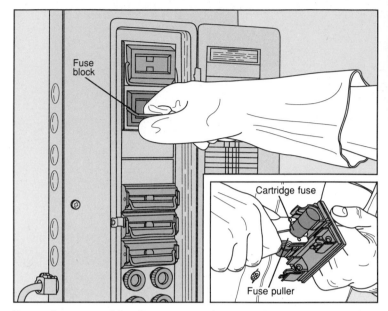

Removing a plug fuse. If the circuit is controlled by a circuit breaker, shut it off *(page 83)*. If the circuit is controlled by a cartridge fuse, remove it *(step right)*. Otherwise, locate the plug fuse controlling the circuit; if the circuits are not labeled, shut off power at the main fuse block, service disconnect breaker *(page 83)* or main circuit breaker *(page 82)*. Working in safe conditions *(page 82)*, wear a rubber glove to grasp the fuse only by its insulated rim and unscrew it *(above)*, shutting off electricity to the circuit. A broken metal strip inside the fuse indicates an overloaded circuit; a discolored fuse indicates a short circuit *(inset)*. If necessary, use a continuity tester to test the fuse *(page 86)*. Before replacing the fuse, calculate the electrical load and check for a short circuit *(page 85)*. To restore electricity to the circuit, replace the fuse with one of identical amperage. Ensure each circuit is labeled for easy identification in the event of a future emergency *(step below)*.

Removing a cartridge fuse. If the circuit is controlled by a circuit breaker, shut it off *(page 83)*. If the circuit is controlled by a plug fuse, remove it *(step left)*. Otherwise, locate the fuse block of the cartridge fuse; if the circuits are not labeled, shut off power at the main fuse block, service disconnect breaker *(page 83)* or main circuit breaker *(page 82)*. Working in safe conditions *(page 82)*, grip the handle of the fuse block and pull it straight out *(above)*, shutting off electricity to the circuit. If the circuit is overloaded or shorted, the fuse will blow—and not look damaged; pull it out using a fuse puller *(inset)* or by hand and use a continuity tester to test it *(page 86)*. Before replacing the fuse, calculate the electrical load and check for a short circuit *(page 85)*. To restore electricity to the circuit, replace the fuse with one of identical amperage, then put back the fuse block. Ensure each circuit is labeled for easy identification in the event of a future emergency *(step below)*.

LABELING YOUR SERVICE PANEL

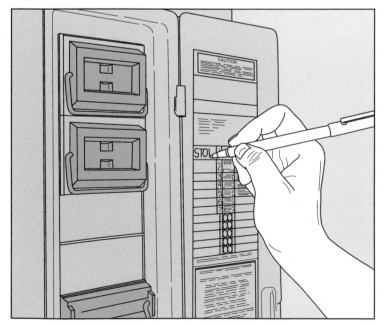

Mapping your electrical circuits. To respond quickly in the event of an electrical emergency, each circuit in your home must be correctly and clearly labeled on the service panel; often, the labels are missing, outdated or illegible. Begin by sketching a floor plan of the house, then walk around each room, mapping its outlets, switches, major appliances and other electrical fixtures. Turn off each switch and unplug each major appliance. At the service panel, post a new label for each circuit, then designate a number for each circuit and write it on the label. Shut off electricity to circuit number 1, shutting off the circuit breaker *(page 83)* or removing the fuse *(steps above)*. To identify the electrical units on the circuit, find the outlets, switches, major appliances and other electrical fixtures that no longer receive electricity. Turn on each switch, plug in each major appliance and use a working lamp to check the upper and lower receptacle of each outlet; those that do not work are on the circuit. (Note that a circuit can serve more than one room or floor.) On your map, write the circuit number beside each outlet, switch, major appliance and other electrical fixture on the circuit, then return to the service panel and restore electricity to the circuit. Use the information recorded on your floor plan to characterize the circuit and write a short description of it on its label *(left)*. Then, shut off electricity to circuit number 2 and repeat the procedure, continuing until you have mapped each circuit; include each 240-volt circuit controlled by a double circuit breaker or fuse block. Post your map at the service panel for future reference.

CALCULATING ELECTRICAL LOAD

Determining a circuit overload. A circuit is overloaded if it is used beyond its capacity—the amperage rating of its circuit breaker or fuse. If you suspect that a circuit is overloaded, calculate its existing load and compare the result to its capacity. To calculate the existing load on a circuit, list each electrical unit on the circuit along with its wattage rating. The wattage rating is usually printed on a label *(below)* found on the back or bottom panel of an appliance or near the socket of a lamp or lighting fixture. Typical wattage ratings of many household appliances are listed in the chart at right. Add the wattage ratings of the electrical units on the circuit, then divide by 120 volts to convert to amperes. If the result is higher than the amperage rating of the circuit breaker or fuse, the circuit is overloaded; if the load on the circuit is continuous (3 hours or more), it should be limited to 80 per cent of the amperage rating of the circuit breaker or fuse. Move a high-wattage appliance such as a hair dryer or toaster oven to another circuit or have a new circuit run from the service panel.

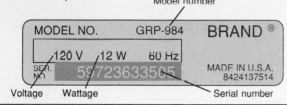

Model number

MODEL NO.   GRP-984   BRAND ®

120 V   12 W   60 Hz

SER. NO.   59723633505   MADE IN U.S.A.
8424137514

Voltage   Wattage   Serial number

TYPICAL WATTAGE RATINGS OF APPLIANCES

APPLIANCE	APPROXIMATE WATTAGE RATING	APPLIANCE	APPROXIMATE WATTAGE RATING
Blender	200-400	Microwave oven	500-800
Coffee maker	600-1000	Portable heater	1500
Computer	150-600	Radio	10-100
Food processor	500	Television	150-450
Hair dryer	400-1500	Toaster	800-1200
Iron	1200	Toaster oven	1500
Kettle	1200-1400	Vacuum cleaner	300-600
Lamp or fixture	25-150	VCR	50

CHECKING FOR A SHORT CIRCUIT

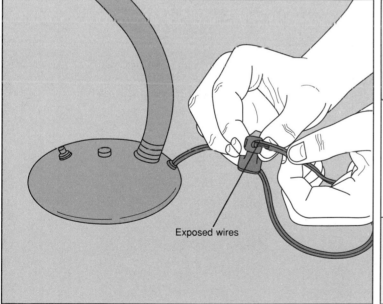

Exposed wires

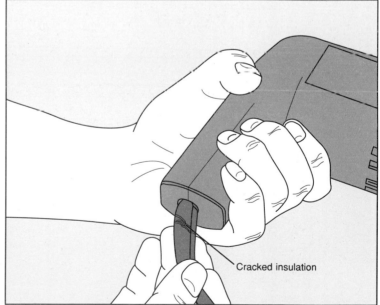

Cracked insulation

Inspecting plugs and cords. If a circuit breaker trips repeatedly or a fuse blows repeatedly, suspect a short circuit—damaged wiring within the circuit. To trace a short circuit, turn on each wall switch and unplug each electrical unit on the circuit, then restore power to the circuit by flipping the circuit breaker to ON *(page 83)* or replacing the fuse *(page 84)*. If the circuit breaker trips or the fuse blows, suspect a short circuit in the wiring behind the ceilings or walls and have it repaired as soon as possible. If the circuit breaker does not trip or the fuse does not blow, suspect a short circuit in the wiring of an electrical unit. Carefully inspect the plug, power cord and any extension cord of each electrical unit for signs of damage. Look for corroded, loose or bent plug prongs;

a plug with a removable insulating disc is unsafe, especially if the disc is missing and the wire ends of the power cord are exposed. Power cords and extension cords tend to crack or fray at the plug, exposing wires *(above, left)*; also check for cracked or frayed insulation *(above, right)*. Have any damaged plug, power cord or extension cord replaced before reusing the electrical unit. Keep power cords and extension cords away from heat and water; do not run them under rugs or carpets or fasten them using tacks, pins or staples. If necessary, isolate the electrical unit causing the short circuit by plugging in and turning on each electrical unit in turn; the faulty electrical unit will trip the circuit breaker or blow the fuse. Have any faulty electrical unit repaired before reusing it.

USING A CONTINUITY TESTER TO TEST A FUSE

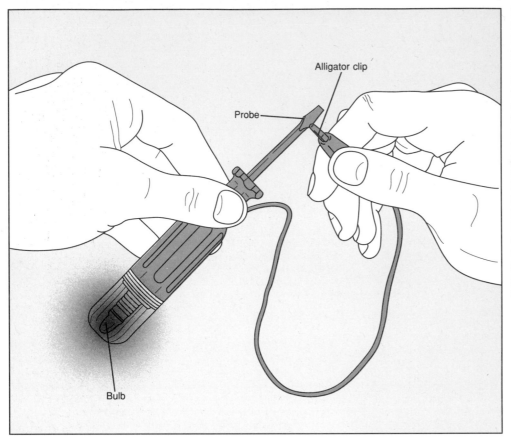

Using a continuity tester. A continuity tester indicates whether a circuit is complete by sending a small electrical current through it. Because the continuity tester is powered by a battery, it must be used only when electricity through the circuit is shut off. Before using the continuity tester, check its battery by touching the alligator clip to the probe *(left)*; the bulb of the continuity tester should glow, as shown. If the bulb of the continuity tester does not glow, replace the battery. To test a circuit (a cartridge fuse, for example) for continuity, touch the alligator clip to one end of the circuit (one end of the fuse) and touch the probe to the other end of the circuit (the other end of the fuse). If the bulb of the continuity tester glows, the circuit is complete—there is continuity. If the bulb of the continuity tester does not glow, the circuit is incomplete—there is not continuity. After using the continuity tester, attach the alligator clip to its plastic insulation to prevent it from accidentally contacting the probe and wearing out the battery.

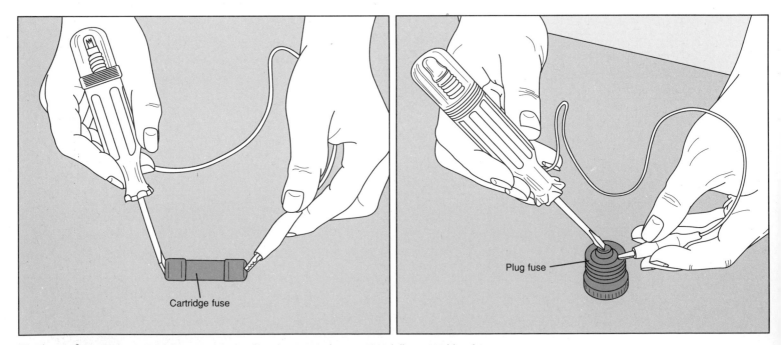

Testing a fuse. Use a continuity tester *(step above)* to test a fuse—especially a cartridge fuse which shows no signs of damage if it blows. To test a cartridge fuse, remove it from the fuse block at the service panel *(page 84)*. Touch the alligator clip to the metal cap at one end of the fuse and touch the probe to the metal cap at the other end of the fuse *(above, left)*. If the fuse is good, the bulb of the continuity tester should glow. To test a plug fuse, remove it from the service panel *(page 84)*. Touch the alligator clip to the metal shell of the fuse and touch the probe to the center contact *(above, right)*. If the fuse is good, the bulb of the continuity tester should glow. If the bulb of the continuity tester does not glow, replace the fuse with one of the same amperage.

SPARKING SWITCHES, OUTLETS AND FIXTURES

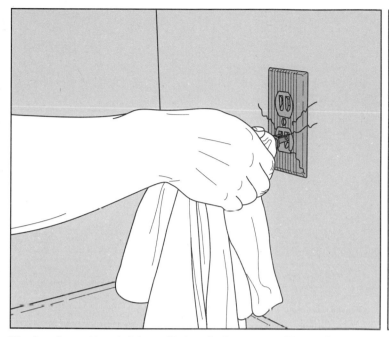

Unplugging and switching off electrical sources of hazards. If a switch, outlet or other electrical unit makes snapping or cracking sounds, or if sparks, smoke or flames appear, immediately shut off electricity to the circuit, shutting off the circuit breaker *(page 83)* or removing the fuse *(page 84)*; if the circuit is not labeled, shut off power at the main circuit breaker *(page 82)*, main fuse block or service disconnect breaker *(page 83)*. If the switch, outlet or other electrical unit is sparking, burning or wet, do not touch it. Use a fire extinguisher rated ABC or BC to put out any flames *(page 61)*. Safely retrieve any electrical unit immersed in water *(step below)*. Work only in dry conditions to pull the plug of an electrical unit out of an outlet or turn off a switch. Protecting your hand with a thick, dry towel or heavy work glove, grasp only the plug or the power cord of the electrical unit and pull it out of the outlet *(above, left)*. Standing to one side of the switch, use a wooden spoon or broom handle to flip off the toggle *(above, right)*. Locate the problem and have it repaired before reusing the electrical unit, outlet or switch.

WATER AND ELECTRICITY

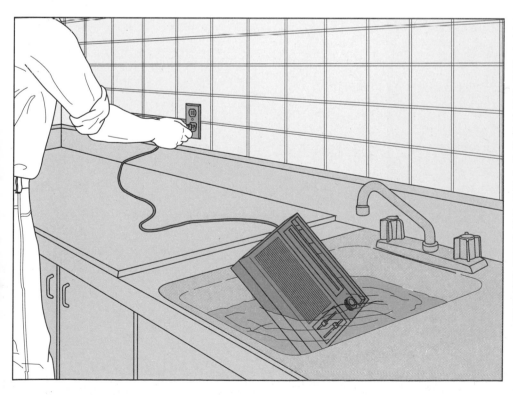

Retrieving an electrical appliance from water. Water can provide an alternative path for the electricity in a circuit. Never use any appliance in damp or wet conditions. A radio, hair dryer or shaver can pose a particular hazard around a sink, bathtub or toilet. If an appliance falls into a sink, bathtub or toilet, do not reach in to retrieve it. If you, the appliance or the area around you or the appliance is wet, immediately shut off electricity to the circuit, shutting off the circuit breaker *(page 83)* or removing the fuse *(page 84)*; if the circuit is not labeled, shut off power at the main circuit breaker *(page 82)*, main fuse block or service disconnect breaker *(page 83)*. Work only in dry conditions to pull the plug of the electrical unit out of the outlet *(left)*. Always turn off and unplug an appliance before cleaning it with a damp cloth, then dry your hands and the appliance thoroughly before plugging it back in. Any outlet near a sink, bathtub or toilet or in an area subject to dampness should be protected by a ground-fault circuit interrupter (GFCI) *(page 79)*.

RESCUING A VICTIM OF ELECTRICAL SHOCK

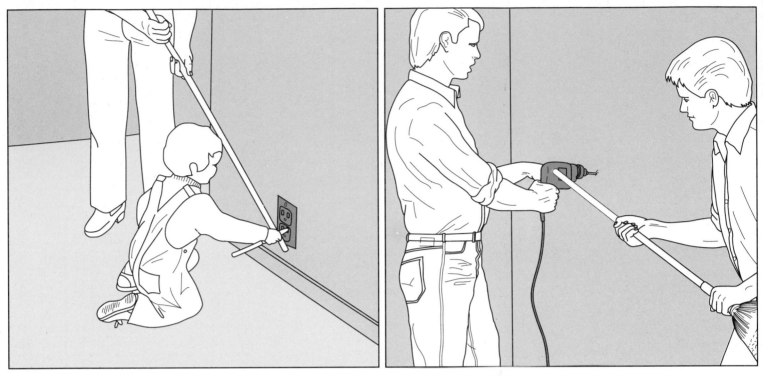

Freeing someone from a live current. Usually a person who contacts live current will be thrown back from the electrical source; sometimes, however, muscles contract involuntarily around the electrical source. Do not touch the victim or the electrical source. Immediately stop the flow of electricity, shutting off power at the main circuit breaker *(page 82)*, main fuse block or service disconnect breaker *(page 83)*. If the power cannot be shut off immediately, unplug or switch off the electrical source of the hazard *(page 87)* or use a wooden broom handle, chair or board to knock the victim free of the electrical source—an outlet *(above, left)* or a tool *(above, right)*, for example. Take measures to prevent electrical emergencies *(page 89)* and install electrical safety devices judiciously throughout your home *(page 79)*.

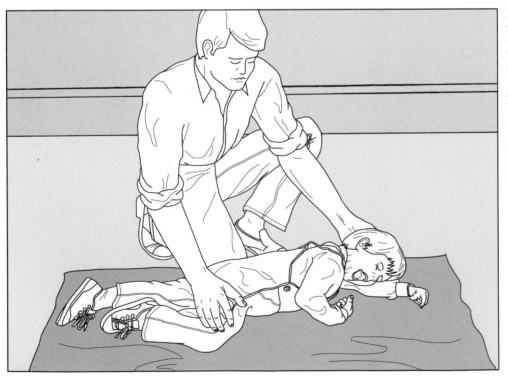

Handling a victim of electrical shock. Call for medical help immediately. Monitor the vital life signs of the victim *(page 16)*, checking for breathing and a pulse. If there is no breathing, administer artificial respiration *(page 17)*; if there is no pulse, administer cardiopulmonary resuscitation (CPR) only if you are qualified. If there is breathing and no back or neck injuries have been sustained, place the victim in the recovery position *(page 20)*. Tilt the head back with the face to one side and the tongue forward to maintain an open airway *(left)*. Keep the victim calm and comfortable until medical help arrives.

PREVENTING ELECTRICAL EMERGENCIES

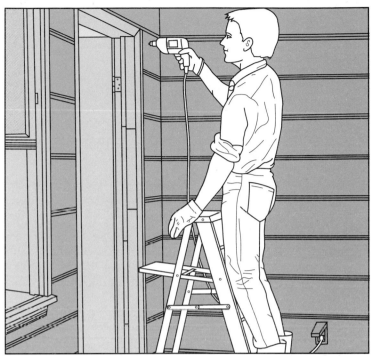

Plugging into your electrical system safely. Install electrical safety devices judiciously throughout your home *(page 79)*. Regularly inspect plugs, power cords and extension cords for signs of damage *(page 85)*. Do not use an "octopus" connector at an outlet *(inset)*; an overloaded circuit can result. Use an extension cord to supply electricity to an area only temporarily; do not use it as permanent wiring. Never try to hide a power cord or an extension cord by running it under a rug or carpet or by fastening it along a baseboard with tacks, pins or staples. When removing a power cord or an extension cord from an outlet, grasp and pull only its plug *(above)*; do not tug the cord. Take special precautions when working in a damp area *(step right)* and to protect children *(step below)*.

Working in a damp area. Any new outlet installed outdoors, in a garage, basement or bathroom, or within 6 feet of a sink or other area subject to moisture must be protected by a ground-fault circuit interrupter (GFCI)—a requirement of the U.S. National Electrical Code. When working outdoors or in any damp area with an electrical tool, make sure it is properly grounded or double-insulated. Use only a heavy-duty, three-prong extension cord rated for outdoor use; plug it into an outlet with a built-in GFCI or use a portable GFCI or an extension cord with a built-in GFCI *(page 79)*. Secure the connection between the power cord of the tool and an extension cord by looping the cords loosely together before plugging in the tool. As an added precaution, use a wooden ladder and wear heavy rubber gloves *(above)*. Be careful not to touch overhead power lines when working on your roof or siding.

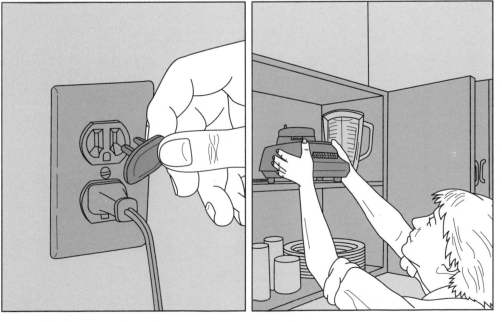

Protecting children. Teach your children to treat electricity with respect; instruct them not to play with power cords, extension cords or wires and never to poke anything into an outlet or appliance. To protect curious fingers, cover any unused outlet with a plastic safety cap, fitting it securely into the slots *(far left)*. Avoid leaving appliances such as blenders, toasters and irons unattended. Unplug an appliance when it is not in use and store it well out of reach *(near left)*. Do not leave the power cord of an appliance dangling from a counter or shelf; a small child may grab the cord and pull the appliance down on him. A kettle and an iron are particular hazards because the water in them can remain hot enough to scald long after they are turned off.

GAS

Natural gas, also known as methane, and propane gas, also called liquefied-petroleum (LP) gas, are efficient and reliable fuels used by millions of homeowners in North America. Natural gas is distributed through an underground network of supply pipes to which the main gas supply pipe of a home is connected; the main shutoff valve controlling the flow of gas into the supply pipes inside the home is usually located near the gas meter, outdoors or in the basement, utility room or garage. Propane is delivered by truck and stored in a tank or cylinder above or below the ground outside a home; the main shutoff valve controlling the flow of gas into the supply pipes inside the home is usually located under a hinged cover on the tank or cylinder. Each appliance that uses gas also has its own shutoff valve located near it. Tag the main gas shutoff valve and the shutoff valve for each appliance for easy identification in the event of an emergency.

Both natural gas and propane gas are colorless and odorless in their natural state; a sulphur-based chemical is commercially added to give them a strong odor similar to rotten eggs, enabling any leak to be easily detected. Make sure you and your family members are familiar with the distinctive odor of gas; as an added precaution, install a gas detector near each gas appliance *(page 44)*. If you detect a strong odor of gas, take action quickly. **Caution:** A spark from lighting a match, turning a switch on or off, or even picking up a telephone receiver can set off an explosion or cause a fire; leave the house immediately and call the gas company or the fire department from the home of a neighbor. Carbon monoxide, another colorless and odorless gas, is produced when a gas burner has inadequate air supply for proper combustion. To guard against carbon monoxide poisoning, install a carbon monoxide detector *(page 44)* and have each gas appliance serviced professionally at least once annually. Many gas companies and fire departments will measure the level of carbon monoxide in your house.

The Troubleshooting Guide *(page 91)* lists quick-action steps to take in the event of an emergency; some involve routine techniques for relighting a pilot *(page 94)*. Always follow the manufacturer's instructions for the appliance; in some instances, instructions for relighting the pilot may be found on a label of the appliance. Do not attempt to relight a pilot with electrical ignition. **Caution:** If you detect a strong odor of gas, do not attempt to relight the pilot; leave the house immediately and call the gas company or the fire department from the home of a neighbor. The list of Safety Tips at right provides basic precautions to follow in helping you and your family live safely with gas. When in doubt about your ability to handle an emergency, do not hesitate to call for help. Post the telephone number for the gas company and the fire department near the telephone; even in non-emergency situations, qualified professionals can answer questions about the safety of your gas system.

SAFETY TIPS

1. Locate and tag the main gas shutoff valve and the shutoff valve for each gas appliance; in the event of an emergency, you will want anyone to be able to find them quickly.

2. Natural gas and propane gas are treated with a sulphur-based chemical to give them a strong odor similar to rotten eggs. Make sure that you and your family members are familiar with the distinctive odor of gas; as an added precaution, install a gas detector near each appliance *(page 44)*.

3. If you return home and detect the odor of gas, **do not** enter the house; call the gas company or the fire department immediately from the home of a neighbor.

4. If you detect the odor of gas, do not use any electrical switch or outlet, light a match or use the telephone—a spark could cause an explosion or a fire. Leave the house immediately, then call the gas company or the fire department from the home of a neighbor.

5. Call the gas company to locate underground gas supply pipes before excavating on your property or building an addition to your home.

6. Use only gas appliances approved by a nationally recognized testing laboratory such as the American Gas Association or Canadian Gas Association; have older appliances approved by your gas supplier.

7. Always read the manufacturer's instructions for the appliance before attempting to light its pilot; follow the instructions carefully. In some instances, instructions for relighting the pilot are printed on a label of the appliance.

8. Do not attempt to relight the pilot of an appliance with electrical ignition; if there is any problem with the pilot, shut off the gas supply to the appliance *(page 92)* and have it professionally serviced as soon as possible.

9. Keep gas appliances clean and have them serviced regularly; to prevent rusting-causing condensation inside a gas furnace, turn off the pilot at the end of each heating season.

10. Make sure that each gas appliance has adequate air supply for proper combustion; check that the burner assembly on a gas water heater and a gas furnace is properly vented.

11. Install a carbon monoxide detector *(page 44)* or have your home tested for the presence of carbon monoxide.

12. Store paints, solvents and other flammable materials away from gas appliances. Never apply contact cement, paint stripper or any other flammable substance near a gas appliance; a buildup of fumes can trigger an explosion.

13 Keep at least one fire extinguisher rated ABC *(page 55)* in your home and know how to use it in the event of a fire.

14. Do not apply excessive force or use a tool to set any control on a gas appliance; any built-in safety mechanism is sensitive and can be easily damaged.

15. Never use a gas range to heat the house; the amount of oxygen consumed can create a health hazard.

TROUBLESHOOTING GUIDE

SYMPTOM	PROCEDURE
Strong gas odor	Do not use any switch, outlet or telephone or light any flame
	Leave house immediately and call gas company or fire department from home of neighbor
Faint gas odor; not localized near an appliance	Do not use any switch, outlet or telephone or light any flame
	Shut off main gas supply *(p. 92)*; propane *(p. 93)*
	Ventilate room *(p. 93)*
	If propane level of tank or cylinder low, call for delivery
	When gas odor dissipates, restore gas supply and relight pilots *(p. 94)*
	If gas odor persists, leave house and call gas company or fire department from home of neighbor
Faint gas odor; localized near an appliance	Do not use any switch, outlet or telephone or light any flame
	Shut off gas supply to appliance *(p. 92)*
	Ventilate room *(p. 93)*
	If gas odor persists, shut off main gas supply *(p. 92)*; propane *(p. 93)*
	If propane level of tank or cylinder low, call for delivery
	When gas odor dissipates, restore gas supply and relight pilots *(p. 94)*
	If gas odor persists, leave house and call gas company or fire department from home of neighbor
Exposure to carbon monoxide: headache, dizziness, faintness or nausea near gas	Leave house immediately and treat exposure to carbon monoxide *(p. 93)*
	Call gas company or fire department from home of neighbor; also call for medical help
	Have someone ventilate room *(p. 93)* and shut off main gas supply *(p. 92)*; propane *(p. 93)*
No gas appliance works	Shut off main gas supply *(p. 92)*; propane *(p. 93)*
	If propane level of tank or cylinder low, call for delivery
	If gas odor detected, ventilate room *(p. 93)*
	If gas odor persists, leave house and call gas company or fire department from home of neighbor
Range does not work; no heat from stove or oven	Relight stove or oven pilot *(p. 94)*; if electrical ignition, reset circuit breaker or replace fuse *(p. 83)*
	If problem persists, shut off gas supply to range *(p. 92)*
	If gas odor detected, ventilate room *(p. 93)* and shut off main gas supply *(p. 92)*; propane *(p. 93)*
	If propane level of tank or cylinder low, shut off main gas supply *(p. 93)* and call for delivery
	If gas odor persists, leave house and call gas company or fire department from home of neighbor
No hot water	Relight water heater pilot *(p. 94)*; if electrical ignition, reset circuit breaker or replace fuse *(p. 83)*
	If problem persists, shut off gas supply to water heater *(p. 92)*
	If gas odor detected, ventilate room *(p. 93)* and shut off main gas supply *(p. 92)*; propane *(p. 93)*
	If propane level of tank or cylinder low, shut off main gas supply *(p. 93)* and call for delivery
	If gas odor persists, leave house and call gas company or fire department from home of neighbor
No heat	Relight furnace pilot *(p. 94)*; if electrical ignition, reset circuit breaker or replace fuse *(p. 83)*
	If problem persists, shut off gas supply to furnace *(p. 92)*
	If gas odor detected, ventilate room *(p. 93)* and shut off main gas supply *(p. 92)*; propane *(p. 93)*
	If propane level of tank or cylinder low, shut off main gas supply *(p. 93)* and call for delivery
	If gas odor persists, leave house and call gas company or fire department from home of neighbor
Pilot does not light and stay lit	Shut off gas supply to appliance *(p. 92)*
	If gas odor detected, ventilate room *(p. 93)* and shut off main gas supply *(p. 92)*; propane *(p. 93)*
	If propane level of tank or cylinder low, shut off main gas supply *(p. 93)* and call for delivery
	If gas odor persists, leave house and call gas company or fire department from home of neighbor
Underground gas pipe broken during excavation	Extinguish any flame and do not light any flame
	Leave area and warn others to stay away
	Call gas company or fire department immediately

SHUTTING OFF THE MAIN GAS SUPPLY

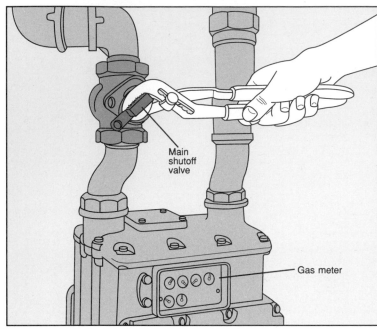

SHUTOFF VALVE CLOSED

SHUTOFF VALVE OPEN

Turning off the main gas supply. Locate the main shutoff valve on the main gas supply pipe for the house; usually it is found at the entry point of the main gas supply pipe near the gas meter, outdoors or in the basement, utility room or garage. To shut off the gas supply, close the valve using adjustable pliers *(left)* or a wrench, turning the handle perpendicular to the supply pipe *(above, left)*. To restore the gas supply, open the valve by turning the handle parallel to the supply pipe *(above, right)*; then, relight each pilot *(page 94)*. Tag the valve for easy identification in the event of a future emergency.

SHUTTING OFF THE GAS SUPPLY TO AN APPLIANCE

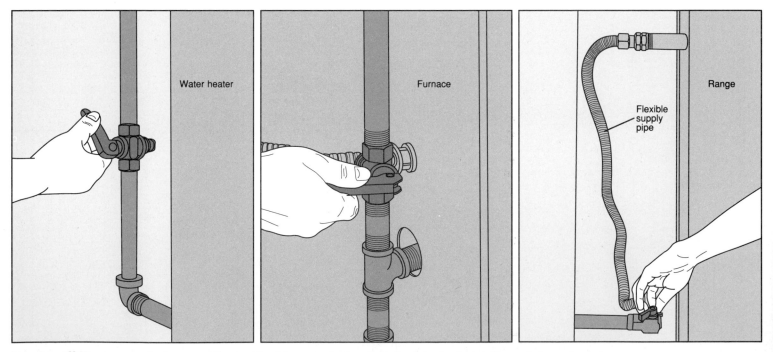

Turning off the gas supply to an appliance. Read the manufacturer's instructions for the appliance before attempting to shut off its gas supply. Locate the shutoff valve on the supply pipe to the appliance and close it by turning the handle perpendicular to the supply pipe; the shutoff valve is usually found near a water heater *(above, left)* or a furnace *(above, center)* or on the connector at the end of the flexible supply pipe on a range *(above, right)*. If there is no shutoff valve on the supply pipe to the appliance, shut off the main gas supply *(step above)* or the main propane gas supply *(page 93)*. To restore the gas supply to the appliance, open the valve by turning the handle parallel to the supply pipe; then, relight each pilot *(page 94)*. Tag the valve for easy identification in the event of a future emergency.

GETTING FRESH AIR

Ventilating a gas-filled room. Caution: Do not use any electrical switch, outlet or telephone or light any flame—a spark could ignite the gas. If there is a strong odor of gas, leave the house immediately and call the gas company or the fire department. If there is a faint odor of gas near an appliance, turn off the gas supply to it *(page 92)*. Ventilate the room to reduce the concentration of gas, opening each window *(above)* and door. When the gas is fully dissipated, restore the gas supply to the appliance and relight each pilot *(page 94)*. As a safety measure, install a gas detector near each gas appliance *(page 44)*.

Treating exposure to carbon monoxide gas. Improper combustion of gas produces carbon monoxide which can cause headache, dizziness, faintness, nausea and, in extreme circumstances, unconsciousness. At the first sign of any symptom indicating possible exposure to carbon monoxide, leave the house immediately and get fresh air. Loosen your clothing at the waist, chest and neck. If you feel faint, sit with your head lowered between your knees *(above)*. Do not re-enter the house. Have someone call the gas company or the fire department immediately. As a preventive measure, install a carbon monoxide detector *(page 44)*.

PROPANE GAS

Using propane gas safely. Propane gas stored as a liquid under pressure in a tank or a cylinder can be used to fuel indoor gas appliances and outdoor gas barbecues. Propane is odorless in its natural state; a sulphur-based chemical is added commercially to give it a strong odor similar to rotten eggs, enabling any leak to be easily detected. Make sure all the members of your family are familiar with the distinctive odor of propane. A safe and efficient fuel when used properly, propane can be dangerous if it is not handled carefully; follow the list of precautions presented below to prevent an emergency:

• If you have a poor sense of smell, install a gas detector *(page 44)* near the base of each appliance that uses propane.

• Never store or set up a propane cylinder indoors; keep it outdoors at least 10 feet from the house and other structures in an upright position away from sources of heat.

• If you disconnect a propane cylinder, seal off the fuel pipe with a plug to prevent any propane from leaking if the shutoff valve is accidentally opened.

• Do not light any flame or smoke near the location of a propane tank or cylinder.

• Use only a government-approved propane tank or cylinder that is in good condition. Have your propane tank or cylinder inspected annually by your propane supplier and replace it if it is rusted, dented or otherwise damaged.

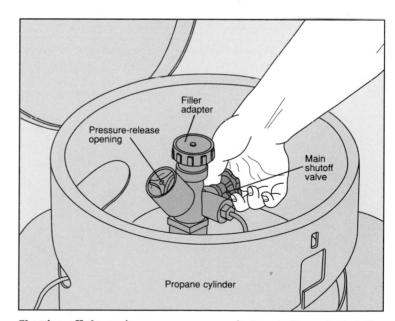

Filler adapter

Pressure-release opening

Main shutoff valve

Propane cylinder

Shutting off the main propane gas supply. Locate the main shutoff valve, usually found under a hinged cover on the propane tank or cylinder; if you cannot locate it, call your propane supplier. To shut off the supply of propane, close the valve by turning the handle fully clockwise *(above)*. To restore the supply of propane, open the valve by turning the handle fully counterclockwise; then, relight each pilot *(page 94)*. Tag the valve for easy identification in the event of a future emergency.

RELIGHTING A PILOT

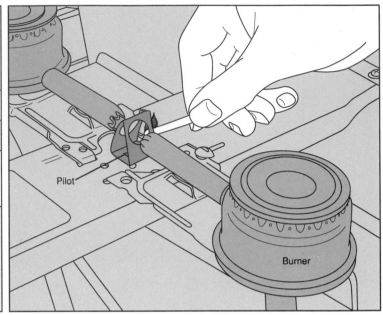

Relighting a stove pilot. Read the manufacturer's instructions for the range before relighting the stove pilots; do not attempt to relight a pilot with electrical ignition. Turn off each range control and ventilate the room, if necessary *(page 93)*. Remove the burner grates, then grasp the cooktop by its front edge or the front burner wells and lift it up, propping it open with the support rod *(above, left)*. Locate each pilot opening, usually between two burners, and hold a lighted match near it *(above,* *right)*. If the pilot does not light and stay lit, clean it with a wooden toothpick. Fit the toothpick into the pilot opening and gently move it up and down; be careful not to enlarge or deform the pilot opening. Then, relight the pilot; if it still does not light and stay lit, shut off the gas supply to the range *(page 92)*. To reassemble the range, lift the cooktop off its support rod, lower it slowly into place to avoid blowing out any pilot and reinstall the burner grates.

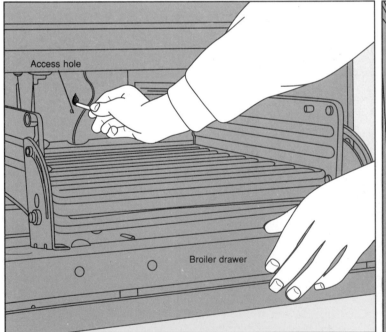

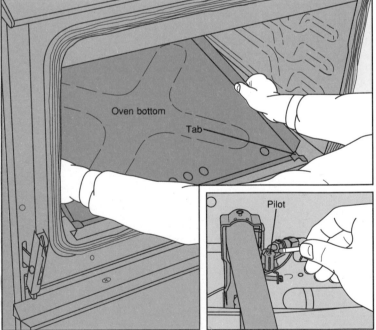

Relighting an oven pilot. Read the manufacturer's instructions for the range before relighting the oven pilot; do not attempt to relight a pilot with electrical ignition. Turn off each range control and ventilate the room, if necessary *(page 93)*. Open the broiler drawer and reach through the access hole at the back of the broiler with a lighted match, holding it near the tip of the pilot on the burner assembly *(above, left)*. If you cannot reach through the access hole with a match or there is no access hole, open the oven door and lift out the oven bottom; slide it out from under any tabs *(above, right)* or loosen any screws holding it and lift it out. If there is a burner plate in the way, unscrew its wing nut and lift it out. Then, hold a lighted match near the tip of the pilot on the burner assembly *(inset)*; on an older range, you may also need to depress a pilot ignition button on the side of the oven or on the oven thermostat. If the pilot does not light and stay lit, shut off the gas supply to the range *(page 92)*. To reassemble the range, reinstall the burner plate and the oven bottom.

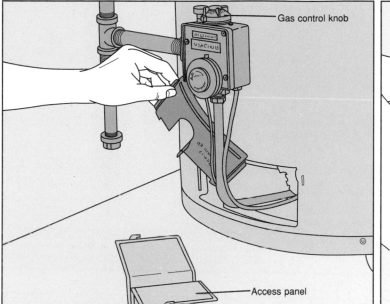

Gas control knob

Access panel

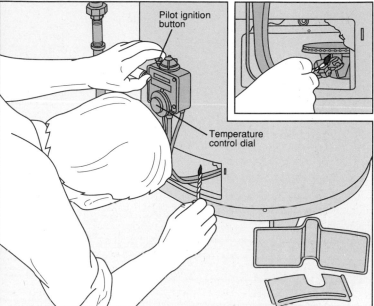

Pilot ignition button

Temperature control dial

Relighting a water heater pilot. Read the manufacturer's instructions for the water heater before relighting the pilot; do not attempt to relight a pilot with electrical ignition. Ventilate the room, if necessary *(page 93)*, then remove each access panel from the water heater, lifting it vertically or sliding it horizontally *(above, left)*. Turn the temperature control dial to its lowest setting and the gas control knob to OFF. Then, turn the gas control knob to PILOT, hold a lighted match or twist of paper near the tip of the pilot on the burner assembly *(inset)* and depress the pilot

ignition button *(above, right)*; if there is no pilot ignition button, depress the gas control knob. When the pilot lights, keep depressing the pilot ignition button or the gas control knob and extinguish the match or twist of paper. Release the pilot ignition button or the gas control knob after 1 minute, turn the gas control knob to ON and reset the temperature control dial. If the pilot does not light and stay lit, shut off the gas supply to the water heater *(page 92)*. To reassemble the water heater, reinstall the access panels.

Access panel

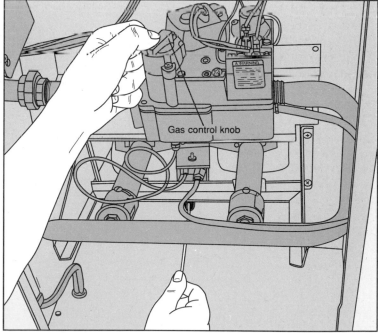

Gas control knob

Relighting a furnace pilot. Read the manufacturer's instructions for the furnace before relighting the pilot; do not attempt to relight a pilot with electrical ignition. Ventilate the room, if necessary *(page 93)*, then unscrew the access panel and slide it up and off the furnace *(above, left)*; if it sticks, rap it gently at the bottom. Set the gas control knob, usually red, to OFF. Then, set the gas control knob to PILOT, hold a lighted match or twist of paper near the tip of the pilot on the burner assembly and depress the pilot ignition button; if there is no pilot ignition

button, depress the gas control knob *(above, right)*. When the pilot lights, keep depressing the pilot ignition button or the gas control knob and extinguish the match or twist of paper. Release the pilot ignition button or the gas control knob after 30 seconds and turn the gas control knob to ON. If the pilot goes out, repeat the procedure, depressing the pilot ignition button or the gas control knob for 1 minute. If the pilot does not light and stay lit, shut off the gas supply to the furnace *(page 92)*. To reassemble the furnace, reinstall the access panel.

PLUMBING

Your home's plumbing system consists of two basic pipelines: supply pipes that carry potable water under high pressure throughout the house and drainpipes that depend on gravity to carry waste water out of the house; to prevent sewer gases from entering the house, each drainpipe is fitted with a P- or S-shaped trap that refills with water every time waste water is carried through it. The same principles of high pressure used to carry in potable water and low pressure used to carry out waste water are responsible for most plumbing emergencies. Keep a well-stocked emergency plumbing kit on hand *(page 97)*; know where the main water shutoff valve for your home is located and tag it for easy identification in the event of an emergency. Consult the Troubleshooting Guide *(page 98)* to have emergency procedures at your fingertips and to help you respond quickly in an emergency situation when a permanent repair cannot be undertaken.

The high pressure that carries potable water to a fixture also forces it out of a faulty supply pipe. Use a pencil tip and electrical tape or a pipe-leak clamp to temporarily seal a small leak in a supply pipe *(page 101)*. A damaged section of a supply pipe can be temporarily repaired with replacement polybutylene (PB) pipe and adapters—designed to connect it with undamaged copper, chlorinated polyvinyl chloride (CPVC) or PB pipes *(page 102)* or galvanized steel pipes *(page 103)*. To determine if a supply pipe is frozen, run a damp rag or sponge along it; a frozen area will frost over. Use a hair dryer or heating tape to thaw a frozen supply pipe *(page 101)*; never use a propane torch. If you suspect a supply pipe behind a wall or ceiling is frozen, you can help minimize any damage if it bursts by opening the faucet nearest to it and turning off the main water supply *(page 99)*. The low-pressure pull of gravity may not be enough to carry waste water through a drain clogged with debris. Use a plunger or an auger to clear any blockage in a toilet *(page 105)*, sink *(page 106)* or bathtub *(page 107)*. Always wear rubber gloves when working on a drain to prevent contact with waste water.

The list of Safety Tips at right reviews basic precautions to follow in preventing plumbing emergencies in your home and in working safely on your plumbing system. Water can turn a small electrical fault into a deadly hazard by making your body a convenient path for electrical current; do not touch any electrical device, even a switch or a power cord, in wet conditions. If your water has a peculiar taste, odor or color, or if members of your household suffer frequent illnesses that may be water-borne, have your water professionally tested *(page 107)*. When in doubt about the safety of your plumbing system or your ability to handle an emergency, do not hesitate to call for help. Post the telephone number for your water utility and a 24-hour plumber near the telephone; even in non-emergency situations, qualified professionals can answer questions concerning your plumbing system.

SAFETY TIPS

1. Locate and tag the main shutoff valve for your home's water supply as well as the shutoff valve or valves for each fixture; in the event of an emergency, you will want anyone to be able to find them quickly.

2. When working with electricity, do not touch a metal faucet, pipe, fixture or other object that may form part of your electrical grounding route.

3. If your plumbing system is of metal, it may provide the electrical grounding for your home; if you replace a metal pipe with a plastic pipe or otherwise interrupt the integrity of any electrical grounding through a plumbing system of metal, install an electrical jumper wire *(page 103)*.

4. If no hot water is used in your home within a period as short as 2 weeks, hydrogen can build up in the water heater and the hot-water supply pipes; before using any hot water, open each hot-water faucet in the house and allow the water to run for at least 2 minutes.

5. Wear rubber gloves when working on clogged drains or traps and safety goggles when working overhead.

6. Do not rinse foods, grease, fats or coffee grounds down a sink and avoid using a toilet as a waste basket.

7. If a drain is completely blocked, do not use a caustic chemical drain opener—especially one that contains lye; if it does not clear the drain, you will be exposed to it as you use a plunger or an auger.

8. Light and ventilate your work area well and do not reach into any area you cannot see clearly.

9. To prevent pipes from freezing during an extended power outage in cold weather, open the faucets enough to allow a trickle of water to flow; running water is less likely to freeze than water left standing in a pipe.

10. Do not leave a hand-held shower attachment in a filled bathtub or a garden hose in a filled swimming pool; back-siphonage, the reverse flow of contaminated water into supply pipes, could occur. If you suspect supply pipes contain contaminated water, call your local or state department of health to have your water tested *(page 107)*.

11. When leaving your home vacant for an extended period of time during the winter, call your water utility to shut off the main water supply at the curb valve (near the street). Close the main shutoff valve *(page 99)* and open the faucets to drain the supply pipes. Also drain the water heater *(page 71)*. Pour a small amount of plumber's antifreeze into the drain of each toilet, sink, bathtub and shower to protect the trap.

12. At the end of autumn in northern climates, turn off the water supply to each exterior faucet; the shutoff valve is located on the supply pipe inside the house. Then, open each exterior faucet to drain the water in the supply pipe.

13. Have a septic tank cleaned every 2 years or according to its specific installation instructions.

14. Know how to work safely with gas *(page 90)* or electricity *(page 78)* before attempting any repair on a gas or electrical water heater.

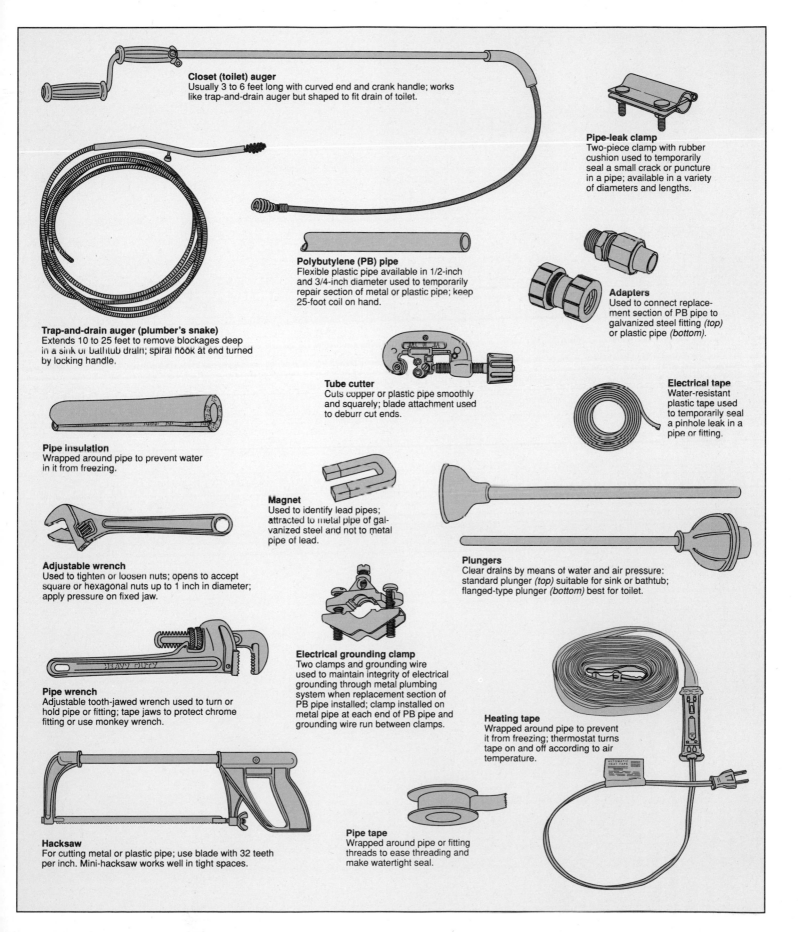

Closet (toilet) auger
Usually 3 to 6 feet long with curved end and crank handle; works like trap-and-drain auger but shaped to fit drain of toilet.

Pipe-leak clamp
Two-piece clamp with rubber cushion used to temporarily seal a small crack or puncture in a pipe; available in a variety of diameters and lengths.

Polybutylene (PB) pipe
Flexible plastic pipe available in 1/2-inch and 3/4-inch diameter used to temporarily repair section of metal or plastic pipe; keep 25-foot coil on hand.

Trap-and-drain auger (plumber's snake)
Extends 10 to 25 feet to remove blockages deep in a sink or bathtub drain; spiral hook at end turned by locking handle.

Adapters
Used to connect replacement section of PB pipe to galvanized steel fitting *(top)* or plastic pipe *(bottom)*.

Tube cutter
Cuts copper or plastic pipe smoothly and squarely; blade attachment used to deburr cut ends.

Electrical tape
Water-resistant plastic tape used to temporarily seal a pinhole leak in a pipe or fitting.

Pipe insulation
Wrapped around pipe to prevent water in it from freezing.

Magnet
Used to identify lead pipes; attracted to metal pipe of galvanized steel and not to metal pipe of lead.

Adjustable wrench
Used to tighten or loosen nuts; opens to accept square or hexagonal nuts up to 1 inch in diameter; apply pressure on fixed jaw.

Plungers
Clear drains by means of water and air pressure: standard plunger *(top)* suitable for sink or bathtub; flanged-type plunger *(bottom)* best for toilet.

Pipe wrench
Adjustable tooth-jawed wrench used to turn or hold pipe or fitting; tape jaws to protect chrome fitting or use monkey wrench.

Electrical grounding clamp
Two clamps and grounding wire used to maintain integrity of electrical grounding through metal plumbing system when replacement section of PB pipe installed; clamp installed on metal pipe at each end of PB pipe and grounding wire run between clamps.

Heating tape
Wrapped around pipe to prevent it from freezing; thermostat turns tape on and off according to air temperature.

Hacksaw
For cutting metal or plastic pipe; use blade with 32 teeth per inch. Mini-hacksaw works well in tight spaces.

Pipe tape
Wrapped around pipe or fitting threads to ease threading and make watertight seal.

TROUBLESHOOTING GUIDE

SYMPTOM	PROCEDURE
Pipe bursts	Shut off main water supply *(p. 99)*
	Temporarily repair copper, chlorinated polyvinyl chloride (CPVC) or polybutylene (PB) pipe *(p. 102)* or galvanized steel pipe *(p. 103)*
	Have permanent repair undertaken as soon as possible
Pipe leaks	Shut off main water supply *(p. 99)*
	Temporarily stop pipe leak *(p. 101)*
	Have permanent repair undertaken as soon as possible
Ceiling or wall wet	Suspect damaged pipe behind ceiling or wall; shut off water supply to fixtures above ceiling or wall *(p. 100)* or shut off main water supply *(p. 99)*
	Have pipe repaired or replaced as soon as possible
Faucet bursts or leaks	Shut off water supply to fixture *(p. 100)* or shut off main water supply *(p. 99)*
	Have faucet repaired or replaced as soon as possible
Toilet overflows	Shut off water supply to toilet *(p. 100)*
	Unblock toilet *(p. 105)*
	If problem persists, have toilet drain repaired or replaced as soon as possible
Toilet blocked	Do not flush toilet
	Unblock toilet *(p. 105)*
	If problem persists, have toilet drain repaired or replaced as soon as possible
Toilet leaks	Shut off water supply to toilet *(p. 100)*
	Have toilet repaired or replaced as soon as possible
Sink overflows or does not drain	Turn off faucets
	Unclog sink drain *(p. 106)*
	If problem persists, have sink drain repaired or replaced as soon as possible
Sink drains slowly	Mix together 1/4 cup of baking soda, 1/4 cup of salt and 1/16 cup cream of tartar, spoon into drain and flush with 1 quart of water
Sink leaks	Shut off water supply to sink *(p. 100)*
	Have sink repaired or replaced as soon as possible
Bathtub overflows or does not drain	Turn off faucets
	Unclog bathtub drain *(p. 107)*
	If problem persists, have bathtub drain repaired or replaced as soon as possible
Bathtub drains slowly	Mix together 1/4 cup of baking soda, 1/4 cup of salt and 1/16 cup cream of tartar, spoon into drain and flush with 1 quart of water
Appliance, water heater or water boiler overflows or leaks	Shut off water supply to fixture *(p. 100)*
	Drain appliance, water heater *(p. 71)* or water boiler and mop up standing water *(p. 72)*
	Have appliance, water heater or water boiler repaired or replaced as soon as possible
No water from any faucet	If temperature below freezing, check for frozen main water supply pipe by running damp rag or sponge along it; if it frosts over, thaw frozen pipe *(p. 101)* and turn up heat in house
	If temperature below freezing and main water supply pipe inaccessible, shut off main water supply *(p. 99)* and open faucet nearest to pipe to minimize damage if pipe bursts; turn up heat in house
	Call water utility to service curb valve or main supply pipe outside house
No water from one faucet	If temperature below freezing, check for frozen water supply pipe by running damp rag or sponge along it; if it frosts over, thaw frozen pipe *(p. 101)* and turn up heat in house
Low water pressure from one faucet	If temperature below freezing, suspect partially frozen water supply pipe; turn up heat in house
	Raise temperature of pipes by opening faucets
	When water pressure restored, take interim preventive measure to keep pipe from freezing *(p. 101)*
Extended power outage in cold weather	Take interim preventive measure to keep pipes from freezing *(p. 101)*

SYMPTOM	PROCEDURE
No hot water	Relight pilot of gas water heater *(p. 94)*; reset circuit breaker or replace fuse of electrical water heater *(p. 83)*
	If problem persists, have water heater repaired or replaced as soon as possible
Sewage backs up into house	Do not flush any toilet or drain any fixture
	Shut off main water supply *(p. 99)*
	Call municipality to service municipal sewer line
	Have house main drain serviced as soon as possible
Sewage fumes from toilet, sink or bathtub	Flush toilet or open sink or bathtub faucet to refill drain trap
	If problem persists, have house drains serviced professionally as soon as possible
Basement floor drain backs up	Mop up standing water *(p. 72)*
	Check that any sump pump plugged into working outlet; reset circuit breaker or replace fuse *(p. 83)*
	Have floor drain unblocked as soon as possible
Object dropped into toilet or sink	Do not flush toilet or open sink faucet
	Retrieve object with wire or coat hanger
	Have toilet removed to retrieve object from trap; remove trap bend of sink to retrieve object *(p. 106)*
Main shutoff valve broken	Call water utility to shut off water at curb valve
	Have main shutoff valve repaired or replaced as soon as possible
Water contamination suspected	Call local or state department of health to have water tested *(p. 107)*
	Do not use water from supply pipes for drinking or cooking; use bottled water or water purification tablets or boil water for at least 10 minutes

SHUTTING OFF THE MAIN WATER SUPPLY

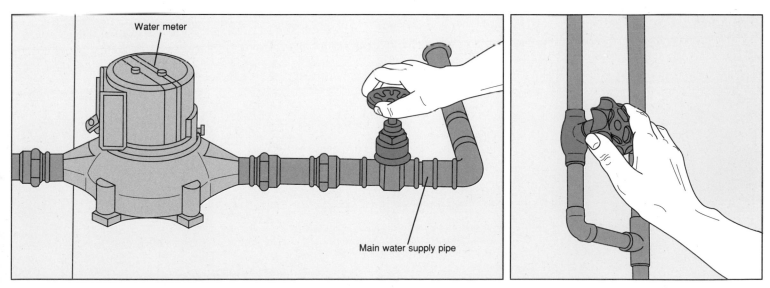

Water meter

Main water supply pipe

Turning off the main water supply. Locate the main shutoff valve on the main water supply pipe for the house and close it; usually it is found at the entry point of the main water supply pipe, indoors near the water meter *(above, left)* or in the basement, utility room or crawl space *(above, right)*. If your water supply is provided by a well, look for the main shutoff valve on the main water supply pipe near the pressure gauge or water pump. Turn the handle fully clockwise to close the valve, shutting off the water supply. If the water meter has two valves, close the valve on the supply side (before the water meter). To drain the water supply pipes in the house, open all the faucets. To restore the water supply, open the valve by turning the handle fully counterclockwise; turn it slowly to avoid a large pressure surge. Allow the water to run for several minutes to remove the air in the water supply pipes, then close all the faucets. Tag the valve for easy identification in the event of a future emergency.

SHUTTING OFF THE WATER SUPPLY TO A FIXTURE

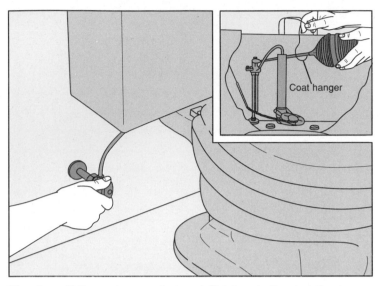

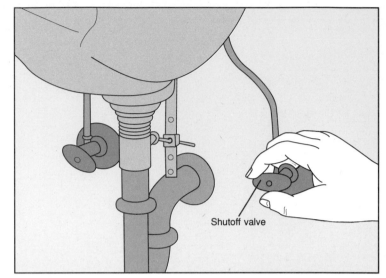

Turning off the water supply to a toilet. Locate the shutoff valve on the supply pipe under the toilet tank and turn the handle fully clockwise *(above)*, shutting off the water supply to the toilet. If the valve leaks or there is no valve, turn off the main water supply *(page 99)* or support the float ball. To support the float ball, lift the lid off the toilet tank, gently raise the float ball to its highest position, and hook a coat hanger under its arm and over the edge of the toilet tank *(inset)*. To restore the water supply, slowly turn the handle of the valve fully counterclockwise; or, turn on the main water supply or remove the hanger, reposition the float ball and put the lid back on the toilet tank. Tag each valve for easy identification in the event of a future emergency.

Turning off the water supply to a sink. Locate the shutoff valve for each faucet on its supply pipe under the sink. Turn the handle of each valve fully clockwise *(above)*, shutting off the water supply to the sink. Open the faucets to drain the water supply pipes to the sink. If a valve leaks or there is no valve, turn off the main water supply *(page 99)*. To restore the water supply, slowly turn the handle of each valve fully counterclockwise or turn on the main water supply. Allow the water to run for several minutes to remove the air in the water supply pipes, then close the faucets. Tag each valve for easy identification in the event of a future emergency.

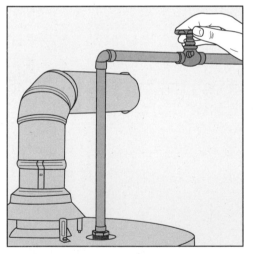

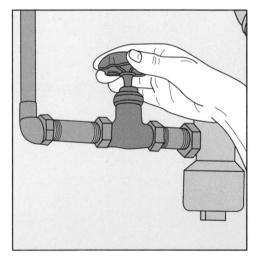

Turning off the water supply to an appliance. Locate the shutoff valve on each supply pipe and turn the handle fully clockwise: for a clothes washer, usually the valves behind it *(above)*; for a dishwasher, usually a valve under the sink. For a portable appliance, turn off the sink faucets. If a valve leaks or there is no valve, turn off the main water supply *(page 99)*. To restore the water supply, slowly turn the handle of each valve fully counterclockwise; or, turn on the faucets, the water supply to the sink or the main water supply. Tag each valve for easy identification in the event of a future emergency.

Turning off the water supply to a water heater. Locate the shutoff valve on the supply pipe to the water heater, usually found near and above it. Turn the handle fully clockwise *(above)*, shutting off the water supply to the water heater (and the hot water supply to the house). If the valve leaks or there is no valve, turn off the main water supply *(page 99)*. To restore the water supply, slowly turn the handle of the valve fully counterclockwise or turn on the main water supply. Tag each valve for easy identification in the event of a future emergency.

Turning off the water supply to a water boiler. Locate the shutoff valve on the supply pipe to the water boiler, usually found near and above it. Turn the handle fully clockwise *(above)*, shutting off the water supply to the water boiler (and the hot water supply of the heating system). If the valve leaks or there is no valve, turn off the main water supply *(page 99)*. To restore the water supply, slowly turn the handle of the valve fully counterclockwise or turn on the main water supply. Tag each valve for easy identification in the event of a future emergency.

THAWING A FROZEN PIPE

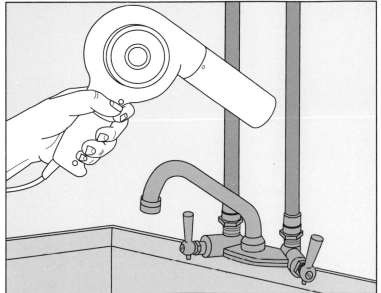

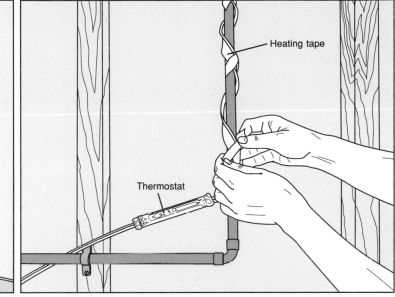

Heating tape

Thermostat

Warming a frozen pipe. Turn the main water supply about 3/4 of the way off *(page 99)*. To allow melting ice to drain, open the faucet nearest to the frozen section of pipe. Using a hair dryer, slowly warm the pipe, working from the faucet to the frozen section *(above, left)* to prevent water trapped by ice from heating up and bursting the pipe; keep the hair dryer moving and 3 to 4 inches from the pipe. When water begins to trickle from the faucet, open the main shutoff valve, turning the handle fully counterclockwise; the flow of water helps to speed the thawing. After thawing the pipe, turn off the faucet; undertake a temporary preventive measure if there is a risk of the pipe freezing again.

Using heating tape, warm a frozen pipe the same way. Wrap the heating tape tightly every 1 1/2 to 2 inches around the pipe, secure it every 6 inches with plastic tape *(above, right)* and plug it into an outlet; it draws electrical current, warming the pipe. To prevent the freezing of a pipe, use heating tape equipped with a thermostat to maintain a constant temperature. To prevent the freezing of a pipe inside a cabinet, keep the doors open, allowing heat from the room to warm it or set up and turn on a lamp beside it. To prevent the freezing of a pipe in an electrical power outage, open the faucet enough to allow water to flow or wrap pipe insulation tightly around the pipe and secure it with duct tape.

STOPPING A PIPE LEAK

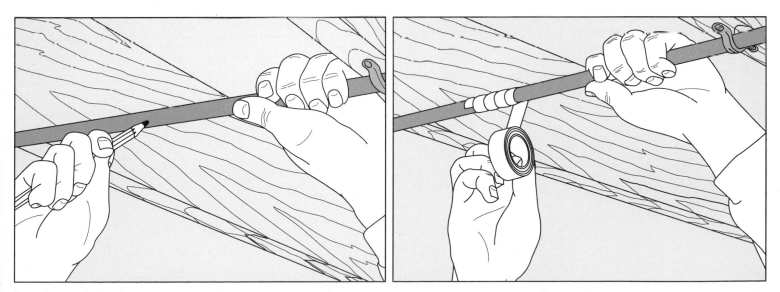

Plugging a pinhole leak. To temporarily seal a crack or puncture, install a pipe-leak clamp *(page 102)*. To temporarily plug a pinhole leak, turn off the main water supply *(page 99)* and open the faucet nearest to the damaged section of pipe to drain it. Jam the tip of a pencil into the pinhole *(above, left)* and break it off. Dry off the damaged section of pipe with a cloth, then wrap electrical tape around it, overlapping the tape by about 1/2 of its width each turn *(above, right)* and extending it 3 to 4 inches on each side of the plug. Apply 3 or 4 layers of tape the same way. To temporarily plug a pinhole leak at a fitting, use the same procedure, wrapping tape around it and the pipe. Turn on the main water supply, turn off the faucet and periodically inspect the repair; if water leaks from it, reinforce it by wrapping 3 or 4 layers of duct tape around it.

STOPPING A PIPE LEAK (continued)

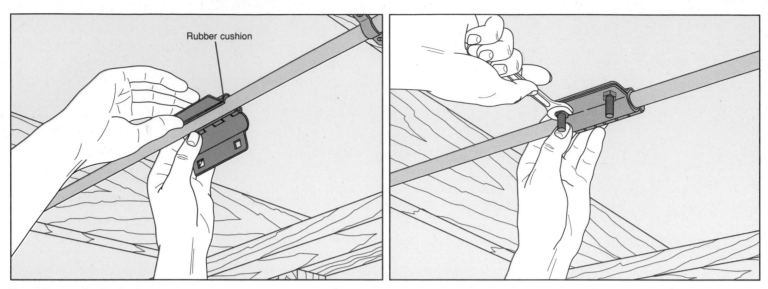

Installing a pipe-leak clamp. If the leak is from a pinhole, temporarily plug it *(page 101)*. To temporarily seal a crack or a puncture, install a pipe-leak clamp. Turn off the main water supply *(page 99)* and open the faucet nearest to the damaged section of pipe to drain it. Dry off the damaged section of pipe with a cloth. Using a wrench, remove the nuts and slide out the bolts holding the clamp together. Fit the clamp around the pipe, centering it on the damaged section, with the rubber cushion completely covering the hole *(above, left)*. To secure the clamp, insert the bolts and tighten each nut in turn with a wrench until the rubber cushion sits firmly against the pipe *(above, right)*. Turn on the main water supply and turn off the faucet.

REPAIRING A COPPER, CPVC OR PB PIPE

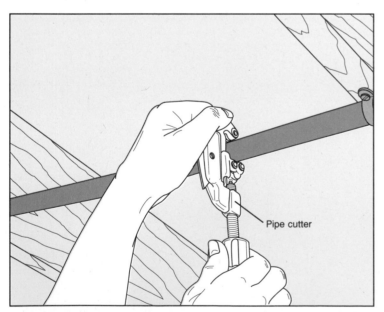

1 **Removing the damaged section.** Turn off the main water supply *(page 99)* and open the faucet nearest to the damaged section of pipe to drain it. If the damaged pipe is of galvanized steel, repair it *(page 103)*. To temporarily repair a damaged pipe of copper, CPVC (chlorinated polyvinyl chloride) or PB (polybutylene), install a replacement section of PB pipe. Set a bucket under each end of the damaged section of pipe to catch any water that has not drained. Wearing safety goggles, cut off each end of the damaged section of pipe using a pipe cutter *(above)* or a hacksaw. To remove the damaged section of pipe, unscrew any hangers holding it to joists or studs.

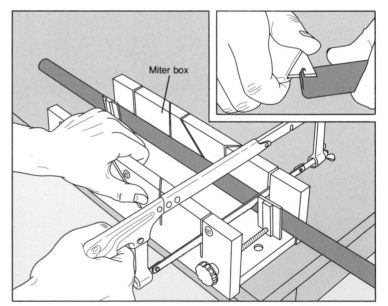

2 **Preparing the replacement pipe.** At the end of each undamaged pipe, scrape off any burrs using a utility knife or emery paper, apply a thin coat of petroleum jelly and push on an adapter until the pipe bottoms out inside its socket. Use a measuring tape to measure the distance between the midpoint of each adapter, then mark the measurement on a replacement PB pipe. To cut the pipe to length, secure it in a miter box, lining up the mark with the saw guides, and use a hacksaw *(above)*; or, hold the pipe firmly against a flat surface and press down squarely with a sharp knife. Scrape any burrs off each end of the pipe, then bevel its outside edge slightly with a utility knife *(inset)*.

REPAIRING A COPPER, CPVC OR PB PIPE (continued)

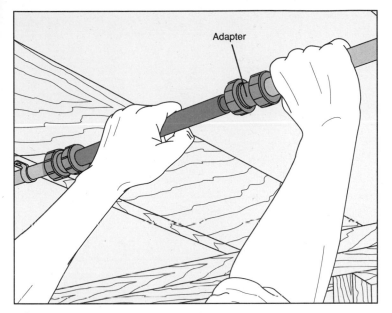

3 **Installing the replacement pipe.** Position the replacement pipe against the adapters, centering it, and mark the midpoint of each adapter on it. Apply a thin coat of petroleum jelly on each end of the pipe and push one end into an adapter until it bottoms out inside the adapter socket, using the mark as a guide; push the other end into the other adapter the same way *(above)*, moving the end of the undamaged section of pipe to position it, if necessary. Tighten each adapter by hand, then replace any hangers removed. Turn on the main water supply and turn off the faucet.

4 **Installing an electrical jumper wire.** To maintain the integrity of electrical grounding through a plumbing system of metal pipes, the undamaged section of metal pipe on each side of the repair must be linked together with grounding clamps and a grounding wire. To install a clamp at each end of the undamaged section of pipe, loosen its screws enough to fit it around the pipe, then tighten the screws. To connect the wire to each clamp, loosen the grounding screw and fit the wire into the clamp, then tighten the grounding screw *(above)*.

REPAIRING A GALVANIZED STEEL PIPE

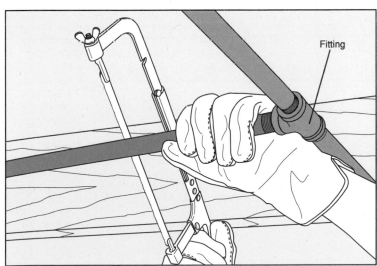

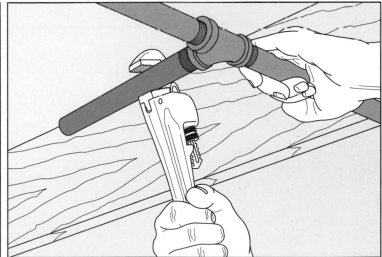

1 **Removing the damaged pipe.** Turn off the main water supply *(page 99)* and open the faucet nearest to the damaged section of pipe to drain it. If the damaged pipe is of copper, CPVC (chlorinated polyvinyl chloride) or PB (polybutylene), repair it *(page 102)*. To temporarily repair a damaged pipe of galvanized steel, replace it with PB pipe. Set a bucket under the fitting at each end of the damaged pipe to catch any water that has not drained. Wearing work gloves and safety goggles, use a hacksaw to cut off each end of the damaged pipe 6 to 8 inches from the fitting *(above, left)*. To remove the section of damaged pipe, unscrew any hangers holding it to joists or studs. To remove each threaded section of the damaged pipe from its fitting, grip it with a pipe wrench and turn it counterclockwise *(above, right)*; apply pressure only with the top, fixed jaw of the pipe wrench, repositioning it as necessary.

REPAIRING A GALVANIZED STEEL PIPE (continued)

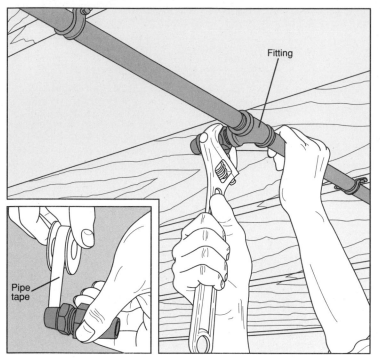

Fitting

Pipe tape

2 **Installing the adapters.** Install an adapter at each fitting using pipe tape to ease the threading of it and provide it with a water-tight seal. Wrap the pipe tape tightly around the threads of the adapter 1 1/2 turns counterclockwise *(inset)*; the threads should be visible through the pipe tape. Screw the adapter clockwise into the fitting.by hand, then tighten it by gripping its fixed nut securely with an adjustable wrench and turning it *(above)*.

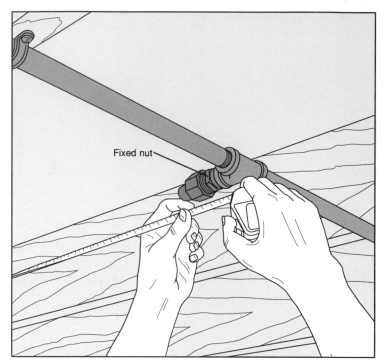

Fixed nut

3 **Preparing the replacement pipe.** Measure the distance between the base of each fixed nut *(above)*, then mark the measurement on a replacement PB pipe. To cut the pipe to length, secure it in a miter box, lining up the mark with the saw guides, and use a hacksaw; or, hold the pipe firmly against a flat surface and press down squarely with a sharp knife. Scrape any burrs off each end of the pipe using a utility knife or emery paper, then bevel its outside edge slightly with a utility knife.

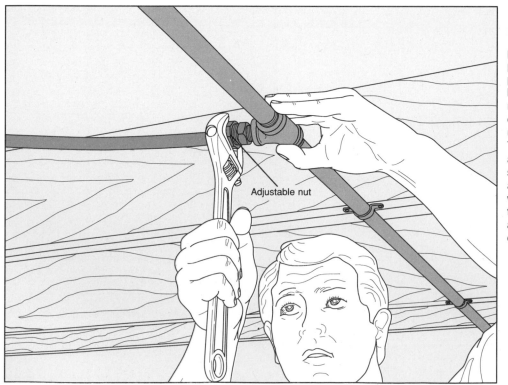

Adjustable nut

4 **Installing the replacement pipe.** Position the replacement pipe against the adapters, centering it, and mark the midpoint of each adapter on it. Apply a thin coat of petroleum jelly on each end of the replacement pipe and push one end into an adapter until it bottoms out inside the adapter socket, using the mark as a guide; push the other end into the other adapter the same way, moving it or the undamaged pipe to position it, if necessary. Tighten each adapter by hand, then using an adjustable wrench, gripping its adjustable nut securely and turning it clockwise *(left)*. Replace any hangers removed, then turn on the main water supply and turn off the faucet. To maintain the integrity of electrical grounding through a plumbing system of metal pipes, install an electrical jumper wire *(page 103)*.

UNBLOCKING A TOILET

1 Preparing to clear the blockage. Do not flush the toilet. If the bowl is overflowing, turn off the water supply to the toilet *(page 100)*. Spread old newspapers or rags around the toilet to absorb water spilled from the bowl. Wearing rubber gloves, use a plastic container to bail water out of the bowl until it is half full *(above)*. If the bowl is less than half full, add water until it is half full. Locate the drain opening—the larger one, if there are two openings.

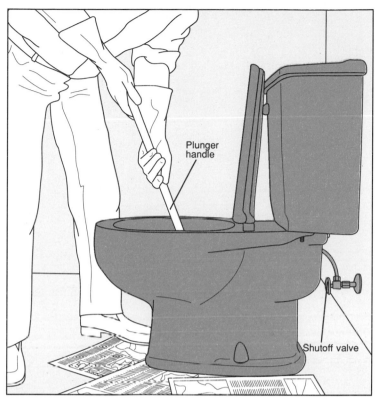

2 Using a flange-type plunger. Wearing rubber gloves, fit the cup of a flange-type plunger over the drain opening. Keeping the cup below the water level, pump the plunger up and down vigorously 8 to 10 times *(above)*, then lift it out. If the bowl does not drain freely, repeat the procedure; or, use a closet auger to break up or snag the blockage *(step 3)*. When the bowl drains freely, the blockage is cleared; if you turned off the water supply to the toilet, turn it back on.

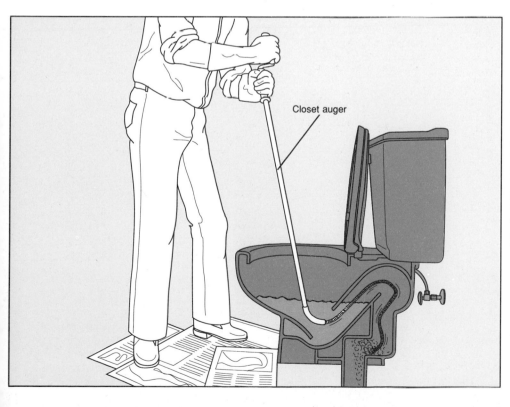

3 Using a closet auger. Use a closet auger, shaped to fit a toilet; its curved sleeve allows it to be fed into the drain opening without scratching the porcelain. Wearing rubber gloves, feed the auger into the drain opening and crank the handle clockwise; the auger should move freely until it reaches the blockage. Crank the handle until the auger tightens, indicating it is as far into the drain opening as possible *(left)*; then, still cranking the handle, pull the auger slowly out of the drain opening. If the bowl does not drain freely, repeat the procedure; if the blockage cannot be cleared using the auger, have the toilet taken off and the blockage removed. When the bowl drains freely, the blockage is cleared; if you turned off the water supply to the toilet, turn it back on.

CLEARING A CLOGGED SINK DRAIN

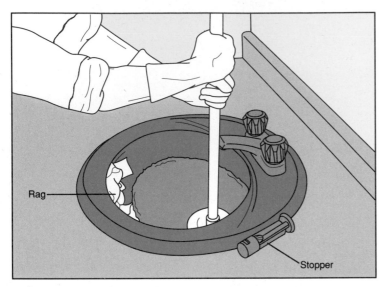

1 **Using a plunger.** If there is a drain stopper, open it, then pull it out or turn it counterclockwise and lift it out; if it does not come out easily, first remove any retaining nut holding it under the sink. Block any overflow opening by packing a wet rag into it; with a double sink, close the stopper or install the plug of the other drain. Fill the sink with 4 to 6 inches of water—enough to cover the cup of a plunger. Wearing rubber gloves, fit the plunger over the drain opening, angling the cup to avoid trapping air. Keeping the cup below the water level, pump the plunger up and down vigorously 8 to 10 times *(above)*, then lift it out. If the sink drains freely, the blockage is cleared; put back any drain stopper you removed.

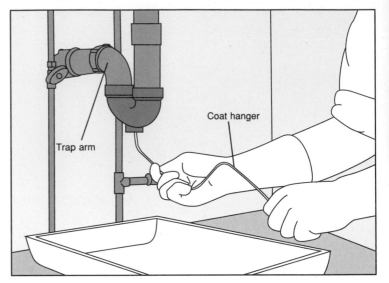

2 **Removing the cleanout plug and clearing the trap.** If the sink does not drain freely, remove the cleanout plug to clear the trap; if the trap does not have a cleanout plug, remove the trap bend to clear it *(step 3)*. Set a pan or bucket under the trap. Wearing rubber gloves, use an adjustable wrench to loosen the cleanout plug, then remove it by hand. To dislodge any blockage, probe through the cleanout opening into the trap arm using a coat hanger *(above)*; or, use a trap-and-drain auger, loosening the screw on its handle to feed in the coil and tightening the screw to turn the handle clockwise. Use the pan or bucket to catch any debris. Then, put back the cleanout plug and any drain stopper you removed. Run hot water to flush the trap.

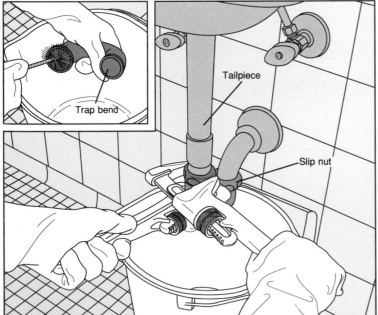

3 **Removing the trap bend and clearing the trap.** Set a bucket or pan under the trap. Wearing rubber gloves, support the trap bend with one hand and loosen the slip nut at each end of it using a monkey wrench *(above, left)* or tape-covered adjustable wrench. Then, unscrew each slip nut by hand and slide it off the trap bend. Pull the trap bend off the trap arm and the tailpiece, then empty out any water in it. To clean out the trap bend, scrub it thoroughly using a bottle brush *(inset)* and rinse it in another sink.

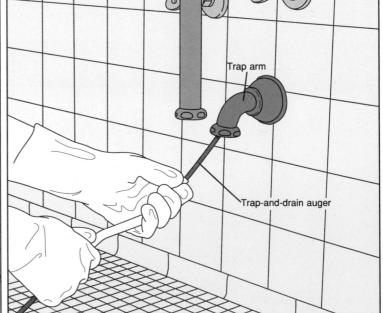

To clean out the trap arm, use a trap-and-drain auger, loosening the screw on its handle to feed in the coil as far as possible *(above, right)* and tightening the screw to turn the handle clockwise. Repeat the procedure until any blockage is dislodged, then pull out the auger, catching any debris in the bucket or pan. To reinstall the trap bend, push it onto the tailpiece and the trap arm. Slide each slip nut onto the trap bend and tighten it by hand, then using the monkey wrench or adjustable wrench. Put back any drain stopper you removed.

CLEARING A CLOGGED BATHTUB DRAIN

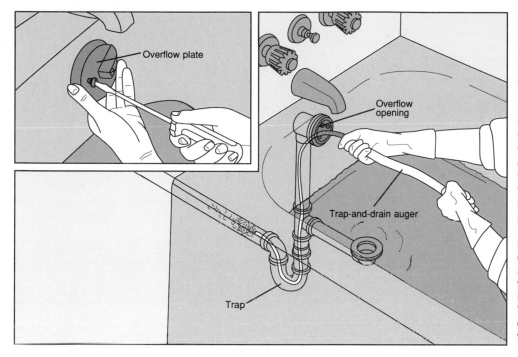

Clearing the trap. If there is a drain stopper, open it and pull it out, working its rocker arm free of the drain opening; note the orientation of the rocker arm for reassembly. Unscrew the overflow plate *(inset)* and remove it, pulling the lift assembly out of the overflow opening.

To use a plunger, block off the overflow opening by packing a wet rag into it, then fill the bathtub with 4 to 6 inches of water—enough to cover the cup of the plunger. Wearing rubber gloves, fit the plunger over the drain opening, angling the cup to avoid trapping air. Keeping the cup below the water level, pump the plunger up and down vigorously 8 to 10 times, then lift it out. If the bathtub does not drain freely, repeat the procedure or use a trap-and-drain auger.

To use a trap-and-drain auger, loosen the screw on its handle to feed the coil through the overflow opening as far as possible into the trap and tighten the screw to turn the handle clockwise. Repeat the procedure until the blockage is dislodged *(left)*, then slowly pull out the auger. When the bathtub drains freely, put back the overflow plate and any stopper you removed, then run hot water to flush the trap.

TESTING YOUR DRINKING WATER

Checking your water for contaminants. If your water has a peculiar taste, odor or color, or if members of your household suffer frequent illnesses that may be water-borne, have your water professionally tested. Two types of standard lab tests for water are available: bacteria analysis and chemical analysis—which determines levels of toxins and corrosives. Maximum safe levels of water contaminants are set by the U.S. Environmental Protection Agency. For a list of certified testing labs in your area, consult your local or state department of health; the testing lab should provide you with containers and instructions for drawing water samples.

One common source of household water contamination is lead ions leached from lead supply pipes or lead solder used to join copper supply pipes. Symptoms of lead poisoning include: fatigue and irritability, insomnia, loss of appetite, constipation or diarrhea, and pain in the joints and abdomen. In June 1986, the U.S. Safe Drinking Water Act prohibited the use of lead pipes, solder and flux in the repair or installation of any plumbing system connected to a public water supply. The plumbing system of an older house or a home supplied with water by a private well, however, may contain lead—identifiable by its lack of magnetism, softness and dark gray color.

If you suspect your household water is contaminated, have any problem with your plumbing system remedied as soon as possible and take interim preventive measures. For drinking and cooking, buy bottled water, if possible. If you suspect your water is contained with bacteria, you can use water purification tablets or boil the water for at least 10 minutes before drinking it or cooking with it. If you suspect your water is contaminated with lead ions, you can minimize the amount of lead you ingest by letting the water run for at least 3 minutes before drawing any for drinking or cooking.

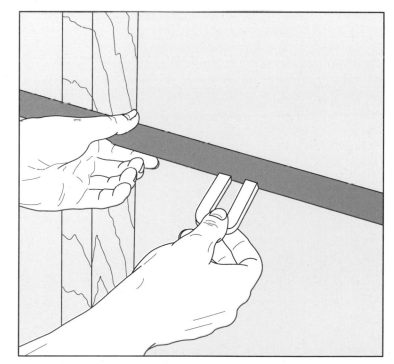

Checking for lead pipes and lead solder. To check if any metal supply pipe in your home is of lead, use a magnet *(above)*; it will be attracted to a pipe of galvanized steel and will not be attracted to a pipe of lead. To check if any metal supply pipe has solder containing lead, use a utility knife to shave off a thin sliver of solder; if it is very soft and dark gray in color, it may contain lead. If you suspect your plumbing system contains lead pipes or lead solder, have it inspected and, if necessary, updated as soon as possible.

HEATING AND COOLING

The heating and cooling systems of your home play a key role in the comfort of you and your family, controlling the indoor climate against the fall and rise of the temperature outdoors. Well-maintained heating and cooling systems can offer safe, reliable, uninterrupted service—with little risk of failure at the peak of your need for them. Although heating and cooling systems can be of many different types, with different parts assembled in different ways, each one is comprised of four basic components: a heat or cool-air producer, a heat exchanger, a distribution system and a thermostat.

With a heating system, the heat producer can be a gas burner, an electrical heating element, an oil burner or a heat pump. The heat exchanger can be a furnace or a water boiler. Heat can be circulated throughout the house by a water distribution system, a network of concealed pipes and radiators or convectors, or by an air distribution system, a network of concealed ducts and registers. The thermostat monitors the temperature indoors and regulates it, turning on and off the heating system.

With a cooling system, the cool-air producer can be a central air conditioning unit, a window air conditioner or a heat pump—because of the flow of refrigerant used to transfer heat, a heat pump can be used for cooling as well as heating. Evaporator coils serve as the heat exchanger and cool air usually is circulated throughout the house by an air distribution system. The thermostat operates the same way and provides the same function as with a heating system.

The Troubleshooting Guide on pages 109 and 110 lists quick-action steps to take in the event of an emergency and refers you to pages 111 to 117 for more detailed instructions. In some instances, you may need to shut off power to the heating or cooling system, shutting off the unit disconnect switch *(page 111)* and the circuit *(page 83)*—and then shut off the gas supply to the gas burner *(page 92)*, the oil supply to the oil burner *(page 111)* or the water supply to the water boiler *(page 112)*. In other instances, you may be able to try a stopgap measure: relighting the pilot of a gas burner *(page 95)*; replacing a fuse of an electrical heating element *(page 112)*; resetting an oil burner or cleaning its photocell *(page 113)*; checking the defrost system of a heat pump *(page 114)*; jumpering a low-voltage thermostat *(page 116)*.

The list of Safety Tips at right covers basic guidelines to help you prevent a heating or cooling system emergency in your home. If you are ever in doubt about your ability to handle an emergency, do not hesitate to call for help. Post the telephone numbers for the fire department and each of your heating and cooling system utilities, including the gas or oil company, near the telephone; even in non-emergency situations, qualified professionals can answer questions about the safety of your heating or cooling systems. In most regions, dial 911 in the event of a life-threatening emergency.

SAFETY TIPS

1. Locate and label or tag the main shutoff for each utility in your home: electricity *(page 82)*; gas *(page 92)*; propane *(page 93)*; water *(page 99)*; oil *(page 111)*; in the event of an emergency, you will want anyone to be able to find them quickly.

2. Natural gas and propane gas are treated with a sulphur-based chemical to give them a strong odor of rotten eggs. If your heating system has a gas burner, make sure you and your family members are familiar with the distinctive odor of gas; as an added precaution, install a gas detector near the gas burner *(page 44)*.

3. If you return home and detect the odor of gas, **do not** enter the house; call the gas company or the fire department immediately from the home of a neighbor.

4. If you detect the odor of gas, do not use any electrical switch or outlet, light a match or use the telephone—a spark could cause an explosion or a fire. Leave the house immediately, then call the gas company or the fire department from the home of a neighbor.

5. Call your heating and cooling system utilities, including the electricity utility and the gas or oil company, before excavating on your property or building an addition to your home.

6. Ask the gas or oil company for an annual checkup of your heating system, including a measurement of the carbon monoxide level in your home; as an added precaution, install a carbon monoxide detector *(page 44)*.

7. Collect any leaking oil or water in a bucket or basin and clean up any oil spill immediately *(page 111)*. Dispose of any oil-soaked waste material following the recommendations of your local fire department or environmental protection agency.

8. Keep furniture and curtains away from electrical baseboard heaters and make sure the registers of an air distribution system are unobstructed. Use an electrician's fish tape or a long stiff wire to pull any blockage out of a duct.

9. Store paints, solvents and other flammable materials away from gas or oil burners and electrical heating elements. Never apply contact cement, paint stripper or any other flammable substance near a gas or oil burner; a buildup of fumes can trigger an explosion.

10. Ensure your heating and cooling systems are installed according to local building codes and serviced according to the manufacturer's instructions. Inform your insurance agent of any major changes made to your heating or cooling system.

11. When undertaking a repair, use only replacement parts and wiring of the same specifications as the original. Look for the UL (Underwriters Laboratories) or CSA (Canadian Standards Association) label on new parts.

12. Keep at least one fire extinguisher rated ABC *(page 55)* in your home and know how to use it in the event of a fire.

13. Never work with electricity in damp or wet conditions. Know how to work safely at the service panel *(page 82)*.

14. Do not attempt to temporarily bypass the high-voltage thermostat of an electrical baseboard heater. Before servicing any low-voltage thermostat, shut off power to the heating or cooling system, shutting off the unit disconnect switch *(page 111)* and the circuit *(page 83)*.

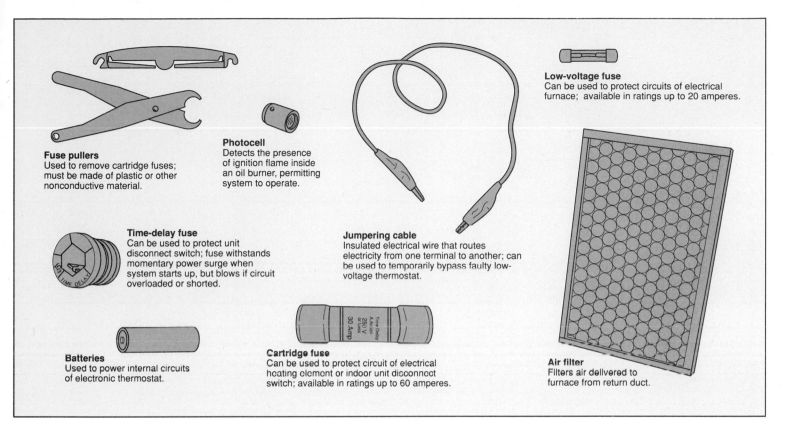

Fuse pullers
Used to remove cartridge fuses; must be made of plastic or other nonconductive material.

Photocell
Detects the presence of ignition flame inside an oil burner, permitting system to operate.

Low-voltage fuse
Can be used to protect circuits of electrical furnace; available in ratings up to 20 amperes.

Time-delay fuse
Can be used to protect unit disconnect switch; fuse withstands momentary power surge when system starts up, but blows if circuit overloaded or shorted.

Jumpering cable
Insulated electrical wire that routes electricity from one terminal to another; can be used to temporarily bypass faulty low-voltage thermostat.

Batteries
Used to power internal circuits of electronic thermostat.

Cartridge fuse
Can be used to protect circuit of electrical heating element or indoor unit disconnect switch; available in ratings up to 60 amperes.

Air filter
Filters air delivered to furnace from return duct.

TROUBLESHOOTING GUIDE

continued ►

SYMPTOM	PROCEDURE
Heating system does not work	Raise thermostat setting
	Restore power to heating system, turning on circuit *(p. 83)* and unit disconnect switch *(p. 111)*
	Service heat pump *(p. 114)*
	If oil or propane level of tank low, call for delivery
	Relight gas pilot *(p. 94)*; service electrical heating element *(p. 112)*; service oil burner *(p. 113)*
	Service water distribution system *(p. 114)*; service air distribution system *(p. 115)*
	Service low-voltage thermostat *(p. 116)*
	Have heating system inspected and repaired as soon as possible
Cooling system does not work	Lower thermostat setting
	Restore power to cooling system, turning on circuit *(p. 83)* and unit disconnect switch *(p. 111)*
	Service electrical heating element *(p. 112)*
	Service air distribution system *(p. 115)*; service window air conditioner *(p. 115)*
	Service low-voltage thermostat *(p. 116)*
	Have cooling system inspected and repaired as soon as possible
Heating system runs but does not heat	Service heat pump *(p. 114)*
	If oil or propane level of tank low, call for delivery
	Service water distribution system *(p. 114)*; service air distribution system *(p. 115)*
	Have heating system inspected and repaired as soon as possible

TROUBLESHOOTING GUIDE (continued)

SYMPTOM	PROCEDURE
Cooling system runs but does not cool	Service air distribution system *(p. 115)*; service window air conditioner *(p. 115)*
	Have cooling system inspected and repaired as soon as possible
Heating system does not shut off	Lower thermostat setting
	Shut off power to heating system, shutting off unit disconnect switch *(p. 111)* and circuit *(p. 83)*
	Have heating system inspected and repaired as soon as possible
Cooling system does not shut off	Raise thermostat setting
	Shut off power to cooling system, shutting off unit disconnect switch *(p. 111)* and circuit *(p. 83)*
	Have cooling system inspected and repaired as soon as possible
Sparks or burning odor from heating or cooling system	Do not touch any heating or cooling system unit
	Immediately shut off power to heating or cooling system, shutting off unit disconnect switch *(p. 111)* and circuit *(p. 83)*; or, shut off electrical system *(p. 82)*
	If flames or smoke come from heating or cooling system unit, leave house immediately and call fire department from home of neighbor
	Have heating or cooling system inspected and repaired as soon as possible
Shock from heating or cooling system	Do not touch any heating or cooling system unit
	Immediately shut off power to heating or cooling system, shutting off unit disconnect switch *(p. 111)* and circuit *(p. 83)*; or, shut off electrical system *(p. 82)*
	Have heating or cooling system and electrical system inspected and repaired as soon as possible
Strong gas odor	Do not use any switch, outlet or telephone or light any flame
	Leave house immediately and call gas company or fire department from home of neighbor
Faint gas odor; localized near furnace	Do not use any switch, outlet or telephone or light any flame
	Shut off gas supply to gas burner *(p. 92)*
	Ventilate room *(p. 93)*
	If gas odor persists, shut off main gas supply *(p. 92)*; propane *(p. 93)*
	If propane level of tank low, call for delivery
	When gas odor dissipates, restore gas supply and relight pilots *(p. 94)*
	If gas odor persists, leave house and call gas company or fire department from home of neighbor
	Have heating system inspected and repaired as soon as possible
Gas pilot does not light and stay lit	Shut off gas supply to gas burner *(p. 92)*
	If gas odor detected, ventilate room *(p. 93)* and shut off main gas supply *(p. 92)*; propane *(p. 93)*
	If propane level of tank low, shut off main gas supply *(p. 93)* and call for delivery
	If gas odor persists, leave house and call gas company or fire department from home of neighbor
	Have heating system inspected and repaired as soon as possible
Oil burner or oil supply pipe leaks	Cope with oil emergency *(p. 111)*
	Have heating system inspected and repaired as soon as possible
Heat pump, central air conditioning unit or window air conditioner leaks refrigerant (oily fluid)	Do not touch refrigerant or any exposed refrigerant pipe
	Shut off power to cooling system, shutting off unit disconnect switch *(p. 111)* and circuit *(p. 83)*; turn off and unplug window air conditioner
	Have cooling system inspected and repaired as soon as possible
Water boiler or water supply pipe leaks	Cope with water emergency *(p. 112)*
	Have heating system inspected and repaired as soon as possible
Radiator, convector or water distribution pipe leaks	Cope with water emergency *(p. 112)*
	Have heating system inspected and repaired as soon as possible
Auxiliary light of heat pump indoor thermostat glows continuously	Service heat pump *(p. 114)*
	If problem persists, have heat pump inspected and repaired as soon as possible

SHUTTING OFF ELECTRICITY TO THE HEATING OR COOLING SYSTEM

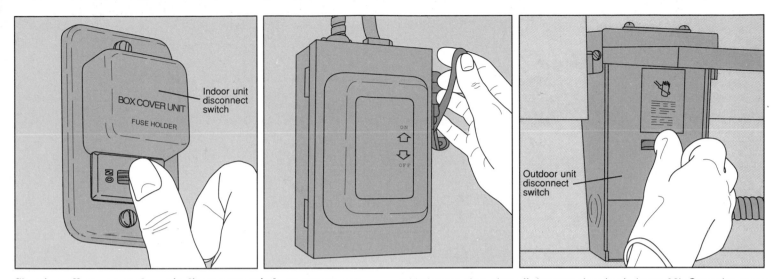

Shutting off power at the unit disconnect switch. Locate the unit disconnect switch: for a furnace or a water boiler, usually indoors near it; for a heat pump or a central air conditioning unit, usually outdoors near it. If the area around the unit disconnect switch is damp, wear rubber gloves and stand on a dry board or wear dry rubber boots. At an indoor unit disconnect switch, set the switch to OFF *(above, left)*, shutting off electricity; if the unit disconnect switch is controlled by a lever, set it to OFF *(above, center)*. At an outdoor unit disconnect switch, raise the weatherproof cover and set the switch to OFF *(above, right)*. As an

added precaution, shut off power to the circuit *(page 83)*. Open the cover of the unit disconnect switch to check any fuse protecting it; if necessary, remove each fuse as you would at a service panel *(page 84)* and use a continuity tester to test it *(page 86)*. If a fuse is faulty, replace it with an identical fuse of the same amperage. Close the cover of the unit disconnect switch and restore electricity, turning on power to the circuit *(page 83)* and setting the unit disconnect switch to ON; at an outdoor unit disconnect switch, also lower the weatherproof cover back into place.

COPING WITH AN OIL EMERGENCY

Shutting off the oil supply to the oil burner. Shut off power to the furnace, shutting off the unit disconnect switch *(step above)* and the circuit *(page 83)*. Locate the valve on the oil supply pipe between the oil burner and the oil tank, usually found near the oil burner or the oil tank. Turn the handle fully clockwise *(above)*, shutting off the oil supply to the oil burner. To restore the oil supply, slowly turn the handle of the valve fully counterclockwise. Turn on power to the furnace, turning on the circuit *(page 83)* and the unit disconnect switch *(step above)*. Tag the valve for easy identification in the event of a future emergency.

Cleaning up an oil spill. Caution: Do not light any flame or smoke. Shut off the oil supply to the oil burner *(step left)*. To temporarily plug a pinhole leak, wipe off the damaged section of pipe with a cloth, then wrap electrical tape tightly around it, overlapping the tape by about 1/2 of its width each turn and extending it 3 to 4 inches on each side of the leak. Wipe up any small oil spill with a cloth. Soak up any large oil spill by pouring an absorbent material such as cat litter or vermiculite on it *(above)*; when the oil spill is soaked up, scoop up the absorbent material with a shovel or a broom and dust pan. Dispose of oil-soaked cloths and absorbent material following the recommendations of your local fire department or environmental protection agency.

COPING WITH A WATER EMERGENCY

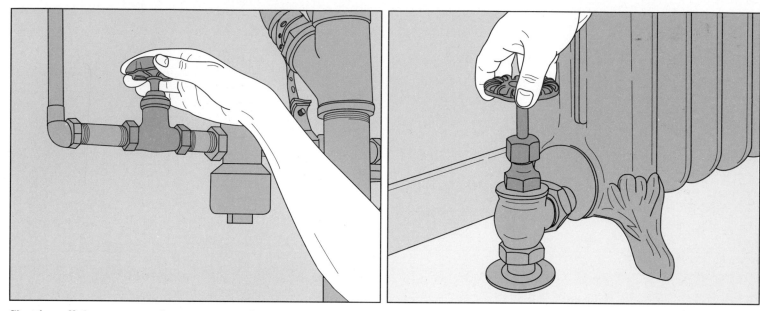

Shutting off the water supply to a water boiler. Locate the shutoff valve on the supply pipe to the water boiler, usually found near and above it. Turn the handle fully clockwise *(above)*, shutting off the water supply to the water boiler (and the hot water supply of the heating system). If the valve leaks or there is no valve, turn off the main water supply *(page 99)*. To restore the water supply, slowly turn the valve fully counterclockwise or turn on the main water supply. Tag each valve for easy identification in the event of a future emergency.

Shutting off the water supply to a radiator or convector. Locate the shutoff valve on the supply pipe to the radiator, usually found near it at floor level; with a convector, remove or reach under the front panel. Turn the handle fully clockwise *(above)*, shutting off the water supply. If the valve leaks or there is no valve, turn off the water supply to the water boiler *(step left)*. To restore the water supply, slowly turn the valve fully counterclockwise or turn on the water supply to the water boiler; put back any convector front panel you removed.

SERVICING AN ELECTRICAL HEATING ELEMENT

Testing and replacing the fuses. Shut off power to the furnace, shutting off the unit disconnect switch *(page 111)* and the circuit *(page 83)*. To remove the front panel of the furnace, grasp its slotted handles, then tug it sharply upward and pull it off *(above, left)*. Locate the control box cover, a hinged metal plate near the top of the furnace; unscrew it *(above, center)* and flip it down, then locate the fuses in a fuse block near the transformer or connected to a panel in the control box. Gently pry out each fuse with a fuse puller *(above, right)*. Use a continuity tester to test each fuse *(page 86)*; the bulb should glow if the fuse is good. If a fuse is faulty, replace it with an identical fuse of the same amperage. Gently push each fuse into place by hand. Flip up the control box cover, put back its screws and reinstall the front panel of the furnace. Turn on power to the furnace, turning on the circuit *(page 83)* and the unit disconnect switch *(page 111)*. If the problem persists, turn off power to the furnace and have it repaired as soon as possible.

SERVICING AN OIL BURNER

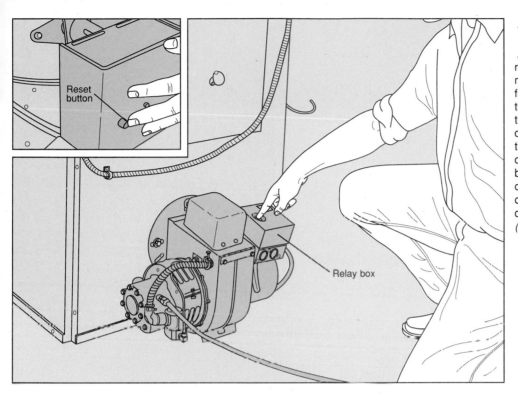

1 Resetting the oil burner. To check if the heat sensor is tripped and reset the oil burner, depress the reset button on the relay box and hold it for about 3 seconds. On most models, the relay box is mounted on the front of the furnace *(left)*; on some older models, the relay box may be mounted on the stack at the back of the furnace *(inset)*. If the oil burner does not start, wait 1 minute, then depress the reset button once again. **Caution:** Never depress the reset button more than twice; unburned oil pumped into the combustion chamber of the furnace can accumulate and may explode or overheat when ignited. If the oil burner still does not start, open the ignition transfomer *(step 2)* to check the photocell.

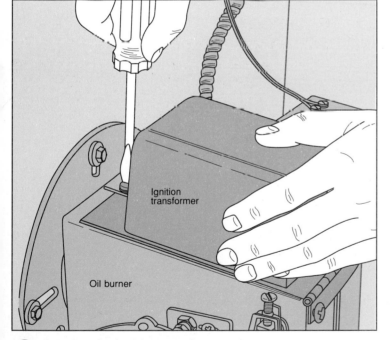

2 Opening the ignition transformer. Shut off power to the furnace, shutting off the unit disconnect switch *(page 111)* and the circuit *(page 83)*. As a safety mechanism, a photocell inside the ignition transformer shuts off the oil burner if its flame goes out; a dirty or faulty photocell, however, can shut off the oil burner when its flame is lit. To check the photocell, locate the ignition transformer—a hinged box usually on the top of the oil burner. Remove the screw holding the ignition transformer to the oil burner *(above)*, then open the ignition transformer and locate the photocell.

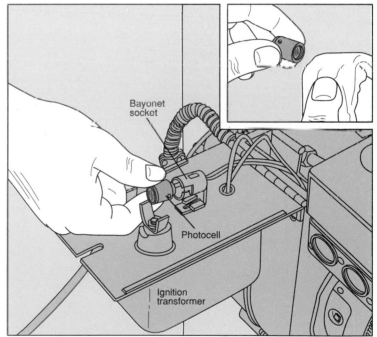

3 Cleaning the photocell. Push the photocell and twist it counterclockwise to remove it from a bayonet socket *(above)*; pull out a plug-in photocell. Wipe any soot off the eye of the photocell using a clean cloth moistened with water *(inset)*. Reinstall the photocell, reversing the procedure used to remove it, then close the ignition transformer and put back its screw. Turn on power to the furnace, turning on the circuit *(page 83)* and the unit disconnect switch *(page 111)*. If the problem persists, turn off power to the furnace and replace the photocell with an exact dupicate. If the problem still persists, turn off power to the furnace and have the oil burner repaired as soon as possible.

SERVICING A HEAT PUMP

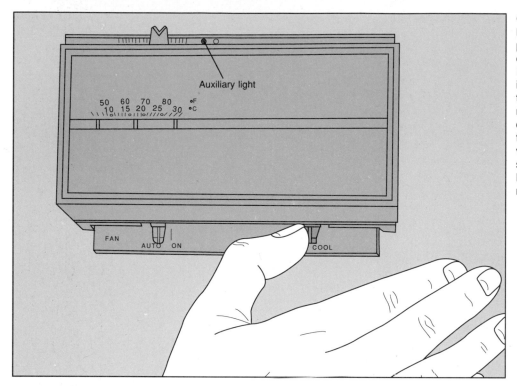

Checking the defrost system. The auxiliary light of the indoor thermostat glows if the heat pump is in defrost mode or if a low temperature outdoors activates the auxiliary heating system. If the auxiliary light glows continuously and there is ice buildup on the outdoor coils, set the indoor thermostat to COOL *(left)*, sending warm refrigerant from the indoor coils to the outdoor coils to melt the ice. Wait at least 30 minutes for the ice to melt. If the ice melts, the reversing valve inside the heat pump may have been stuck temporarily; reset the indoor thermostat to HEAT. If the ice does not melt or the problem recurs, turn off power to the heat pump *(page 111)* and have it repaired as soon as possible.

SERVICING A WATER DISTRIBUTION SYSTEM

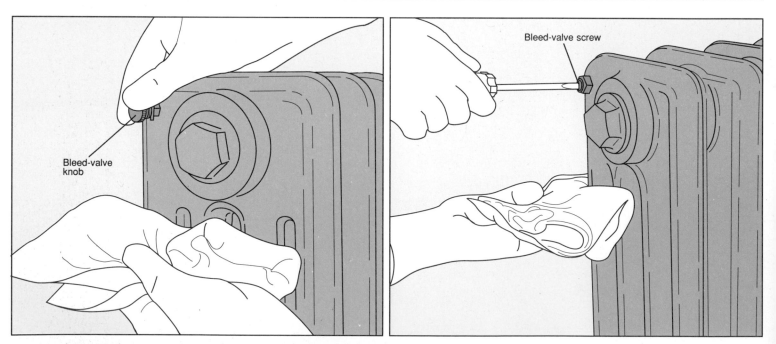

Bleeding radiators and convectors. Air trapped in radiators and convectors can obstruct the delivery of heat. To bleed the air out of a water distribution system, work through the house from room to room, starting on the top floor. Use a cloth or a small container to catch escaping water. At a radiator with a bleed-valve knob, turn the knob counterclockwise 1 full revolution, bleeding the trapped air *(above, left)*. At a radiator with a bleed-valve screw, turn the screw counterclockwise 1 full revolution using a screwdriver *(above, right)*. At a radiator with an automatic bleed valve, unscrew the cap, then turn it upside down and push it into the valve—as you would to let air out of a tire. At a convector, unscrew and lift off the front panel to reach the bleed valve, then use the same procedure. Keep the valve open, bleeding the trapped air, until a steady stream of water flows from it—indicating all the trapped air is purged. Then, close the bleed valve, reversing the procedure used to open it.

SERVICING AN AIR DISTRIBUTION SYSTEM

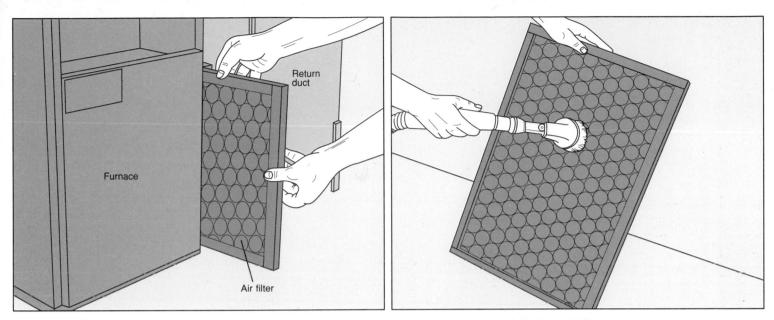

Cleaning a disposable air filter. Shut off power to the furnace, shutting off the unit disconnect switch *(page 111)* and the circuit *(page 83)*. Locate the air filter in its slot on the side, front or top of the furnace and pull it out *(above, left)*. To inspect the air filter for dirt, hold it up to a light or shine a flashlight at it. If no light or only a little light can be seen through the air filter, it is clogged with dirt and should be replaced with an exact duplicate. If there is no replacement air filter on hand, clean it as a stopgap measure. Using a vacuum cleaner fitted with a soft-bristled brush attachment, gently remove dirt embedded in the fibers of the air filter *(above, right)*. Slide the air filter into its slot, then turn on power to the furnace, turning on the circuit *(page 83)* and the unit disconnect switch *(page 111)*.

SERVICING A WINDOW AIR CONDITIONER

1 **Removing the front panel.** Turn off the air conditioner and unplug it from the outlet. To reach the air filter, leave the air conditioner in place and take off the front panel. Remove the bolts or screws holding the front panel and lift it off the air conditioner. If there are no bolts or screws holding the front panel, grip each side of it and pull it off the air conditioner, releasing it from the retaining clips *(above)*.

2 **Removing the air filter.** Locate the air filter in front of the evaporator coils or the blower fan. Release any retaining clips holding the air filter, then pull it off the air conditioner *(above)*. If the air filter is dirty, clean it *(step 3)*. If the air filter is damaged, replace it with an exact duplicate, reversing the procedure used to remove it; put back the front panel, then plug in and turn on the air conditioner.

SERVICING A WINDOW AIR CONDITIONER (continued)

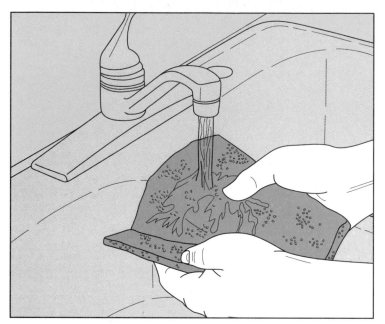

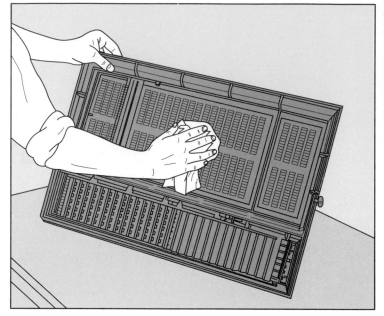

3 **Cleaning the air filter.** Using a vacuum cleaner fitted with a soft-bristled brush attachment, gently remove loose dirt from the fibers of the air filter. Soak the air filter in a solution of mild household detergent and water to wash embedded dirt out of the fibers, then rinse it thoroughly with clean water *(above)* and wring it dry. Reinstall the air filter, reversing the procedure used to remove it. Clean the air filter of the air conditioner the same way at the beginning of the season and at least once each month it is in operation.

4 **Cleaning the front panel.** Clean off each side of the front panel, using a cloth moistened with water or a stiff-bristled brush to remove dust and dirt from the grille *(above)*; dislodge stubborn particles with a toothpick or an old toothbrush. To remove greasy dirt off the front panel, soak it in a solution of mild household detergent and water, then rinse it thoroughly with clean water and dry it with a clean cloth. Put back the front panel, reversing the procedure used to remove it; then, plug in and turn on the air conditioner.

SERVICING A LOW-VOLTAGE THERMOSTAT

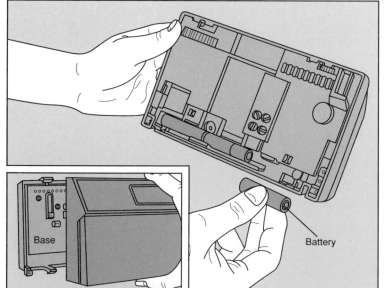

Base

Battery

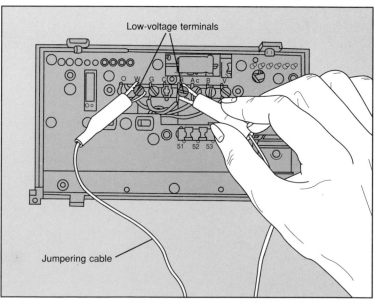

Low-voltage terminals

Jumpering cable

Jumpering a low-voltage thermostat (electronic model). Shut off power to the system, shutting off the unit disconnect switch *(page 111)* and the circuit *(page 83)*. If the low-battery light of the thermostat is glowing, pull the cover off the base *(inset)* and replace each battery with an exact duplicate *(above, left)*; then, reinstall the cover and turn on power to the system, turning on the circuit *(page 83)* and the unit disconnect switch *(page 111)*. Otherwise, pull the cover off the base and use a

jumpering cable to temporarily bypass the thermostat. **Caution:** Do not attempt to jumper the thermostat of an electrical baseboard heater. Set the thermostat to AUTO and HEAT. Locate the terminals of the red and white wires on the base—marked R and W. Connect one clip of the jumpering cable to each terminal *(above, right)*, then turn on power to the system. Do not leave the house unattended; when the indoor temperature reaches a comfortable level, shut off power to the system.

SERVICING A LOW-VOLTAGE THERMOSTAT (continued)

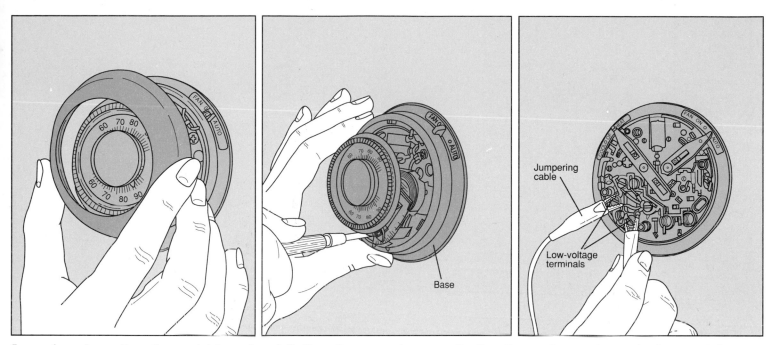

Jumpering a low-voltage thermostat (round model). Shut off power to the system, shutting off the unit disconnect switch *(page 111)* and the circuit *(page 83)*. Pull the cover of the thermostat off the base *(above, left)* and use a soft-bristled brush to clean off dust and dirt, adjusting the dial to help dislodge particles. Put back the cover, then turn on power to the system, turning on the circuit *(page 83)* and the unit disconnect switch *(page 111)*. If the problem persists, shut off power to the system, pull off the cover and use a jumpering cable to temporarily bypass the thermostat. **Caution:** Do not attempt to jumper the thermostat of an electrical baseboard heater. Unscrew the dial *(above, center)* and lift it off the base. Set the thermostat to AUTO and HEAT. Locate the terminals of the red and white wires on the base—marked R and W. Connect one clip of the jumpering cable to each terminal *(above, right)*, then turn on power to the system. Do not leave the house unattended; when the indoor temperature reaches a comfortable level, shut off power to the system.

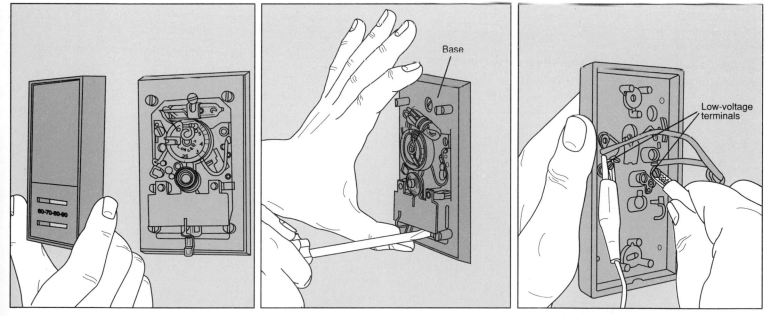

Jumpering a low-voltage thermostat (rectangular model). Shut off power to the system, shutting off the unit disconnect switch *(page 111)* and the circuit *(page 83)*. Pull the cover of the thermostat off the base *(above, left)* and use a soft-bristled brush to clean off dust and dirt, adjusting the dial to help dislodge particles. Put back the cover, then turn on power to the system, turning on the circuit *(page 83)* and the unit disconnect switch *(page 111)*. If the problem persists, shut off power to the system, pull off the cover and use a jumpering cable to temporarily bypass the thermostat. **Caution:** Do not attempt to jumper the thermostat of an electrical baseboard heater. Unscrew the base *(above, center)* and gently lift it away from the wall, exposing the wires connected behind it. Set the thermostat to AUTO and HEAT. Locate the terminals of the red and white wires—marked R and W. Connect one clip of the jumpering cable to each terminal *(above, right)*, then turn on power to the system. Do not leave the house unattended; when the indoor temperature reaches a comfortable level, shut off power to the system.

ENVIRONMENTAL DISASTERS

An environmental disaster is a natural force that can strike anywhere at any time, carving a deadly path of destruction through a region and causing billions of dollars in damages. Environmental disasters such as earthquakes, tornadoes and flash floods can be unpredictable and may strike with little or no warning; be prepared to take shelter quickly (page 122). Other environmental disasters such as hurricanes and severe winter storms or blizzards are seasonal and can be tracked in advance—providing time for local emergency management authorities to issue warnings. In many communities, sirens sound as an alert to an impending environmental emergency. If you hear a siren, immediately tune in an emergency broadcast station on your radio or television and follow the instructions of your local emergency management authorities; be prepared to evacuate (page 123). Keep a well-stocked emergency survival kit in a convenient, accessible location in your home (page 122); refer to page 119 for temporary sources of lighting and heating you may need in the event of an environmental disaster.

The Troubleshooting Guide on pages 120 and 121 places procedures for coping with an environmental emergency at your fingertips, listing quick-action steps to take and referring you to pages 122 to 131 for more detailed information; read the instructions before you need them. In the event you must evacuate your house, be prepared to safeguard your possessions (page 124)—if there is time. For example, prepare plywood panels to cover windows against high winds (page 127); or, in an emergency, use tape to help protect them (page 126). Or, to help minimize water damage, anchor your water heater (page 125) and elevate major appliances onto platforms (page 125) or wrap them in plastic sheeting (page 126). In the event of an environmental emergency such as an airborne hazardous material, you may be advised to take shelter indoors (page 131). You may also need to seek refuge indoors during a heating system failure, eliminating drafts around doors and windows (page 129); or, during a heat wave, installing window shields (page 129).

The list of Safety Tips at right provides basic guidelines to follow in preparing for and coping with an environmental disaster. If you must evacuate your house, do not return until you are advised by your local or federal authorities that any danger is past. Call your insurance agent as soon as possible; an insurance adjuster will be assigned to assess the damage. Prepare to re-enter your house safely (page 135); if you have any doubt about its structural safety, do not enter it until it is inspected by a local or federal building authority or a certified home inspector. When your house is safe to enter and upon permission of your insurance agent, begin your cleaning-up operation as soon as possible (page 132).

SAFETY TIPS

1. Keep a well-stocked emergency survival kit on hand (page 122) and store it in a convenient, accessible place; in the event of an environmental emergency, you will want anyone to be able to find it quickly.

2. Locate and label or tag the main shutoff for each utility in your home: electricity (page 82); gas (page 92); propane (page 93); water (page 99); oil (page 111); in the event of an emergency, you will want anyone to be able to find them quickly.

3. Find out about the emergency warning system in your community. If you are unsure if there is a warning system or what do if it is activated, call your local fire department.

4. Call your local emergency management authorities to find out about the recommended evacuation routes in your area. Obtain the location of all nearby public shelters and post a map of them in a convenient place in your home.

5. Conduct regular drills with your family on the correct procedure to follow in the event of different environmental emergencies—taking shelter quickly during an earthquake (page 122), evacuating before a hurricane (page 123) and taking shelter indoors following release of an airborne hazardous material (page 131), for example.

6. Ask an out-of-town relative or friend to serve as a contact person in the event family members are separated during an emergency. Make sure all family members know the name and memorize the telephone number of the contact person.

7. During an impending environmental emergency, keep your car filled with fuel. If there is a widespread power outage, gas stations may not be able to operate their pumps. Do not store gasoline in your garage or the trunk of your car.

8. Make sure your house and possessions are protected by an appropriate homeowner insurance policy; consider obtaining additional coverage for any environmental disaster to which the region you live in may be vulnerable.

9. Make a comprehensive list of all your possessions, including their model and serial numbers. Keep the list in a convenient location at home and store a copy of it outside the house—with a relative or friend or in a safety deposit box.

10. Keep important documents such as birth certificates, passports and insurance policies in a safe, accessible location at home; in the event of an evacuation, you will want anyone to be able to find them quickly. As a precaution, store a copy of important documents outside the house, preferably in a safety deposit box.

11. If you must evacuate your house during an environmental emergency, do not return until the area is declared safe by your local or federal authorities. If you doubt the structural safety of your house, do not enter it until it is inspected by a local or federal building authority or a certified home inspector.

12. If you return home and detect the odor of gas, **do not** enter the house; call the gas company or the fire department immediately. Do not light any flame or smoke in the house until it is aired out; pockets of gas may be trapped in areas of it.

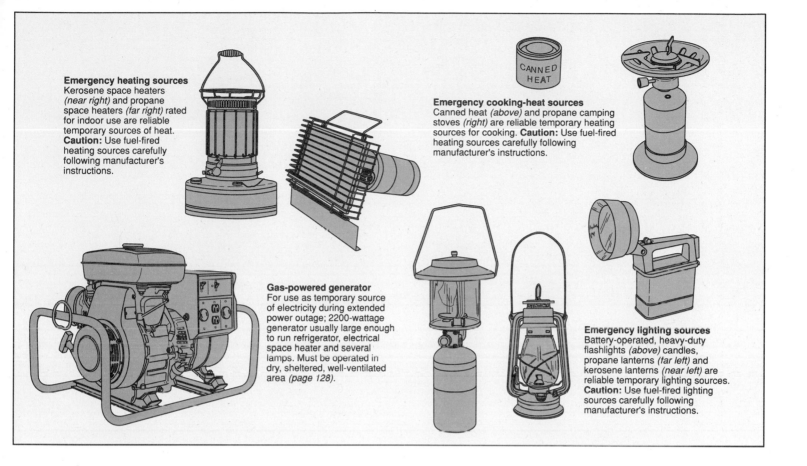

Emergency heating sources
Kerosene space heaters *(near right)* and propane space heaters *(far right)* rated for indoor use are reliable temporary sources of heat. **Caution:** Use fuel-fired heating sources carefully following manufacturer's instructions.

Emergency cooking-heat sources
Canned heat *(above)* and propane camping stoves *(right)* are reliable temporary heating sources for cooking. **Caution:** Use fuel-fired heating sources carefully following manufacturer's instructions.

Gas-powered generator
For use as temporary source of electricity during extended power outage; 2200-wattage generator usually large enough to run refrigerator, electrical space heater and several lamps. Must be operated in dry, sheltered, well-ventilated area *(page 128)*.

Emergency lighting sources
Battery-operated, heavy-duty flashlights *(above)* candles, propane lanterns *(far left)* and kerosene lanterns *(near left)* are reliable temporary lighting sources. **Caution:** Use fuel-fired lighting sources carefully following manufacturer's instructions.

ENVIRONMENTAL TERMS

The National Weather Service of the National Oceanic and Atmospheric Administration (NOAA) in the United States uses specific terms when forecasting weather activity and reporting emergencies on emergency broadcast radio and television stations. An understanding of these terms can help you prepare for an approaching environmental emergency:

• Tornado: Violent storm with winds up to 300 miles per hour. Likely months for a tornado are May and June—especially in the Great Plains area of the U.S.

• Tornado watch: Issued 6 to 8 hours before an expected tornado.

• Tornado warning: Issued when a tornado is sighted in an area.

• Hurricane: Violent storm with winds between 75 and 155 miles per hour, heavy rainfall and tidal flooding. Hurricane season in the U.S. lasts from June 1 to November 30.

• Hurricane watch: Issued 24 to 36 hours before an expected hurricane.

• Hurricane warning: Issued 12 to 24 hours before an expected hurricane.

• Tropical storm warning: Issued when storm with winds between 39 and 73 miles per hour is expected.

• Flood warning: Issued 18 to 24 hours before expected flooding; includes severity of flooding anticipated.

• Flash flood: Usually caused by a torrential rainfall, melting snow or a dam failure.

• Flash flood watch: Issued when conditions are conducive to a flash flood.

• Flash flood warning: Issued when a flash flood is imminent or flooding is sighted.

• Winter storm watch: Issued 12 to 24 hours before expected severe winter conditions—including freezing rain or heavy snowfall.

• Winter storm warning: Issued 12 hours before expected severe winter conditions.

• Blizzard warning: Issued 6 hours before expected heavy snowfall with winds of 35 miles per hour or more.

TROUBLESHOOTING GUIDE

SYMPTOM	PROCEDURE
Earthquake	Take shelter immediately *(p. 122)*
	Tune in emergency broadcast station on radio or television and follow instructions of emergency management authorities
	Have emergency survival kit on hand *(p. 122)*
	Shut off utilities *(p. 123)*
	Remain indoors until area declared safe by authorities
	Cope with power outage *(p. 128)* and water shortage *(p. 130)*
	Clean up *(p. 132)*
Tornado	Take shelter immediately *(p. 122)*
	Tune in emergency broadcast station on radio or television and follow instructions of emergency management authorities
	Have emergency survival kit on hand *(p. 122)*
	Evacuate house if instructed by emergency management authorities *(p. 123)*
	Shut off utilities *(p. 123)*—if there is time
	Safeguard possessions *(p. 124)*—if there is time
	Stay away or remain indoors until area declared safe by authorities
	Cope with power outage *(p. 128)* and water shortage *(p. 130)*
	Clean up *(p. 132)*
Hurricane	Take shelter immediately *(p. 122)*
	Tune in emergency broadcast station on radio or television and follow instructions of emergency management authorities
	Have emergency survival kit on hand *(p. 122)*
	Evacuate house if instructed by emergency management authorities *(p. 123)*
	Shut off utilities *(p. 123)*—if there is time
	Safeguard possessions *(p. 124)*—if there is time
	Stay away or remain indoors until area declared safe by authorities
	Cope with power outage *(p. 128)* and water shortage *(p. 130)*
	Clean up *(p. 132)*
Flood	Take shelter immediately *(p. 122)*
	Tune in emergency broadcast station on radio or television and follow instructions of emergency management authorities
	Have emergency survival kit on hand *(p. 122)*
	Evacuate house if instructed by emergency management authorities *(p. 123)*
	Shut off utilities *(p. 123)*—if there is time
	Safeguard possessions *(p. 124)*—if there is time
	Prepare for water shortage by filling bathtubs, sinks and containers with water—if there is time
	Stay away or remain indoors until area declared safe by authorities
	Cope with power outage *(p. 128)* and water shortage *(p. 130)*
	Clean up *(p. 132)*
Tropical storm	Take shelter immediately *(p. 122)*
	Tune in emergency broadcast station on radio or television and follow instructions of emergency management authorities
	Have emergency survival kit on hand *(p. 122)*
	Remain indoors until danger past
	Cope with power outage *(p. 128)*
	Clean up *(p. 132)*

SYMPTOM	PROCEDURE
Thunderstorm	Take shelter immediately *(p. 122)*
	Remain indoors until danger past
	Cope with power outage *(p. 128)*
	Clean up *(p. 132)*
Snowstorm or blizzard	Take shelter immediately *(p. 122)*
	Tune in emergency broadcast station on radio or television and follow instructions of emergency management authorities
	Have emergency survival kit on hand *(p. 122)*
	Remain indoors until area declared safe by authorities
	Cope with power outage *(p. 128)* and heating system failure *(p. 129)*
Heat wave	Cope with heat wave *(p. 129)*
Forest fire	Tune in emergency broadcast station on radio or television and follow instructions of emergency management authorities
	Have emergency survival kit on hand *(p. 122)*
	Evacuate house if instructed by emergency management authorities *(p. 123)*
	Shut off utilities *(p. 123)*—if there is time
	Stay away until area declared safe by authorities
	Cope with power outage *(p. 128)* and water shortage *(p. 130)*
	Clean up *(p. 132)*
	Safeguard house against forest fires *(p. 131)*
Airborne hazardous material	Take shelter indoors immediately *(p. 131)*
	Tune in emergency broadcast station on radio or television and follow instructions of emergency management authorities
	Have emergency survival kit on hand *(p. 122)*
	Evacuate house if instructed by emergency management authorities *(p. 123)*
	Shut off utilities *(p. 123)*—if there is time
	Stay away or remain indoors until area declared safe by authorities
	Clean up *(p. 132)*
Dust storm	Take shelter indoors immediately *(p. 131)*
	Tune in emergency broadcast station on radio or television and follow instructions of emergency management authorities
	Have emergency survival kit on hand *(p. 122)*
	Remain indoors until area declared safe by authorities
	Clean up *(p. 132)*
Power outage	Have emergency survival kit on hand *(p. 122)*
	Turn off or unplug appliances and other electrical units to prevent overloading of system when power restored; turn on lamp or lighting fixture to know when power restored
	Cope with power outage *(p. 128)*
Heating system failure	Have emergency survival kit on hand *(p. 122)*
	Cope with heating system failure *(p. 129)*
Water shortage	Have emergency survival kit on hand *(p. 122)*
	Prepare for water shortage by filling bathtubs, sinks and containers with water—if there is time
	Cope with water shortage *(p. 130)*

COPING WITH AN ENVIRONMENTAL EMERGENCY

Taking shelter in an environmental emergency. Take action at the earliest warning of an emergency. Have an emergency survival kit on hand *(below)* and be ready to evacuate *(page 123)*; if there is time, safeguard your possessions *(page 124)*. Stay calm; the first step in coping with the emergency is clear thinking and an unpanicked response. Tune in an emergency broadcast station on a radio or television. Follow the instructions of your local emergency management authorities and use the guidelines below:

• **Earthquake.** If you are indoors, stand in an interior doorway and brace yourself against the door frame, crouch under a heavy piece of furniture or brace yourself against a supporting wall; do not stand near a window or a bookcase or other object that can topple over. If you are outdoors, move to an open area away from any structure or overhead utility line. If you are in a car, stay in it.

• **Tornado or hurricane.** Seek shelter close to the ground away from any window in the lowest level of the house—the basement or a closet or bathroom in the center of the house. If possible, crouch under a heavy piece of furniture. If you cannot move indoors, take refuge close to the ground in a ditch or ravine and try to anchor yourself to a secure tree or structure. If you are in a car, abandon it and take refuge close to the ground.

• **Flood.** Evacuate your house immediately if you are advised. Otherwise, seek shelter indoors or outdoors at the highest level possible. Avoid drinking tap water that may be contaminated by floodwater. If you are outdoors, stay away from any natural waterway and do not attempt to cross it. If you are in a car, drive carefully; if floodwater stalls the car, abandon it and move by foot to higher ground.

• **Winter storm or blizzard.** A winter storm or blizzard can result in a power outage and isolation at home. Stock extra supplies of non-perishable food during the winter; have emergency lighting and heating sources on hand *(page 128)*. If you are trapped in a car during a winter storm or blizzard, stay in the car and flash your emergency lights or hang a cloth from the aerial or window; if you run the engine, open a window to prevent carbon monoxide poisoning.

• **Thunderstorm.** Seek shelter indoors away from any window, electrical unit, fireplace, radiator, pipe or plumbing fixture. Turn off and unplug electrical units with electronic components; avoid using the telephone. If you cannot move indoors, seek shelter close to the ground at a low level—in a ditch or ravine or under a thick growth of small trees. Do not stand near an isolated tree, a telephone pole or a body of water; avoid being the tallest object in an open area. If you are in a car, stay in it.

• **Forest fire.** Safeguard your house *(page 131)* and follow the instructions of local emergency management authorities.

• **Airborne hazardous material.** Take shelter indoors *(page 131)*; follow the instructions of local emergency management authorities.

ENVIRONMENTAL EMERGENCY SURVIVAL KIT

Clothing, toiletries and blankets. Keep a complete change of warm clothing for each family member. Stock supplies of soap, towels, toothbrushes, tissue paper and other personal hygiene items. Include a blanket or sleeping bag for each family member.

Non-perishable food. Stock a 7-day supply of canned, dehydrated or precooked food for each family member; it should require no refrigeration and little heat and water to prepare. Consider infants, pets and others with special diet needs. Include a bottle opener, a mechanical can opener, plates, drinking glasses, cooking and eating utensils, and garbage bags.

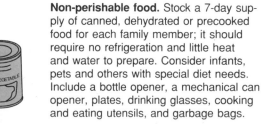

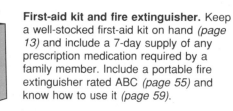

First-aid kit and fire extinguisher. Keep a well-stocked first-aid kit on hand *(page 13)* and include a 7-day supply of any prescription medication required by a family member. Include a portable fire extinguisher rated ABC *(page 55)* and know how to use it *(page 59)*.

Potable water. Stock a 7-day supply of drinking water for each family member (1 gallon per person each day). Bottled water can be stored for an extended period of time; replace stored tap water every 2 months. To store tap water, disinfect each container using a solution of 1 tablespoon of household bleach per gallon of warm water; fill each container with the solution, empty it after 15 minutes and rinse it thoroughly. Refill each container with fresh water, then label and date it.

Battery-powered radio. Rely on a battery-powered radio to tune in local emergency broadcast stations for updates on an emergency situation. Stock extra batteries for the radio.

Lighting, heating and cooking equipment. Store a battery-powered flashlight, candles, matches and canned heat for cooking food. Fuel-powered lanterns, heaters and stoves can be used *(page 128)* if carefully stored and operated according to the manufacturer's instructions.

PREPARING AN EVACUATION PLAN

Planning to evacuate safely. Be prepared to evacuate your house immediately, following the instructions of your local emergency management authorities. Have an emergency survival kit on hand *(page 122)* and take measures in advance to safeguard your possessions *(page 124)*.

• Call your local emergency management authorities to find out the recommended evacuation routes in your area—especially if you live in a region prone to tornadoes, hurricanes, floods or forest fires. Have your local emergency management authorities help you map out the best evacuation route from your house.

• Obtain the location of all public shelters in your community. Inquire about the geographical site of your house; for example: its elevation in relation to nearby waterways or its location in relation to wind patterns.

• Find out if your community uses emergency warning signals; be sure you know what they sound like, what they mean and what to do when they are heard.

• Practice family evacuation drills to ensure each family member knows how to respond safely and quickly in the event of an environmental emergency that calls for evacuation.

Study the history of environmental disasters in your area and learn the time of year an emergency is most likely to occur; in many coastal areas frequently subjected to severe storms and floods, storm surge maps are available. Use the following guidelines to help you prepare a safe evacuation plan:

• Have an emergency survival kit on hand *(page 122)* to take with you if you evacuate; make sure each family member knows where it is located.

• Locate and label or tag the main shutoff for each utility in your home: electricity *(page 82)*; gas *(page 92)*; propane *(page 93)*; water *(page 99)*; oil *(page 111)*; in an emergency, you will want anyone to be able to find them quickly and shut them off.

• Keep important documents in a convenient, accessible location; in the event of an evacuation, you will want anyone to be able to find them quickly.

• Do not wait until the last minute of an emergency to evacuate; you could face hazardous and congested road conditions. Stay tuned to your local emergency broadcast station and use your designated evacuation route. As you leave the house, lock all the windows and doors behind you.

SHUTTING OFF UTILITIES

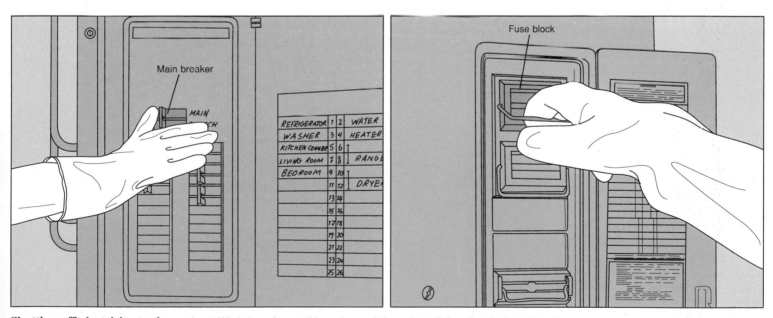

Shutting off electricity to the system. Work in safe conditions *(page 82)* to shut off the electrical system. If your electrical system is protected by a service disconnect breaker, shut off electricity at it *(page 83)*. Otherwise, locate the main circuit breaker or the main fuse block at the service panel and shut off electricity. If your electrical system is protected by a main circuit breaker, wear a rubber glove to flip it to OFF *(above, left)*. If your electrical system is protected by a main fuse block, wear a rubber glove to grip its handle and pull it straight out *(above, right)*; if there is more than one main fuse block, pull out each one the same way. If there is a shutoff lever instead of a main fuse block, pull it down to shut off electricity. To restore electricity, reset the service disconnect breaker *(page 83)* or the main circuit breaker *(page 82)*, reinstall the main fuse block *(page 83)* or push the shutoff lever up.

SHUTTING OFF UTILITIES (continued)

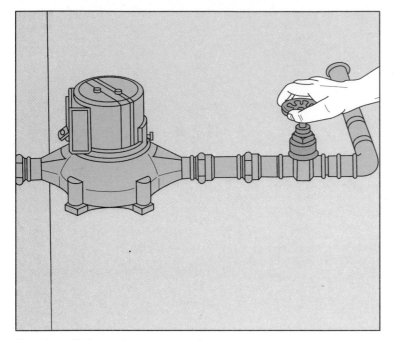

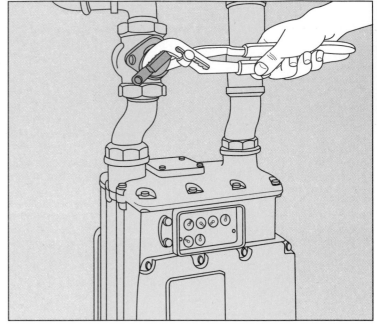

Turning off the main water supply. Locate the main shutoff valve on the main water supply pipe for the house and close it; usually it is found at the entry point of the main water supply pipe, indoors near the water meter or in the basement, utility room or crawl space. Turn the handle fully clockwise to close the valve *(above)*, shutting off the water supply; if the water meter has two valves, close the valve on the supply side (before the water meter). To restore the water supply, open the valve by slowly turning the handle fully counterclockwise.

Turning off the main gas supply. Locate the main shutoff valve on the main gas supply pipe for the house; usually it is found at the entry point of the main gas supply pipe near the gas meter, outdoors or in the basement, utility room or garage. To shut off the gas supply, close the valve using adjustable pliers *(above)* or a wrench, turning the handle perpendicular to the supply pipe. To restore the gas supply, open the valve by turning the handle parallel to the supply pipe. With propane, shut off or restore the gas supply at the tank or cylinder *(page 93)*.

SAFEGUARDING YOUR POSSESSIONS

Minimizing disaster aftermath. If your area is prone to disasters such as earthquakes, tornadoes, hurricanes or floods, take measures to protect your house before an emergency occurs. Listen to weather forecasts and learn the warning signs of an impending emergency; during the summer, for example, a fast-moving, turbulent, green-gray cloud front preceded by a sudden drop in temperature may mean imminent hail or heavy rain. Evacuate immediately on the instructions of your local emergency management authorities, even if you feel your own house is safe—do not waste valuable time attempting to safeguard your possessions. The following guidelines list ways you can help to safeguard your possessions in advance of an emergency, as well as at the first sign of its approach:

• Consider purchasing special insurance coverage for earthquakes, tornadoes, hurricanes, floods or other environmental disasters common to your region. For example, the U.S. government-sponsored National Flood Insurance Program protects homeowners against losses suffered from a flood.

• An earthquake can collapse a chimney, causing extensive damage. Most new houses built within an earthquake zone have chimneys reinforced with steel ties; if your chimney is not reinforced, use steel straps to anchor it to floor and ceiling joists.

• High winds can lift a mobile home off its footings; use metal cables or straps to anchor it to concrete posts or the ground.

• Consider installing a lightning protection system if you live in an area of frequent lightning storms—especially if your house is isolated or the tallest one in the neighborhood. Ensure any roof-mounted antenna is grounded.

• Anchor your water heater *(page 125)*. Prepare plywood panels to cover windows *(page 127)*; or, tape them *(page 126)*.

• At the first sign of an emergency, bring indoors your outdoor furniture, barbecues, garbage cans, garden tools and other movable objects. Stake to the ground sheds, birdbaths, small trees, freestanding plants and other immovable objects outdoors.

• Keep a supply of old sheets or burlap on hand to anchor with rocks over valuable plants, affording them some protection against heavy rain, hail or frost. Cover large freestanding plants with inverted cardboard boxes.

• If there is a risk of flooding, move your furniture and other household possessions to the highest level of your house. Turn off and unplug all electrical appliances; elevate a heavy major appliance onto a platform *(page 125)* or wrap it in plastic sheeting *(page 126)*.

SAFEGUARDING YOUR POSSESSIONS (continued)

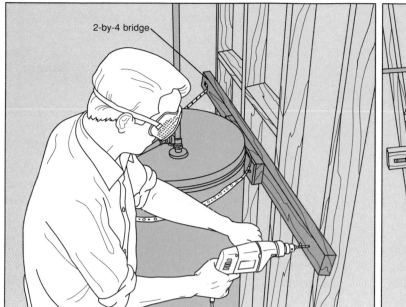

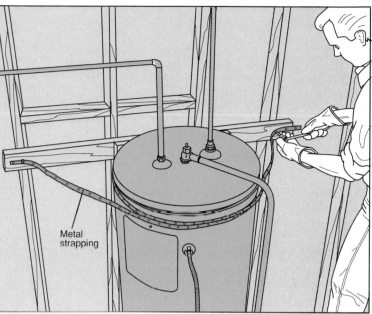

Anchoring a water heater. Use metal strapping to anchor the water heater to the studs behind it. If the studs are not exposed, locate them by tapping along the wall, listening for a change from a hollow to a solid sound; or, use a magnetic stud finder or a density sensor. Nail 2-by-4s or other wood as a horizontal bridge between the studs, filling the gap between them and the water heater. Wearing safety goggles, use a drill fitted with a bit of a diameter slightly smaller than a lag bolt to bore a hole through one end of the bridge and partway into the stud; mark the hole depth on the bit with tape. Wearing work gloves, fit a washer onto

the lag bolt, then insert the lag bolt through the strapping and screw it into the hole using a socket wrench. Wrap the strapping 1 1/2 turns around the water heater, pull it to the other end of the bridge and use tin snips to cut off any excess. Secure the end of the strapping at the end of the bridge the same way, boring a hole for a lag bolt *(above, left)*, pulling the strapping tightly and fitting the lag bolt through a washer and it, and screwing in the lag bolt *(above, right)*. Use the same procedure to anchor the bottom of the water heater.

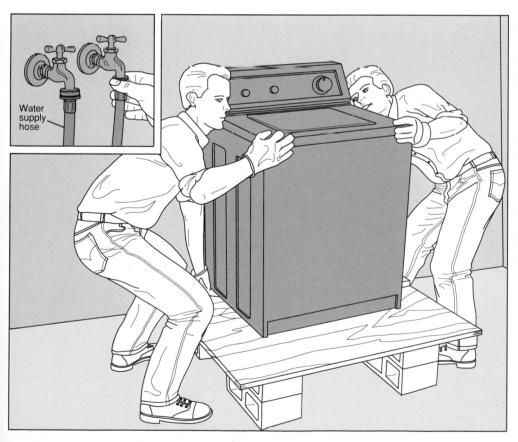

Elevating a major appliance onto a platform. To help protect a major appliance from floodwater, wrap it in plastic sheeting *(page 126)* or elevate it onto a platform of plywood and concrete blocks. Turn off and unplug the appliance. With a clothes washer, also shut off the water supply to it *(page 100)* and remove the water supply hoses from the faucets *(inset)*; with a clothes dryer, take off the exhaust hose. Place concrete blocks on the floor near the appliance, stacking them to the height you need; avoid stacking more than 3 blocks together. Then, cover the blocks with a plywood panel thick enough to support the weight of the appliance; if necessary, stack plywood panels. Working with a helper, lift the appliance and set it down on the platform *(left)*. **Caution:** To avoid back strain while lifting and lowering the appliance, bend at your knees, keeping your back straight.

SAFEGUARDING YOUR POSSESSIONS (continued)

Wrapping a major appliance in plastic sheeting. To help protect a major appliance from floodwater, elevate it onto a platform of plywood and concrete blocks *(page 125)* or wrap it in plastic sheeting. Turn off and unplug the appliance. With a clothes washer, also shut off the water supply to it *(page 100)* and remove the water supply hoses from the faucets; with a clothes dryer, take off the exhaust hose. Working with a helper, tilt the appliance back enough to slide the sheeting under it

(above, left), then tilt it forward and pull the sheeting up and around it; work carefully to avoid tearing the sheeting. To help prevent the appliance from floating, wrap garbage bags around sandbags and place them inside it as ballast; or, with a clothes washer or top-loading dishwasher, fill it with clean water. Continue wrapping the sheeting around the appliance, overlapping sections of it, if necessary, and using duct tape to seal the seams completely *(above, right)*.

PROTECTING WINDOWS

Duct tape

Protecting windows with tape. To protect a window during a strong wind, prepare a plywood panel in advance to cover it *(page 127)*; in an emergency, use duct tape. Working indoors, first apply strips of tape along the top, bottom and each side of the window. Then, start at one corner of the window and apply strips of tape about every 4 inches diagonally across it. Finally, apply strips of tape about every 4 inches diagonally across the window in the other direction *(left)*. Use the same procedure to protect each window of the house.

BOARDING UP WINDOWS

1 **Preparing a plywood panel.** In an emergency, use duct tape to protect windows during a strong wind *(page 126)*; otherwise, prepare a plywood panel in advance to cover each window. Measure the length *(above, left)* and height of the window, then add about 6 inches to each dimension. Using a circular saw, cut a plywood panel at least 1/2 inch thick to the size needed; if necessary, join 2 plywood panels with a wood batten and nails. Position the panel on the window, resting it on the sill, and temporarily nail it in place. Mark a

hole for a fastener every 24 inches along the top and each side of the panel about 1 inch from the edge *(above, right)*; avoid locating a fastener at any mortar joint. If the wall is masonry, install lag bolt shields *(step 2)*. If the wall is other than masonry, bore a hole at each mark through the panel and partway into the wall using a drill fitted with a bit of a diameter slightly smaller than a screw; mark the length of a screw on the bit with tape. Then, secure the panel *(step 3)*.

2 **Installing lag bolt shields.** With the panel still in position, wear safety goggles and bore a hole at each mark through the panel using a drill fitted with a bit of the same diameter as a lag bolt; mark the thickness of the panel on the bit with tape. Mark each hole on the wall, take down the panel and use a drill fitted with a masonry bit of the same diameter as a lag bolt shield to drill a hole in the wall at each mark *(above)*; mark the length of the shield on the bit with tape. Using a ball-peen hammer, tap a lag bolt shield into each hole until it is flush with the wall *(inset)*. Then, reposition the panel on the window.

3 **Securing the plywood panel.** Holding the panel in position, secure it with lag bolts or screws. To secure the panel with lag bolts, fit a lag bolt with a washer and use a socket wrench to drive it through a hole in the panel into the shield; repeat the procedure at each hole in the panel *(above)*. To secure the panel with screws, drive a screw through each hole in the panel and into the wall with a screwdriver. Unscrew the panel, take it down and label it; leave the shields or holes in the wall for reinstallation of the panel in the event of an emergency. Store panels for windows in a dry, accessible location.

COPING WITH A POWER OUTAGE

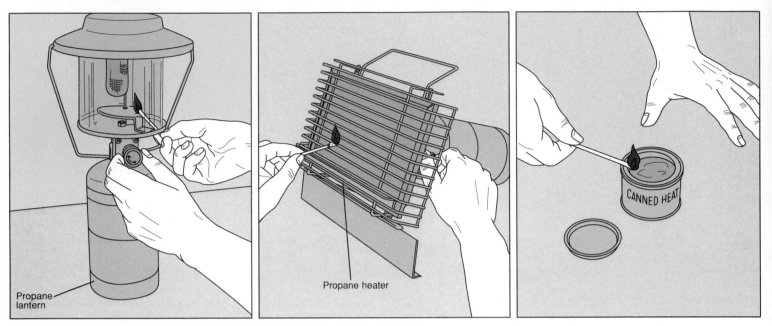

Propane lantern

Propane heater

CANNED HEAT

Equipping yourself with emergency energy sources. Plan in advance for a power outage or heating system failure—have alternate sources of lighting and heating on hand. A gas-powered generator can be purchased or rented to cope with an extended power outage *(step below)*. Stock candles, matches and a flashlight in a convenient, accessible location; candles are a reliable source of light and can provide a surprising amount of warmth. A propane lantern *(above, left)* or a kerosene lantern can provide bright, long-lasting light, a propane space heater *(above, center)* or a kerosene space heater rated for indoor use can

provide heat for a room and canned heat *(above, right)* or a propane camping stove can provide heat for cooking—but each must be used carefully following the manufacturer's instructions. **Caution:** If you use any fuel-fired lighting or heating source indoors, open a window or door slightly for proper ventilation. Set up any temporary lighting or heating source on a sturdy, flat surface at least 3 feet away from combustible materials; never leave it unattended. Do not use a propane or charcoal barbecue indoors. Keep a portable fire extinguisher rated ABC *(page 55)* on hand and know how to use it *(page 59)*.

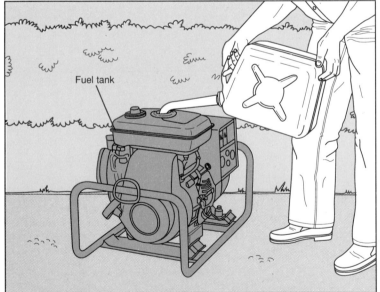

Fuel tank

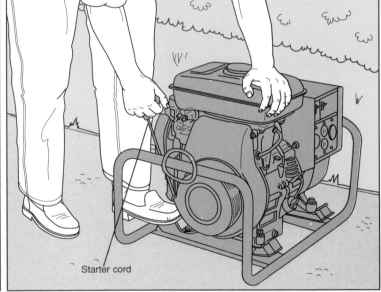

Starter cord

Using a portable gas-powered generator. Purchase or rent a gas-powered generator to provide a temporary source of electricity. Choose a generator of sufficient wattage, calculating the electrical load you need *(page 85)*; a 2200-wattage generator is usually enough to run a refrigerator or freezer, an electrical space heater and several lamps. To run an appliance with a compressor, such as a refrigerator or freezer, a generator with surge capacity is required. Set up the generator on a flat, dry surface in a sheltered location with direct ventilation to the outdoors—a garage, carport or porch, for example. Unscrew the fuel tank cap and fill the fuel tank with gasoline *(above, left)*, then screw

back on the cap. Following the manufacturer's instructions, turn on and start the generator, bracing it firmly with a foot and one hand to pull the starter cord *(above, right)*. When the generator starts, adjust the choke until the engine runs smoothly. Plug extension cords rated for outdoor use into the outlets of the generator, then plug the appliances, tools or other electrical units you need into the outlets of the extension cords and turn them on. To refuel the generator, turn off the appliances, tools and other electrical units, unplug the extension cords and turn off the generator; wait at least 15 minutes for the engine to cool.

COPING WITH A HEATING SYSTEM FAILURE

Eliminating drafts around doors and windows. Plan in advance for a power outage or heating system failure, having alternate sources of heating on hand; a gas-powered generator can be purchased or rented to cope with an extended heating system failure *(page 128)*. Set up any temporary heating source in one room of the house, carefully following the manufacturer's instructions; keep the interior doors to the room closed as much as possible and seal off any vent in the room with towels, cloths or rolled-up newspapers. To help prevent heat from escaping out of an exterior door, seal off the openings around it the same way *(above, left)*. To help prevent heat from escaping through a window, use plastic sheeting to weatherproof it, securing the sheeting to the frame with duct tape *(above, right)* or staples. **Caution:** If you use any fuel-fired lighting or heating source indoors, open a window or door slightly for proper ventilation.

COPING WITH A HEAT WAVE

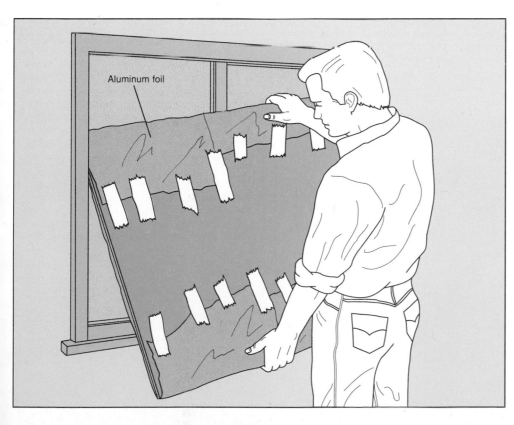

Aluminum foil

Installing a window shield. During a heat wave, stay indoors as much as possible in a well-ventilated, cool room of the house. If you live in an area prone to heat waves, consider having aluminum awnings or shutters that help deflect heat professionally installed or install tinted plastic film on the windows *(page 130)*; in an emergency, temporarily install window shields of cardboard and aluminum foil. To make a window shield, measure the length and height of the window, then use a utility knife to cut a section of cardboard to the size needed. Cover one side of the cardboard with aluminum foil, keeping the shiny side exposed, and secure it to the other side of the cardboard with duct tape or staples. Position the shield over the window *(left)* and use duct tape to hold it in place.

COPING WITH A HEAT WAVE (continued)

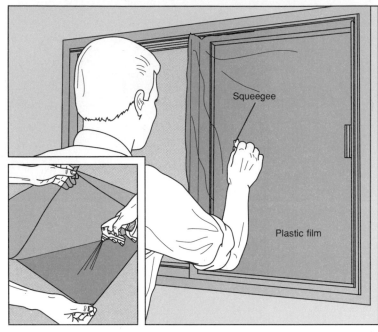

Installing tinted plastic window film. During a heat wave, stay indoors as much as possible in a well-ventilated, cool room of the house; in an emergency, temporarily install window shields of cardboard and aluminum foil *(page 129)*. If you live in an area prone to heat waves, consider having aluminum awnings or shutters that help deflect heat professionally installed or install tinted plastic film on the windows. To install tinted plastic film on a window, wash off the inside of the window using a clean, lint-free cloth and a commercial window cleaner or a solution of mild household detergent and warm water. Measure the length and height of the window, then add about 1 inch to each dimension and use scissors to cut the film to the size needed. Working with a helper, peel the backing off the film and use an atomizer to mist it with water *(inset)*; also mist the inside of the window. Position the film on the window and work from the top to the bottom of it, pressing it into place with your fingertips. Mist the film again and use a hand squeegee to smooth out wrinkles and bubbles *(above, left)*. Trim off the excess film along each side of the window using a carpenter's square and a utility knife *(above, right)*. Mist the film again, remove excess moisture from it using the squeegee and dry it off with a clean, lint-free cloth.

COPING WITH A WATER SHORTAGE

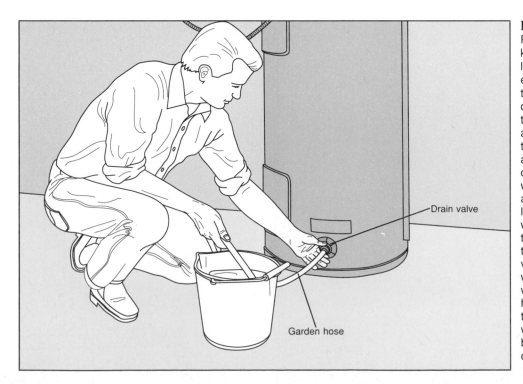

Finding emergency sources of potable water. Plan in advance for a shortage of potable water; keep bottled water on hand or store tap water in labeled and dated containers *(page 122)*. In an emergency, obtain potable water from a toilet tank or the water heater. Use a cup to bail water out of a toilet tank, funneling it into a clean plastic or glass container. To drain the water out of a water heater, shut off power to it *(page 83)* or the system *(page 82)*; with a gas water heater, also turn off the gas supply to it *(page 92)*. Locate the shutoff valve for the water supply to the water heater, usually found near and above it, and turn the handle fully clockwise. If the valve leaks or there is no valve, turn off the main water supply *(page 99)*. Connect a garden hose to the drain valve of the water heater and run it to a clean bucket *(left)*, then open the drain valve by turning the handle fully counterclockwise. Drain as much water as needed from the water heater, then close the valve by turning the handle fully clockwise. As a safety precaution, treat the water taken out of a toilet tank or the water heater using water purification tablets or by boiling it for at least 10 minutes before drinking it or cooking with it.

PROTECTING YOUR HOUSE AGAINST A FOREST FIRE

Safeguarding your home against forest fires. A forest fire can be triggered by a number of causes—including lightning, prolonged hot, dry weather and negligence. Houses located in and near woodland areas are vulnerable to forest fires; hundreds of homes in the U.S. are lost each year. If you live in or near a woodland area, the risk to your house from a forest fire can be reduced by proper landscaping and maintenance. Follow the guidelines below:

• Create a firebreak around the house by clearing away underbrush, leaves, conifer needles and dead vegetation within a 30-foot radius of it—further if it is located on a slope.

• Prune any dead or low-hanging branch within 10 feet of the roof or chimney *(step right)*. If a branch touches a power line, call your electricity utility to have it pruned.

• Sweep leaves, twigs, conifer needles and debris off your roof, deck and porch, and clean out the gutters regularly—especially during periods of hot, dry weather.

• Store firewood away from your house and other structures—including deck, porches, fences and sheds. Do not burn trash in an outdoor incinerator.

• Install a wire-mesh spark arrestor on the top of each chimney to prevent sparks and burning particles from flying out.

• Install smoke detectors throughout your house *(page 58)*; service them regularly *(page 59)*. Have at least one fire extinguisher rated ABC on hand *(page 55)*; know how to use it *(page 59)*.

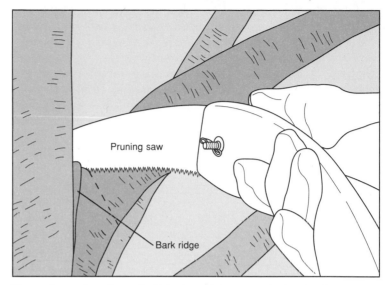

Removing a tree branch. If the branch is over 4 inches in diameter, call a tree professional. For a branch less than 1 1/2 inches in diameter, trim it off using pole shears or lopping shears. For a branch less than 2 inches in diameter, trim it off using a small, curved pruning saw. Wearing work gloves, stand out of the way of the branch and position the blade next to the bark ridge, then saw down through it *(above)*. If the branch is 2 to 4 inches in diameter, trim off its smaller branches. Then, position the pruning saw under the branch about 10 inches from the trunk and saw up about 1/3 of the way through it. Start a second cut on the top of the branch about 1 inch farther from the trunk than the first cut and saw down to it.

COPING WITH AIRBORNE HAZARDOUS MATERIALS

Taking shelter in your house. In the event of an airborne hazardous material emergency, seek shelter indoors immediately and tune in an emergency broadcast station on a radio or television; your local emergency management authorities may recommend that you stay indoors until the danger is past or instruct you to evacuate *(page 123)*. If you are advised to stay indoors, use the guidelines listed below to help minimize the concentration of airborne hazardous material that enters the house:

• Close the doors and windows; use wet towels, cloths or rolled-up newspapers or duct tape to seal the openings around them.

• Turn off the central heating or cooling system; shut off any window air conditioner.

• Turn off any window or attic fan and seal any duct or vent with plastic sheeting or aluminum foil *(step right)*.

• Shut the flue damper of the fireplace.

• Seek shelter in the center of the house, preferably in a windowless room; close interior doors behind you.

• Stay tuned to the emergency broadcast station on your radio or television and follow the instructions of your local emergency management authorities.

• If you must venture outdoors, cover your nose and mouth with a handkerchief or an article of clothing.

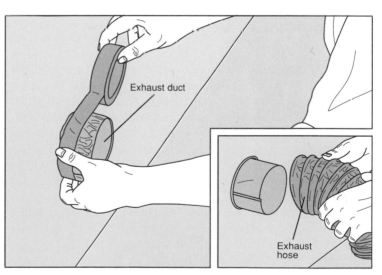

Sealing ducts and vents. To help minimize the amount of airborne hazardous material entering your house, seal all ducts and vents with plastic sheeting or aluminum foil. For example, to seal the exhaust duct of a clothes dryer, turn off and unplug the clothes dryer; if necessary, move it out from the wall to reach the exhaust duct to the outdoors. Loosen any clamp or screws holding the exhaust hose, then pull it off the exhaust duct *(inset)*. Stuff wet towels, cloths or rolled-up newspapers into the exhaust duct, then cover the duct opening with plastic sheeting or aluminum foil and secure it with duct tape *(above)*.

CLEANING UP

Few experiences are as disheartening as coping with the aftermath of a fire or water disaster; the devastation to your home and possessions can cost many thousands of dollars to correct and cleaning up can be an arduous task. If you have evacuated your house due to a natural or environmental disaster, do not return until you are advised by local or federal authorities that any danger is past. Call your insurance agent as soon as possible; an insurance adjuster will be assigned to assess the damage. Prepare to re-enter your house safely *(page 135)*; if you have any doubt about its structural safety, do not enter it until it is inspected by a local or federal building authority or a certified home inspector. When your house is safe to enter and upon permission of your insurance agent, begin your cleaning-up operation as soon as possible; take photographs or use a video camera to record the damage before you start.

The Troubleshooting Guide on page 134 puts emergency procedures for cleaning up after a fire or water disaster at your fingertips and refers you to pages 135 to 141 for quick-action steps to take. Ventilate your house *(page 137)* as soon as possible, opening the windows and doors to allow fresh air to circulate. In addition to basic cleaning tools and supplies, you are likely to require some specialty equipment *(page 133)*, usually available at a tool rental center. Rent a gas-powered generator *(page 128)* to run dehumidifiers, fans and other electrical equipment needed in your cleaning-up operation. Remove standing water using a trash pump *(page 136)*, submersible pump, wet-dry vacuum or mop *(page 72)*. Clean and disinfect the walls, ceilings and floors *(page 138)*. To salvage household possessions, clean and dry them as quickly as possible *(page 139)*. Complete the cleaning up of the house interior before turning your attention to the house exterior *(page 140)* and the yard *(page 141)*.

The list of Safety Tips *(right)* covers guidelines for performing a basic cleaning-up operation after a fire or water disaster. Always wear the proper safety gear recommended for the job, avoiding any risk of contact with the toxins produced by a fire or of infection from contaminated water—both of which can carry long-term detrimental effects to your health. When disposing of any fire- or water-damaged material or any substance resulting from a fire or water disaster, keep in mind its impact on the environment. Recommended safe disposal methods can vary from community to community; call your local department of public works, the mayor's office or an environmental protection agency for the disposal regulations in effect for your community. When in doubt about your ability to handle the aftermath of a fire or water disaster, do not hesitate to call for help. Post the telephone number for your insurance agent, each of your utilities, the fire department and your local or federal building authority near the telephone; qualified professionals can answer questions about your clean-up operation.

SAFETY TIPS

1. Locate and label or tag the main shutoff for each utility in your home: electricity *(page 82)*; gas *(page 92)*; propane *(page 93)*; water *(page 99)*; oil *(page 111);* in the aftermath of a fire or water disaster, you will want anyone to be able to find them quickly.

2. Do not return to your house after a major natural or environmental disaster until the authorities declare the area is safe. If you doubt the structural safety of your house, do not enter it until it is inspected by a local or federal building authority or a certified home inspector.

3. If you are returning to an isolated area, tell someone who will notify the proper authorities if you do not report back.

4. Stay away from fallen power lines; do not enter your house if power lines are touching it. Report any fallen power line to your electricity utility, the fire department or another appropriate authority.

5. If you return home and detect the odor of gas, **do not** enter the house; call the gas company or the fire department immediately. Do not light any flame or smoke in the house until it is thoroughly aired out; pockets of gas may be trapped in areas of it.

6. Before beginning your cleaning-up operation, call the electricity utility to confirm that power to your house is shut off; as an added precaution, shut off power at the service panel *(page 82)*. Shut off the main gas supply *(page 92)*; main propane supply *(page 93)*. If necessary, also shut off the main water supply *(page 99)*. Call your water utility to check if the water supply is contaminated.

7. Wear the proper protective gear for your cleaning-up operation: rubber boots, rubber gloves and rain gear when working with fire- or water-damaged items and materials; safety goggles when working overhead; a hard hat to protect your head against falling debris.

8. Wear a respirator when removing soot or working with chemical products that generate toxic particles or fumes; choose a filter that is specially made to block the particles or fumes and replace it according to the manufacturer's instructions. Wear an anti-bacterial mask to avoid the risk of infection from contaminated water.

9. Ventilate the house as quickly as possible *(page 137)* and keep any area in which you are working well ventilated. If you feel dizzy, faint or sick, leave the house immediately and get fresh air, then improve ventilation before continuing your cleaning-up operation.

10. Keep children and pets away from the work site. When you finish cleaning up for the day, change after leaving the work site and launder your work clothes separately. Rinse off your tools and equipment with clean water and leave them outdoors to dry.

11. Take periodic breaks from your cleaning-up operation to rest and inspect the work that you have done. Never persist with your cleaning-up operation when you are fatigued.

12. When disposing of substances that may be contaminated or any household cleaners, solvents and paints, do not pour them down a house drain or into a septic system. Call your local department of public works, the mayor's office or an environmental protection agency for the disposal regulations in effect for your community.

13. Keep at least one fire extinguisher rated ABC *(page 55)* on hand and know how to use it.

14. Never mix ammonia with household bleach; the solution produces deadly fumes.

15. Have each utility in your house restored only after your system is professionally inspected.

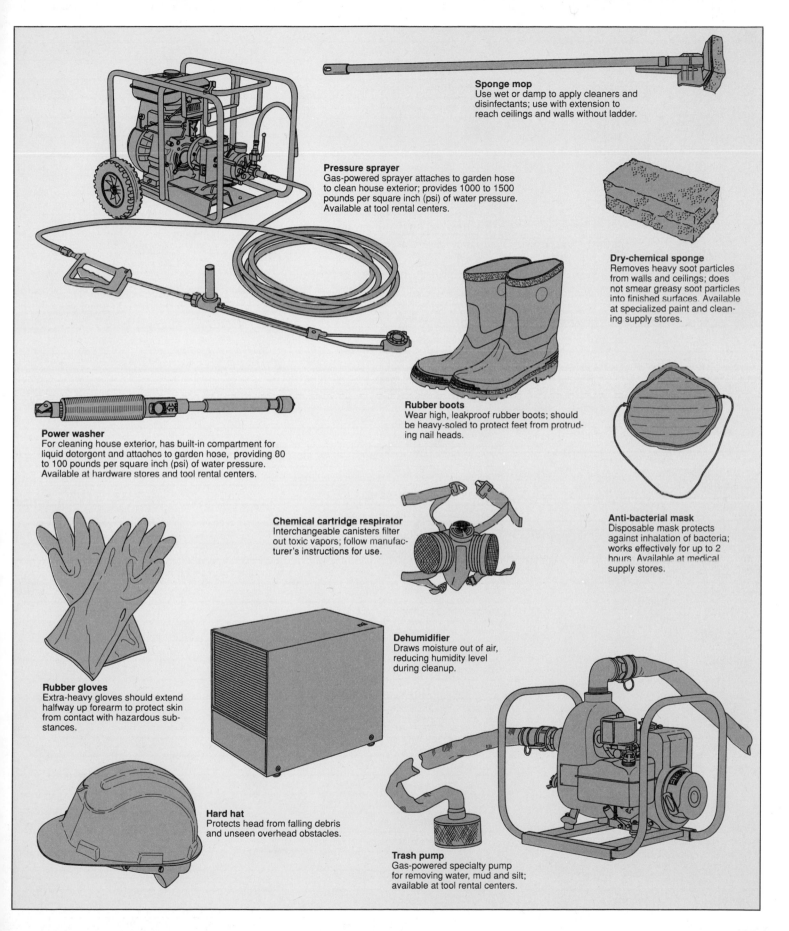

Sponge mop
Use wet or damp to apply cleaners and disinfectants; use with extension to reach ceilings and walls without ladder.

Pressure sprayer
Gas-powered sprayer attaches to garden hose to clean house exterior; provides 1000 to 1500 pounds per square inch (psi) of water pressure. Available at tool rental centers.

Dry-chemical sponge
Removes heavy soot particles from walls and ceilings; does not smear greasy soot particles into finished surfaces. Available at specialized paint and cleaning supply stores.

Power washer
For cleaning house exterior, has built-in compartment for liquid detergent and attaches to garden hose, providing 80 to 100 pounds per square inch (psi) of water pressure. Available at hardware stores and tool rental centers.

Rubber boots
Wear high, leakproof rubber boots; should be heavy-soled to protect feet from protruding nail heads.

Anti-bacterial mask
Disposable mask protects against inhalation of bacteria; works effectively for up to 2 hours. Available at medical supply stores.

Chemical cartridge respirator
Interchangeable canisters filter out toxic vapors; follow manufacturer's instructions for use.

Dehumidifier
Draws moisture out of air, reducing humidity level during cleanup.

Rubber gloves
Extra-heavy gloves should extend halfway up forearm to protect skin from contact with hazardous substances.

Hard hat
Protects head from falling debris and unseen overhead obstacles.

Trash pump
Gas-powered specialty pump for removing water, mud and silt; available at tool rental centers.

TROUBLESHOOTING GUIDE

SYMPTOM	PROCEDURE
Aftermath of fire or water disaster	After natural or environmental disaster, do not return home until authorities declare area safe
	Call insurance agent immediately
	If structural safety of house doubted, do not enter it until inspected
	Re-enter house safely (p. 135)
	Release trapped water from ceilings (p. 135)
	Remove standing water with trash pump (p. 136); submersible pump, wet-dry vacuum, mop (p. 72)
	Clean up mud and debris (p. 137)
	Ventilate house as quickly as possible (p. 137)
	Clean up soot, smoke or fire-extinguisher residue (p. 138)
	Clean and disinfect (p. 138)
	Salvage household possessions (p. 139)
	Clean house exterior (p. 140)
	Clear debris from yard (p. 141)
	Dispose of contaminated materials according to local environmental regulations
Roof or exterior wall buckled or collapsed	Call insurance agent immediately
	Do not enter house until inspected
	Re-enter house safely (p. 135)
	Salvage household possessions (p. 139)
	Dispose of contaminated materials according to local environmental regulations
Ceiling sagging or bulging; water dripping from it	Call insurance agent immediately
	Re-enter house safely (p. 135)
	Release trapped water from ceiling (p. 135)
	Remove standing water with trash pump (p. 136); submersible pump, wet-dry vacuum, mop (p. 72)
	Clean up mud and debris (p. 137)
	Ventilate house as quickly as possible (p. 137)
	Clean and disinfect (p. 138)
	Salvage household possessions (p. 139)
	Dispose of contaminated materials according to local environmental regulations
Standing water	Call insurance agent immediately
	Re-enter house safely (p. 135)
	Remove standing water with trash pump (p. 136); submersible pump, wet-dry vacuum, mop (p. 72)
	Clean up mud and debris (p. 137)
	Ventilate house as quickly as possible (p. 137)
	Clean and disinfect (p. 138)
	Salvage household possessions (p. 139)
	Dispose of contaminated materials according to local environmental regulations
Soot, smoke or fire-extinguisher residue	Call insurance agent immediately
	Re-enter house safely (p. 135)
	Ventilate house as quickly as possible (p. 137)
	Clean up soot, smoke and fire-extinguisher residue (p. 138)
	Clean and disinfect (p. 138)
	Salvage household possessions (p. 139)
	Clean house exterior (p. 140)
	Dispose of contaminated materials according to local environmental regulations
Pervasive odor after clean up	Have house professionally deodorized

RE-ENTERING YOUR HOUSE AFTER A FIRE OR WATER DISASTER

Re-entering your house safely. The water used to fight a fire or from a flood, severe plumbing leak or backed-up drain can result in extensive structural damage to your home—causing floors to buckle and lift, walls to crumble and ceilings to collapse. As well, your home and its contents can be left vulnerable to mildew and fungus growth, wood rot, and pervasive, lingering odors.

Call your insurance agent immediately to have the damage assessed. If you doubt the structural safety of your house, do not enter it until it is inspected by a local or federal building authority or a certified home inspector. When your house is safe to enter and upon permission of your insurance agent, begin your cleaning-up operation following the safety precautions listed below:

• Check with your electricity utility to confirm that power to your house is shut off; to prevent electricity from being restored without your knowledge, shut off power at the service panel *(page 82)*.

• Confirm that the main gas supply is shut off *(page 92)*; that the main propane supply is shut off *(page 93)*.

• Check with your water utility to find out if the water supply is contaminated; wear an anti-bacterial mask to avoid the risk of infection. If necessary, shut off the main water supply *(page 99)*.

• Notify local authorities that you are going into the house and go back only by daylight. Stay away from any fallen power line. Do not light any flame or smoke; any leaked gas may have collected in areas of the house. If you smell gas, leave the area immediately and call the gas company or the fire department to report the leak.

• Wear high, leakproof rubber boots with heavy soles, rubber gloves and rain gear; wear a hard hat to protect your head from unseen overhead obstacles. Bring a battery-operated, heavy-duty flashlight with you to inspect the damage to your house.

• Walk cautiously through the house. Before entering each room, inspect the ceiling; stand in the doorway and use a broom handle to knock down any damage *(step below)*. Check the floor for holes, buckled boards and protruding nail heads. Before climbing any stairs, check the strength of the banister by shaking it; check the strength of each tread by using one foot to place weight on it.

• Ventilate the house, opening the windows and the doors; if necessary, set up fans and dehumidifiers *(page 137)* using a gas-powered generator *(page 128)*.

• Have electricity to the house restored only after any standing water is removed *(page 136)* and your system is professionally inspected. Plug any electrical tool or appliance you need to complete your cleaning-up operation only into an outlet protected by a ground-fault circuit interrupter (GFCI) *(page 79)*.

CHECKING A CEILING

Releasing trapped water. Prepare to re-enter your house safely *(step above)*, making sure that electricity and the gas supply is shut off; as an added precaution, shut off power at the service panel *(page 82)* and shut off the main gas supply *(page 92)*; main propane supply *(page 93)*. If you suspect the water supply is contaminated or there is a leaking pipe, shut off the main water supply *(page 99)*. Before entering each room, check the ceiling for bulges and other signs of damage. Wearing safety goggles and a hard hat, stand in the doorway of the room and poke the ceiling forcefully using the handle of a broom or mop, piercing a hole to release any trapped water, if necessary *(left)*; be prepared to step back quickly in the event a section of the ceiling collapses. If necessary, stand on a stepladder or add an extension onto the handle to reach the ceiling. Enter the room cautiously, piercing as many holes in the ceiling as necessary to release any trapped water; never stand directly under a bulging section. After checking the ceiling of each room and releasing any trapped water, remove any standing water *(page 136)*, then clean up any mud and debris, and ventilate the house *(page 137)*.

REMOVING STANDING WATER WITH A TRASH PUMP

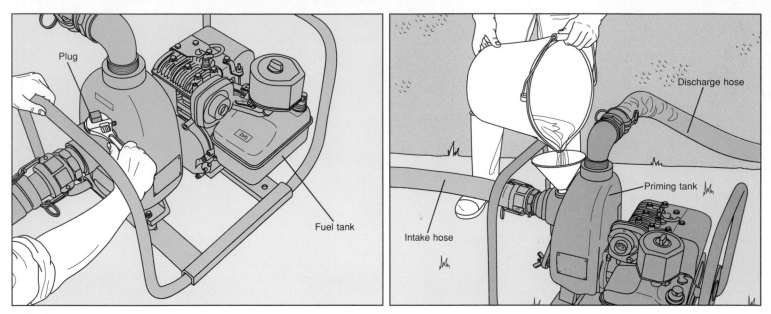

Plug

Fuel tank

Discharge hose

Priming tank

Intake hose

1 **Setting up the trash pump.** Prepare to re-enter the house safely *(page 135)*. To remove less than 18 inches of standing water, use a submersible pump, wet-dry vacuum or mop *(page 72)*. To remove 18 inches or more of standing water, use a gas-powered trash pump, available at a tool rental center; rent an intake nose long enough to reach from outside the house and a discharge hose long enough to reach to an outdoor municipal storm drain. Position the pump on level ground outside the house. Push the intake hose onto the intake pipe and the discharge hose onto the discharge pipe, then close the clamps. Use an adjustable wrench to unscrew the plug of the priming tank *(above, left)*, then fill the priming tank with clean water *(above, right)* and reinstall the plug. Fill the fuel tank with gasoline following the manufacturer's instructions.

Strainer

2 **Pumping out standing water.** Position the discharge hose at the storm drain. Following the manufacturer's instructions, turn on and start the pump, holding it firmly to pull the starter cord *(inset)*. When the pump starts, adjust the choke until the engine runs smoothly. Wearing rubber boots, rubber gloves and an anti-bacterial mask, lower the intake hose through an open window *(left)* until the strainer is submerged. Allow the pump to run, repositioning the intake hose as necessary to keep the strainer submerged; if the engine whines, lift out the intake hose and remove any debris from the strainer. If the pump requires refueling, turn it off and wait at least 15 minutes for the engine to cool. When the water level drops below the strainer, remove the remaining standing water using a submersible pump, wet-dry vacuum or mop *(page 72)*. Clean up any mud and debris, then ventilate the house *(page 137)*.

CLEANING UP MUD AND DEBRIS

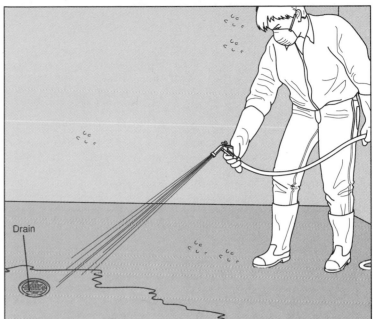

1 **Removing mud and debris.** Prepare to re-enter the house safely *(page 135)*, then remove any standing water using a trash pump *(page 136)*, submersible pump, wet-dry vacuum or mop *(page 72)*. Wearing rubber boots, rubber gloves and an anti-bacterial mask, push the mud and debris into a pile using a broom, mop or squeegee, then scoop it into a garbage can lined with a plastic garbage bag using a shovel *(above)*; fill the bag only halfway, then knot it and take it out of the can. Repeat the procedure until the mud and debris is removed. Dispose of the garbage bags filled with mud and debris according to the regulations of your local municipality.

2 **Rinsing off ceilings, walls and floors.** Use a garden hose to rinse off ceilings, walls and floors with clean water; if necessary, have any plumbing repair undertaken, then turn on the main water supply *(page 99)*. Start on the ceiling, then do each wall in turn, working vertically from top to bottom on a small section at one time; on the floor, work from the perimeter to any drain *(above)* or from one side to the other side of the room. Remove any standing water using a mop or a wet-dry vacuum *(page 72)*; if necessary, set up a gas-powered generator *(page 128)*. Then, ventilate the house *(step below)*.

VENTILATING THE HOUSE

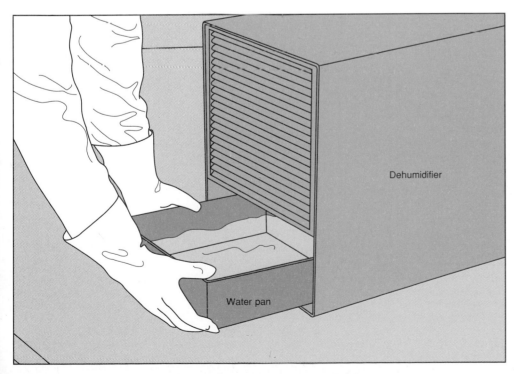

Airing out the house. Prepare to re-enter the house safely *(page 135)*. Remove any standing water using a trash pump *(page 136)* and clean up any mud and debris *(steps above)*, then ventilate the house as quickly as possible. Try to maintain a constant indoor temperature of 70 degrees Fahrenheit; higher temperatures encourage mildew and fungus growth. If necessary, set up a gas-powered generator to run temporary heating sources *(page 128)* and other ventilation equipment. Open the windows and doors; if the weather is too cold to leave them opened, open them periodically as moisture condenses on the windows, then close them after a few minutes. Also open interior closets, cupboards and drawers to air them out. Ventilate each inside *(page 73)* and outside *(page 75)* interior wall damaged by water. To draw excess moisture out of the air, use a dehumidifier, available at a tool rental center; elevate the dehumidifier 3 to 4 feet off the floor and empty the water pan before it fills up *(left)*. Set up fans to increase air circulation and maximize cross-ventilation; do not aim a fan directly at a dehumidifier. Remove any soot, smoke and fire-extinguisher residue, then clean and disinfect *(page 138)*.

CLEANING AND DISINFECTING

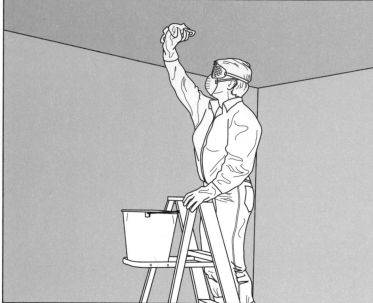

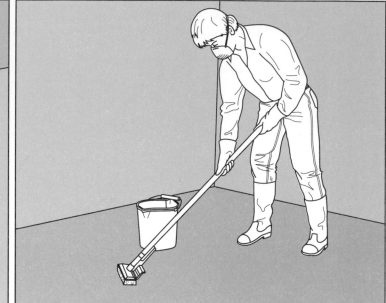

Scrubbing off dirt and bacteria. Prepare to re-enter the house safely *(page 135)*. Remove any standing water using a trash pump *(page 136)*, clean up any mud and debris, then ventilate the house as quickly as possible *(page 137)*. Remove any soot, smoke and fire-extinguisher residue *(step below)*. Wearing rubber boots, rubber gloves and an anti-bacterial mask, clean off dirt using a solution of mild household detergent and warm water; wear safety goggles when working overhead. Use a cloth to scrub the ceiling *(above, left)*, changing often to a clean cloth. Scrub each wall in turn the same way, working vertically from top to bottom on a small section at one time; work from bottom to top if you are cleaning up after a fire to minimize soot stains. Use a squeegee or a sponge mop to scrub the floor, working from the perimeter to any drain or from one side to the other side of the room *(above, right)*; if the floor is concrete, scrub with a stiff-bristled brush. Rinse off the ceiling, walls and floor using clean water. On tough stains, repeat the procedure, mixing 2 to 3 tablespoons of trisodium phosphate (TSP) per gallon of warm water in a plastic bucket. To disinfect, repeat the procedure, mixing 1 to 2 cups of household bleach per gallon of warm water in a plastic bucket.

CLEANING UP AFTER A FIRE

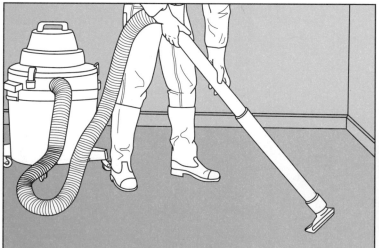

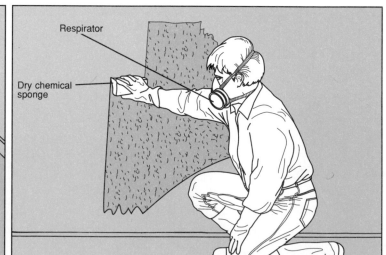

Respirator

Dry chemical sponge

Removing soot, smoke and fire-extinguisher residue. Prepare to re-enter the house safely *(page 135)*. Remove any standing water using a trash pump *(page 136)*, clean up any mud and debris, then ventilate the house as quickly as possible *(page 137)*. Wearing rubber boots, rubber gloves and a respirator fitted with a filter for toxic vapors, use a wet-dry vacuum *(page 72)* to remove soot, smoke and fire-extinguisher residue *(above, left)*; wear safety goggles when working overhead. If necessary, set up a gas-powered generator *(page 128)* to run the wet-dry vacuum. Wipe off ceilings and walls using a dry chemical sponge, also known as a dry painter's sponge, available at a specialty paint or cleaning supply store. Start on the ceiling, then do each wall in turn, working vertically from top to bottom on a small section at one time *(above, right)*; as the outside layer of the sponge becomes soot-stained, use a utility knife to slice it off. Then, clean and disinfect *(step above)*, minimizing soot stains by scrubbing walls from bottom to top.

SALVAGING HOUSEHOLD POSSESSIONS

Salvaging fire- and water-damaged possessions. A fire or water disaster can result in thousands of dollars of damage to household possessions; often, items that are severely damaged cannot be salvaged. Prepare to re-enter your house safely *(page 135)* and call your insurance agent immediately to have the damage assessed.

By acting quickly, you can try to salvage some items that are not severely damaged; for any expensive rug, artwork, antique or family heirloom, immediately call a professional cleaner or restorer. Take photographs or make a video of the damage as proof of loss, then begin your salvage operation using the guidelines listed below.

• **Rugs and carpets.** Clean and let dry, then brush or vacuum *(step below)*; call professional cleaner or restorer.

• **Wooden furniture.** Clean and let dry *(page 140)*; apply furniture oil to protect finish and prevent warping or call professional restorer.

• **Upholstered furniture.** Use wet-dry vacuum *(page 72)* to extract moisture, then let dry; clean using stiff-bristled brush. To remove stains and mildew, call professional cleaner.

• **Bedding.** Use wet-dry vacuum to extract moisture, then let dry; feather pillows can be dried in clothes dryer.

• **Washable clothing and household linens.** Sort by color, then hang to dry away from direct sources of heat; shake or brush, rinse in cool water, then wash and dry according to fabric instructions. To remove stains and mildew from bleachable items, use solution of 1/2 cup of household bleach per gallon of lukewarm water.

• **Leather goods.** Wipe with clean, damp cloth; open items such as suitcases, handbags and purses, stuff them and items such as footwear with crushed paper, and let dry away from direct sources of heat. To remove stains and mildew, use solution of 1 part dena-

tured alcohol and 1 part water, then let dry; apply saddle soap or polish to protect finish.

• **Books and papers.** Place water-soaked items in working freezer to stop mildew growth. Stand damp books on end with pages opened and separate wet papers, then let dry; stack dry books in piles to prevent pages from crumpling.

• **Household appliances and electronic units.** Do not use until professionally serviced. Wipe using solution of mild household detergent and warm water, then disinfect using solution of 1 tablespoon household bleach per gallon of warm water. To prevent corrosion, apply light machine oil to exposed metal parts.

• **Locks and hinges.** Clean and lubricate *(page 140)*.

• **Cooking utensils.** Use fine steel wool to remove rust. Wash using solution of mild household detergent and warm water, then disinfect: soak metal items for 5 minutes in boiling water; soak glassware, porcelain, plastic and enamelware for 10 minutes in solution of 1 tablespoon of household bleach per 1 gallon of hot water. Rinse thoroughly in clean water.

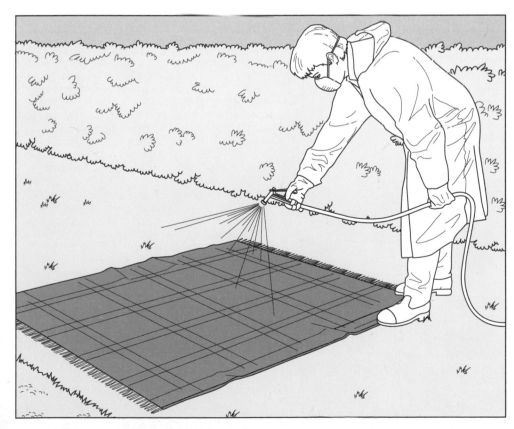

Salvaging rugs and carpets. For a fire-damaged rug or carpet, call a professional cleaner or restorer. To salvage a water-damaged rug or carpet, wear rubber boots and rubber gloves; if you suspect it is contaminated, also wear an anti-bacterial mask. Roll up a rug and any underlayment, and take them outdoors; for a carpet, increase ventilation *(page 137)*. Wash off any mud and debris with clean water; use a garden hose to spray each side of a rug *(left)* and any underlayment. Use a wet-dry vacuum *(page 72)* to extract moisture. Hang up a rug and any underlayment to dry, setting them out on a clothesline, sawhorses or the backs of chairs. Then, clean off any dried residue using a stiff-bristled brush or vacuum. To remove tough stains, use a commercial shampoo or call a professional cleaner or restorer.

SALVAGING HOUSEHOLD POSSESSIONS (continued)

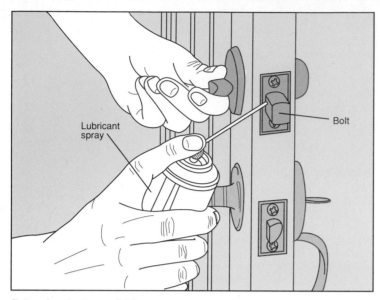

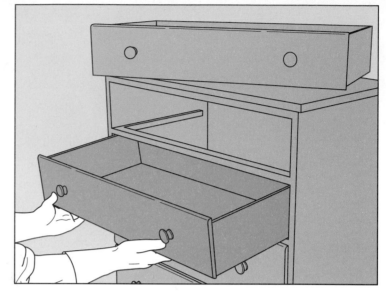

Salvaging locks and hinges. Use a clean towel, cloth or sponge to clean and dry the locks, hinges and other metal hardware of doors, windows, furniture and other household items. For best results, remove the hardware to clean and dry it; or, on an internal mechanism such as a door lock, use compressed air, spraying short bursts through each opening. To remove rust, rub gently with fine steel wool. To lubricate locks, hinges and other metal hardware, use a clean cloth to apply a small amount of light machine oil; or, on an internal mechanism such as a door lock, use a petroleum-based lubricant spray, squirting a small amount around the dead bolt and working the latch back and forth *(above)* or into the keyhole and then turning the key back and forth.

Salvaging wooden furniture. Wearing rubber gloves, take the furniture outdoors to dry, keeping it out of direct sunlight; remove any drawers *(above)* or shelves and open any doors. If the weather is inclement, move the furniture to the garage or carport; otherwise, increase ventilation *(page 137)*. If necessary, elevate the furniture and place plastic sheeting under any metal casters to avoid staining the floor or any rug or carpet. Use a clean towel, cloth or sponge to clean and dry the furniture. To remove mildew, use a solution of 4 to 6 tablespoons of baking soda or trisodium phosphate (TSP) per gallon of water, then rinse with clean water. Apply furniture oil to protect the finish and prevent warping or call a professional restorer.

CLEANING THE HOUSE EXTERIOR

Using a power sprayer. To clean off the house exterior, use a gas-powered pressure washer *(page 141)* or a power sprayer, available at a hardware store or a tool rental center. Close the windows and doors, tape plastic sheeting over lighting fixtures, outlets and vents, and cover nearby vegetation. Following the manufacturer's instructions, connect a garden hose to the power sprayer *(inset)* and fill the soap reservoir with mild liquid detergent.

To use the power sprayer, wear rubber boots, rubber gloves, rain gear and safety goggles; if you are washing off soot or other toxic particles, also wear a respirator fitted with a filter for toxic vapors. Open the faucet, then aim the sprayer at the house exterior, keeping it about 18 inches away from the surface. Holding the sprayer with both hands, turn it on and push the barrel forward for a spray of soap and water. Starting at one end of a wall, wash off the house exterior, working from soffit to foundation in successive 5-foot wide sections *(left)*; do not point the sprayer at doors or windows. To stop the flow of water, turn off the sprayer. Rinse off the house exterior the same way, pulling the barrel back for a spray of only water.

CLEANING THE HOUSE EXTERIOR (continued)

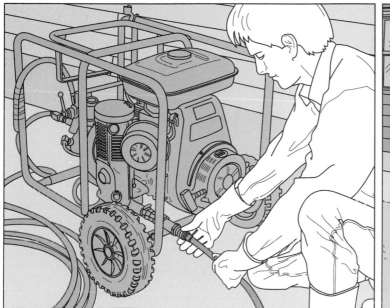

Spray wand

Using a pressure washer. To clean off the house exterior, use a power sprayer *(page 140)* or a gas-powered pressure washer, available at a tool rental center. Close the windows and doors, tape plastic sheeting over lighting fixtures, outlets and vents, and cover nearby vegetation. Following the manufacturer's instructions, connect a garden hose to the pressure washer *(above, left)* and snap a small nozzle onto the end of the spray wand. To use the pressure washer, wear rubber boots, rubber gloves, rain gear and safety goggles; if you are washing off soot or other toxic particles, also wear a respirator fitted with a filter for toxic vapors.

Open the faucet, then aim the spray wand at the ground and squeeze the trigger until a steady stream of water flows; to stop the flow of water, release the trigger. Start the pressure washer following the manufacturer's instructions. Then, holding the spray wand with both hands, aim it at the house exterior, keeping it about 18 inches away from the surface, and squeeze the trigger. Starting at one end of a wall, wash off the house exterior, working from soffit to foundation in successive 5-foot wide sections *(above, right)*; do not point the spray wand at doors or windows. Follow the manufacturer's instructions to turn off the pressure washer.

CLEARING DEBRIS FROM THE YARD

Cleaning up the yard. Allow the ground to dry until it is firm enough to walk on; if necessary, lay down wide boards to walk on to avoid compacting wet soil. To work in the yard, wear rubber boots and work gloves; if you suspect the soil or any vegetation is contaminated, wear rubber gloves. If you suspect a mature tree may fall, set up a temporary barricade to keep others away and call a tree professional. If necessary, support any young tree by tying it to a stake driven into the ground. Use a spade to dig up any severely damaged vegetation; if you suspect the

soil or any vegetation is contaminated, check with your local or state department of health before eating any fruit or vegetable from your garden. Gather up broken branches and other debris by hand *(above, left)* or rake debris into piles *(above, right)* and shovel it into a plastic garbage bag. Wash dirt and debris off vegetation using clean water from a garden hose. If necessary, dilute any excess salts in the soil by soaking it thoroughly with clean water from a garden hose or sprinkler. Dispose of debris from the yard following the regulations of your local municipality.

INDEX

Page references in *italics* indicate an illustration of the subject mentioned. Page references in **bold** indicate a Troubleshooting Guide for the subject mentioned.

ACKNOWLEDGMENTS

The editors wish to thank the following:

Gayle Aitken, Chubb Security Systems, Mississauga, Ont.; Herbert Anderson, Roll-a-way Insulating Security Shutters, St. Petersburg, Fla.; Gerald Arenberg, National Association of Chiefs of Police, Washington, D.C.; Carole Aubry, Canadian Red Cross, Montreal, Que.; Joyce Bagwell, Earthquake Education Center, Charleston, S.C.; Julius Ballanco, Building Officials Code Administrators (BOCA), Country Club Hills, Ill.; Michel Beaulieu, Corporation des maîtres méchaniciens en tuyauterie de Québec, Montreal, Que.; Gilles Beauregard, Inglis Ltd., Laval, Que.; Kevin Belford, American Gas Association, Arlington Va.; Carmel Boisvenue, Centre Du Bébé Plus, Dollard-des-Ormeaux, Que.; Ann Boylan, U.S. Dept. of Transportation, Washington, D.C.; Jim Brodsky, American Insurance Association, Washington, D.C.; Willis Brothers, North Carolina Division of Emergency Management, Raleigh, N.C.; Jim Brown, KPRC Radio, Houston, Tex.; Serge Charbonneau, Gaz Metropolitan, Montreal, Que.; Russell Clanahan and Sandra Farrell, Federal Emergency Management Agency, Washington, D.C.; Dennis Clark, Charleston County EPD, Charleston, S.C.; Hugh Clarke and Barry Coates, Westmount Fire Brigade, Westmount, Que.; Leon Cooper, Home Safeguard Industries, Malibu, Calif.; Ronald Demerjian and Eugene Lecompte, National Committee on Property Insurance, Boston, Mass.; Mario DiDonato, Chubb Security Systems, Montreal, Que; Ann Dioda, American Red Cross, Washington, D.C.; Dr. D.J. Ecobichon, McGill University, Montreal, Que.; Craig Ellis, National Weather Service, Phoenix, Ariz.; Mike Ellis, Corpus Christi, Tex.; Emergency Preparedness Canada, Federal Government of Canada, Ottawa, Ont.; Gerry Feeley, Ronald C. Lister Canada Inc., Montreal, Que.; Fire Prevention Bureau, Birmingham, Ala.; William Fischer, Forest Service—United States Department of Agriculture (USDA), Missoula, Mont.; Guy Gaudreault, Dickie Moore Rentals, St-Laurent, Que.; Gordon Gemeny, Andrew Gemeny and Son, Hyattsville, Md.; Bev Gilbert, Toronto Fire Dept., Toronto, Ont.; Dr. Thomas G. Glass, Jr., San Antonio, Tex.; Dr. Theodore S. Glickman, Resources for the Future, Washington D.C.; Joe Goetz, Brower Brothers Steamatic, Alsip, Ill.; Mark Goldstein, Quantum Group Inc., San Diego, Calif.; Stephen Greenford, Caninspect Inc., Town of Mount Royal, Que.; Spencer Grieco, American Gas Association Laboratories, Cleveland, Ohio; Jamie Haines, National Fire Protection Association, Quincy, Mass.; Janet M. Hanian, Chubb Fire Security Systems, Toronto, Ont.; Wallace R. Hanson, Property Loss Research Bureau, West Shaumburg, Ill.; Hubbell Canada Inc., Brossard, Que.; Robert L. Hughes, Corona Products, Corona, Calif.; Dennis Jensen, Utah Disaster Kleenup, West Midvale, Utah; Ian Johnson, Pittway Corporation of Canada, Rexdale, Ont.; Irwin Kingsbury, Baltimore, Md.; Frank Koutnik, Tallahassee, Fla.; Dick Leppky, Premier Propane, Edmonton, Alta.; Claude Lesage, Giant Factories, Montreal, Que.; Elliot Levine, Levine Brothers Plumbing, Montreal; Dean Lewis and Bill Podd, Refrigeration Service Engineers Society, DesPlaines, Ill.; William Massey, Federal Emergency Management Agency, Atlanta Regional Office, Atlanta, Ga.: Joe A. Mele, National Crime Prevention Institute at University of Louisville, Louisville, Ky.; Marvin Milton, Swerling Milton Winnick Public Insurance Adjusters, Boston, Mass.; Jacques Moreau, Safety First Inc., St. Hubert, Que.; David Palmer, Emergency Response Planning and Management Inc., Princeton, N.J.; Lawrence Tetrilli, Edward H. Marchant Company, Quincy, Mass.; Ronald Passaro, American Society of Home Inspectors Inc., Washington, D.C.; Evan Powell, Chestnut Mountain Research Center, Taylors, S.C.; Gerald Richard, ICG Propane, Longueuil, Que.; Gordon Routley and Thomas Sawyer, Phoenix Fire Dept., Phoenix, Ariz.; Roy Schneider, Woods Wire Products Inc., Carmel, Ind.; Creighton Schwann, Hayward, Calif.; Dr. Earl Schwartz, Bowman Gray School of Medicine, Winston-Salem, N.C; Barry Shanoff, Knopf & Burka, Washington D.C.; Anthony Sillari, T.J. Sillari Inc., Somerville, Mass.; Frank Stanonik, Gas Appliance Manufacturers Association, Arlington, Va.; David H. Stonehill, American Insurance Association, New York, N.Y.; Robert M. Swinford, Forest Service—United States Department of Agriculture (USDA), Washington, D.C.; Roman Talkowski, Dicon Systems Limited, Weston, Ontario; Lee Taylor, Servpro of Lexington/Bedford, Billerica, Mass.; Leonard V. Thibeault, Montreal Fire Dept, Montreal, Que.; Connie R. Thomas, Fernco Connectors Ltd., Davison, Mich.; Bernida J. Trapani, Fernco Connectors Ltd., Sarnia, Ont.; Glen Walsh, Pointe Claire, Que.; Robert L. Warren, National Association of Plumbing, Heating and Cooling Contractors (NAPHCC), Falls Church, Va.; Donald Witten, National Weather Service, Silver Springs, Md.; Charles Zimmerman, Massachusetts Water Resources Authority, Boston, Mass.; Norman Zimmerman, Universal Ship Supply Ltd., Montreal, Que.; Wayne Wood, McGill University Safety Office, Montreal, Que.

The following persons also assisted in the preparation of this book: Kelly Mulcair, Line Roberge, Eve Sévigny.